JOSHUA'S
ALTAR

JOSHUA'S ALTAR

The Dig at Mount Ebal

Milt Machlin

William Morrow and Company, Inc.
New York

Library of Congress Cataloging-in-Publication Data

Machlin, Milt.
    Joshua's altar : the dig at Mount Ebal / by Milt Machlin.
        p.   cm.
    ISBN 0-688-08115-0
    1. Ebal, Mount (West Bank)—Antiquities. 2. Excavations
(Archaeology)—West Bank—Ebal, Mount. 3. Bible. O.T.—
Antiquities. 4. Bible. O.T. Joshua—Criticism, interpreta-
tion, etc. 5. Exodus, The. 6. Joshua (Biblical figure) I. Title.
DS110.E23M33   1990
222'.2093—dc20   90-47878
                                                                       CIP

Printed in the United States of America

First Edition

1 2 3 4 5 6 7 8 9 10

BOOK DESIGN BY M 'N O PRODUCTION SERVICES, INC.

Foreword

This book deals with the story of Exodus and the conquest of Canaan by the armies of Joshua. It is one of the great subjects of controversy in biblical history. In England, this ancient saga has intrigued writers for as long as there has been a written Bible. In the seventeenth century Abraham Cowley, in urging more concentration on biblical subjects rather than classical themes, wrote: "Does not the passage of *Moses* and the *Israelites* into the *Holy Land* yield incomparably more poetical variety than the voyages of *Ulysses* or *Aeneas*?"

In America, from the arrival of the Puritans, the metaphor of a people escaping from bondage into a Promised Land, as did the Israelites, seemed inevitable. The noted preacher Increase Mather described Puritan leader John Winthrop in 1645 as "the American Moses." And there is even some evidence that certain Puritans regarded local Indians as Canaanites to be exterminated and expelled from the land that had been promised by the Lord to his people.

Author Michael Walzer in his book *Exodus and Revolution*, which deals with the political as well as the religious impact of the Exodus story through history, cites more examples of the influence of the story of Exodus and the conquest of the Promised Land on American history. For instance: The Scotch-Irish settlers of Pennsylvania, as well as the Puritans, regarded marauding Indians as the Canaanites of the New World, according to John Bach McMaster, author of *Benjamin Franklin*. "The command laid on Joshua of old," says

5

McMaster, "was binding still. It was the duty of every follower of
the crucified Lord to drive out the heathen from the land." (Actually, it was not the followers of "the crucified Lord" who received
the instructions, but the Israelies, about 1,300 years before Christ.)

As for the blacks of the United States, they identified themselves strongly as the people of Israel, still waiting to cross the
Jordan into the Promised Land, and many of their spirituals reflect
that identification, such as "Swing Low, Sweet Chariot" and "Let
My People Go."

Marc Connelly's play *Green Pastures* is a dramatic expression of the
closeness black Christians felt to the Hebrews and their escape from
the days of slavery in Egypt. The most recent biography of Martin
Luther King, Jr., is called, evocatively, *The Parting of the Waters*.

Place names in the Northeast also reflect the metaphor of America
as Zion—including the innumerable towns and villages named Zion
or New Zion, as well as localities named Canaan in Connecticut
(Canaan *and* New Canaan), New York, Vermont, and New Hamp-
shire.

Probably the first figure of the American Revolution to see a
parallel between the Exodus and U.S. history was Benjamin
Franklin. Franklin believed that the art of poetry was made known
to the Hebrews by Moses. He described the independent colony
on America's shores as "God's new Israel," and proposed that the
Great Seal of the United States should depict Moses with his rod
uplifted and the Egyptian armies drowning in the sea. Jefferson
had a smiliar, though more peaceful, design, still following the
metaphor of the Exodus. He proposed to show on the Great Seal
columns of Israelites marching through the wilderness, led by
God's pillars of cloud and fire. So the connection between the Exodus and the conquest of Canaan had a long history in the Western
world—a direct parallel between the settlement of the United
States and Joshua's settlement is certainly to be found in the concept of Manifest Destiny.

But in reading the Bible as preparation for writing this book, I was
disturbed by the bloodthirsty tone of many of the passages I read in
the Book of Joshua. Were these sanguinary warriors who conquered
Canaan the people from whom our Western culture had descended?
When, according to the Bible, Joshua and the Israelites conquered

Jericho, in one of the two campaigns the Bible says he waged just before proceeding to Mount Ebal, "They exterminated everything in the city with the sword: man and woman, young and old, ox and sheep and ass." [Joshua 6:21]

His next triumph, at Ai, twelve miles northwest of Jericho, was equally grisly, according to the Bible: "When Israel had killed all the inhabitants of Ai who had pursued them into the open wilderness, and all of them, to the last man, had fallen by the sword, all the Israelites turned back to Ai and put it to the sword. The total of those who fell that day, men and women, the entire population of Ai, came to twelve thousand people." [Joshua 8:24–25] Furthermore, they impaled the king of Ai on a stake all day and then left his corpse lying in the entrance to the city gate. The sacking of Ai, according to the Bible, was the last act by Joshua's forces prior to the construction of an altar on Mount Ebal following the instructions in Deuteronomy 11:26–29 (cited in the Epigraph).

I found that I was not the only one to be dismayed by this violent recital. Elie Wiesel, the renowned Jewish historian and Nobel Prize–winner, puzzled over this same anomaly in his *Five Biblical Portraits* (University of Notre Dame Press, 1981).

"His [Joshua's] biography is one long exulting yet bloodchilling adventure, which raises vital questions about Judaism's attitude toward conquest and war. When is violence permitted, when even demanded? When is war justified? When is it a curse? . . . We find Joshua disturbing. Implicated in too many military conflicts, sending too many men to kill or be killed, he seems to personify the victorious but merciless conqueror whom we, naïvely, would prefer not to find among the founders of Jewish history.

"We read the book bearing his name and find ourselves transported from battlefield to battlefield, from execution to hanging, from punishment to vengeance. Lost among cities in ruins and disfigured corpses, we would prefer not to look."

Later, still bewildered by this moral inconsistency, Wiesel, the Holocaust survivor, asks: "Why so much brutality? Why such a lack of magnanimity toward the beaten enemy? Why did all the battles fought and won by Joshua end in mass executions and massacres? One reads Joshua's heroic exploits and admires them, but with embarrassment. Again and again one asks: Why, why? Why did he exterminate all the inhabitants of Jericho? Why did he slay all the citizens of Ai?"

Mark Twain was also bemused by this sanguinary tale. In *The Innocents Abroad* he wrote:

"Then Joshua . . . swept the land like the Genius of Destruction. He slaughtered the people, laid waste their soil, and razed their cities to the ground. He wasted thirty-one kings also . . . though it can hardly be called wasting them, because there was an ample supply of kings in those days and to spare. . . ."

Later, describing the battle of Jabin and his supporters at the waters of Merom [Joshua 11:1–9], he says:

". . . Joshua fell upon them and utterly destroyed them, root and branch. That was his usual policy in war. He never left any chance for newspaper controversies about who won the battle. He made this valley, so quiet now, a reeking slaughter pen."

But despite these doubts about Joshua's moral position, the fascination with the historic basis of the Bible and Joshua's story in particular continues to this day. But whereas fifty years ago any early passage from the Bible was assumed to be mythical or symbolic, the burden of proof has now shifted. Scholars increasingly tend to assume that the text contains at least some germ of truth, and see it as their business to cultivate it. This has not made historical interpretation of the Bible any easier. Both the fundamentalist and the critical or scientific approach were relatively simple compared with the situation today. The discovery of contemporary archives from the third and the second millennia B.C. plus the Dead Sea Scrolls from near the time of Christ (or perhaps earlier, according to recent studies) has thrown new light, and sometimes new confusion, on previously obscure biblical passages. Now many see the Bible texts as very complex and ambiguous guides to the truth, but guides of a sort nonetheless.

Thomas Friedman summed up the inevitable fascination of the Western world with Israel's history in *The New York Times Magazine:* "Israel is the land that, more than anywhere else on earth is soaked with religious meaning and history, and intimately tied to all facets of Western civilization. Because the Jewish return to this particular land unleashes so many passions, touches so many memories, and is relevant to so many people, Israel cannot avoid being interesting. Not here, not now, not tomorrow."

The Exodus, if accepted as arising from a historic event, is the only example of a successful revolt and escape by a slave people recorded in ancient history. Paul Johnson, author of *A History of the Jews* (Harper & Row, 1988), says: "It became an overwhelming memory for the Israelites who participated in it. For those who heard, and later read about it, the Exodus gradually replaced the creation itself as the central determining event in Jewish history. Something happened at the frontiers of Egypt that persuaded the eyewitnesses that God had intervened directly and decisively in their fate. The way it was related and set down convinced subsequent generations that this unique demonstration of God's mightiness on their behalf was the most remarkable event in the whole history of nations."

Like all sciences, biblical archaeology is in a constant state of development. Explorations are taking place and new discoveries are being made every summer at many sites in the world of the Bible. In investigating the archaeological basis of the Exodus and the Book of Joshua, I have been driven by the need to keep up with the latest scientific research, which is multiplying so rapidly that the conclusions of a respected authority whose work has not been revised in the last year or so may no longer be valid. Much of the work cited here has not yet been officially published as this book is written.

Note: In reading this book it is helpful to have a Bible at hand. The one I finally chose was the Tanakh Bible, translated from the original Hebrew, published by the Jewish Publication Society, New York, 1985.

Since I personally detest interrupting the flow of my reading to chase down footnotes, I have left them out and have included sources and parenthetical observations in the text.

Acknowledgments

In a book of this scope so many have helped that in listing them someone of importance is bound to be left out. If I have omitted any of those who offered and supplied help, please accept my sincere apologies.

First: Thanks to my wife for forgoing her honeymoon so that I could go to Israel to research this book, and for her patience with my endless disquisitions at all hours of the day and night concerning my thoughts in composing this work.

Others who were extremely useful, not necessarily in order of their importance, include Dr. Adam Zertal, Dr. Arnold Soloway, Zvi Koenigsberg, Ofra Koenigsberg, Dr. Benjamin Mazar, Amichai Mazar, Dr. Frank Moore-Cross, Dr. Cyrus Gordon, Shmuel Katz, Dr. Zvi Lederman, Nivi Markam, Gad Levy, my original editor, Bruce Lee, and his successor, Randy Ladenheim-Gil, and my agent and friend, Jerry Perles.

Among the volunteers who offered information and photographs are Barbara Lo Bianco, Victoria Dixon, Ruth Whitmer, John Delph, Jane Thomas, J. R. Ensey, Gail Merian, Carolyn J. Robinson, Sharon Beisley, Eugene W. Sucov, Fran A. Stengel, and Frederick E. Wilson.

Contents

13

See, this day I set before you blessing and a curse: blessing, if you obey the commandments of the Lord, your God, that I enjoin on you this day, and curse, if you do not obey the commandments of the Lord your God, but turn away from the path I enjoin on you this day and follow other gods, whom you have not experienced. When the Lord your God brings you into the land which you are about to enter and possess, *you shall pronounce the blessing at Mount Gerizim and the curse at Mount Ebal.* [Deuteronomy 11: 26–29]

JOSHUA'S ALTAR

I

"Then Joshua Built an Altar . . ."

In November 1986 I got a letter from a friend in Israel, who knew of my interest in archaeology, describing a dramatic historic ruin found recently in that country. "The most important biblical archaeological site ever discovered" is the way he described it to me. I was intrigued, to say the least, and my friend promised to keep me informed. A week or so later, in response to my expression of interest in the project, I got a call from Zvi Koenigsberg, a man who had actually worked on Mount Ebal, the site my friend mentioned, almost from the beginning.

I have been deeply interested in archaeology for at least thirty years, and have been involved with underwater archaeological digs at Discovery Bay in Jamaica, at the Well of the Virgins in Yucatán, and off the coast of Yucatán as well as in mainland Mexico. I even sponsored a dig at Tyre, in Lebanon, on behalf of the magazine of which I was then editor, *Argosy*. The Ebal project sounded fascinating to me. A week or so after Koenigsberg called, I invited him to my apartment to discuss his experiences on this important dig.

Zvi arrived at my house, a slim, fit-looking, fortyish man with steel-rimmed glasses, who wore a *kipa*—a small ornamental skullcap worn by Orthodox Jews. He spoke perfect colloquial English, since he had been educated in Brooklyn and went to high school there before immigrating to Israel in 1967. After brief greetings, we got down to the subject of the meeting. Zvi asked me if I had a Bible so that he could show me the scriptural basis of the project we were about to discuss. We were sitting in my study, which has ceiling-to-floor and wall-to-wall bookcases full of volumes dealing with everything from Mafia crime to Phoenician archaeology, but I was embarrassed to find that in all my library there was not a single Bible. Although I was born and raised a Jew, and considered myself a part of the Jewish heritage, I had never been observant religiously, nor had I been particularly interested in the biblical roots of Judaism—or Christianity, for that matter. My feelings of national identity, however, were strong enough that I was one of the first to go overseas to cover the 1967 war in Israel. By the time I got there, the war, which became known as the Six Day War, had been over for several days. I made a tour of the country at that time, including newly occupied territories in the Golan Heights, the Sinai Peninsula, Samaria, and Judea.

It was a moving experience then to be in a country that seemed so idealistic and patriotic in comparison with the United States. In America we have long been used to our freedom and independence to the point where it is taken for granted. In Israel, which had had to fight three times in twenty years for its independence, there was an intensity and dedication the like of which I had never before seen. There was also for me the feeling that I had never until then experienced being in a country in which my own ancestors were rooted.

I had always felt, and still do, that I was not only American by birth, but by spirit and culture. Yet it was uncomfortable for me at times to study the history of the United States from texts in which Jews were rarely mentioned, especially those from eastern Europe. My people had come from the Ukraine at the end of the nineteenth century and the beginning of this one. My father, who arrived at age fifteen, was enormously patriotic about the United States, which he saw, correctly, as the nation that had freed him and the rest of his family from persecution, poverty, and virtual bondage. He enlisted in the U.S. Army at the entry of the United States into World War I, and was proud of having served in the embryo U.S. Air Corps. Later he was an active member of the American Legion, and marched every year in the Memorial Day parade, proudly wearing a shiny chromium-plated World War I–style helmet, as I and my two brothers cheered wildly from the sidelines.

But in my heart I felt that I was an American with certain reservations; what we have come to call a hyphenated American. When the history books spoke of "our forefathers" I knew that they were not speaking of my own ancestors. When I went to Brown University I discovered that Jews could join only one specifically Jewish fraternity. It has become documented since then that Ivy League colleges, and many others, had a quota on the number of Jews admitted. I felt even more outside the mainstream of American culture in chapel (attendance compulsory), where only Christian hymns were sung. I remember intoning, and ultimately learning, "Praise God from Whom All Blessings Flow," and how when I sang the final lines, "Praise Father, Son, and Holy Ghost," I felt a quintessential otherness. I had never previously spoken of these Christian entities except in vain. In the army, during World War II, as a replacement in a largely Texan outfit, I felt even more a stranger, and occasionally had to defend my separateness with my fists.

In Israel, though an alien in a sense, I felt that I was being welcomed home. I experienced a pride in the generations of my people who had over thousands of years kept their roots in this land, perhaps the oldest surviving ethnic and religious group in history.

I was impressed when I met a group of Jewish emigrants from the Atlas Mountains of Morocco, who, though illiterate, had preserved the Jewish tradition orally for such a long time that the written origins were lost in the mists of history—perhaps from before the time that a written Bible ever reached their community. In addition, they were still a pastoral people, who lived in a patriarchal clan structure exactly like that of the early Israelites. Their only connection with modern Israel was their ancient oral tradition, and the rituals that were a part of that heritage.

But in fact, even in this country, there are thousands of people who also know the Bible, or large stretches of it, by heart, some of whom are barely literate, so it is not surprising to think that the early parts of the Bible may well have been known even before they were officially transcribed by priests, and there are many records dating from times of persecution such as the Inquisition when members of the Jewish community remembered rituals, but forgot, or did not have access to, the text of their holy books.

I myself still have no deep feeling for the rituals of Judaism, except in the sense that they are a part of my culture. But I certainly felt a welcoming warmth in Israel as a Jew. There I could truly identify with the forefathers. But I still owned no Bible.

So Zvi, with a look of amused tolerance, opened his briefcase, took out his own King James Bible, and turned to Joshua 8:30, which read:

> Then Joshua built an altar unto the Lord God of Israel in Mount Ebal.
> As Moses the servant of the Lord commanded the children of Israel, as it is written in the book of the law of Moses, an altar of whole stones over which no man hath lift up any iron; and they offered thereon burnt offerings unto the Lord, and sacrificed peace offerings.

I read the passage, which he had highlighted in yellow ink, carefully and looked back at Zvi, who sat waiting for me to finish. This altar, Zvi explained to me, had, according to the Bible, been built just after the end of the Exodus—the flight of the Israelites from Egypt under Moses, and at the beginning of the Israelite occupation of the Promised Land in about 1250 B.C.—a date almost universally accepted.

"Okay," I said. "How are you involved in this?"

Zvi told me that he had been working as a volunteer with a team that had found a site on Mount Ebal, which is in Samaria, in Israel's occupied West Bank, which exactly tallied with the biblical description I had just read of Joshua's altar. The project that led to the discovery of the site was an archaeological survey directed by Adam Zertal, an Israeli archaeologist, who had entered his profession after being severely wounded in the Yom Kippur War in October 1973.

Zertal had done the original survey as his graduate thesis, after learning to walk on crutches. I was impressed by his accomplishment and courage, but skeptical about his identification of the ruin he had found as Joshua's altar. To my knowledge, absolutely no biblical archaeological evidence of this early period in Jewish history had ever been discovered. True, sites of the Settlement Period certainly have been discovered, but none with specific biblical connections. This would be the first site with a clear and specific mention in the Bible relating to Joshua and to a very particular place, time, and event. But I would certainly need more evidence before accepting Zertal's theory concerning his find.

"Suppose I told you," Zvi said, "that we are almost certain that we have found on that site the exact altar that Joshua built, in the place mentioned in the Bible, after more than thirty-two hundred years? Suppose I told you that this is the *only* archaeological evidence relating to the Exodus that ever has been found?"

"I'd say it was one of the most important finds in history. But *have* you found it?"

Zvi held up his hand in a temporizing gesture. "In the first place, it was not *I* who found it, but Adam Zertal.

"As for whether this actually *is* that altar, you can tell me what you think after we have gone over all the evidence we have to date."

At our next meeting Zvi showed me enough archaeological reports, clippings, photos, and letters to convince me that this very well could be the actual site described in the Bible, and certainly merited further investigation. But I had to do a lot of preparatory groundwork before I could start to write the story of the ruin on Ebal. I had to learn to read the technical language of archaeology, though I was familiar with much of it. (An archaeological excavation, for instance, is a "dig." A "cultic site" is a place where religious rites are performed.) And I had to review the biblical text involved and the history behind it.

At Zvi's suggestion, I carefully read the first five books of the Bible—the Pentateuch or Torah (Genesis, Exodus, Leviticus, Numbers, and Deuteronomy), plus the next three, Joshua, Judges, and I and II Samuel. For this purpose I acquired a new Bible called Tanakh, which is a direct translation from the original traditional Hebrew text of the Bible. The King James Version, although written with inspired poetry, was produced two thousand or more years after the original Hebrew biblical texts.

The Tanakh Bible, though prosaic in its style, is precise in its translation. (Tanakh, incidentally, is a Hebrew acronym made up of the first letters of *Torah, Nevi'im,* and *Kethuvim.* Torah is, of course, the first five books reputed to have been written by Moses. Nevi'im are the prophets, and Kethuvim are the rest of the writings, which start with Psalms and end with Chronicles II.) It would be more useful than the King James in determining exactly what was said and meant in the biblical text. Certain passages emerge from different editions of the Bible with interpretations that are not always in agreement. Some of these problems are due to changes that have occurred in the text as it has been translated from one language to another. It is worth noting that official Christian dogma of the late Middle Ages accepted the traditional Jewish interpretation of the Pentateuch.

Bible translation started about 2,200 years ago as the large Jewish population of Alexandria began to come under the influence of Greek conquerors, who had arrived in Egypt with Alexander the Great. When the Greek language replaced Hebrew and Aramaic as the local language, the Bible was no longer understood by the Egyptian Jews, so a translation into Greek was made for the Jewish community of Alexandria. This translation became known as the Septuagint, after the seventy scholars who supposedly composed it.

In the last few centuries before Christ, the Jews who lived in the ancient land of Israel, to the north and east of Judea, also found the Hebrew Bible difficult to understand, for their spoken language had become largely Aramaic. The translation of the Bible into Aramaic became known as the Targum. Incidentally, it is almost certain that Christ and all of his disciples spoke Aramaic and that the Bible they used was the Aramaic version. In the Old Testament, parts of Ezra and Daniel and one verse of Jeremiah were actually written originally in Aramaic, and appeared that way amid the old Hebrew of the rest of the ancient biblical texts.

These are the oldest known translations of the Bible, and the most influential. Virtually every Christian translation has followed the methods of the Jewish translators who created the Septuagint, and generally followed its renderings of Hebrew as well. The Christian translators also were influenced by the Targum, and by the writings of the Jewish philosopher-interpreter Philo of Alexandria, who died in about 45 B.C.

With the growth of Christianity in the first century A.D., the Church adopted the Septuagint as its Bible, and it was also translated into the language of the various Christian communities. As Greek began to give way to Latin, it was only a matter of time before the Latin translation of scripture became the recognized Bible of the

Church, in what became known as the Vulgate—the Bible in the language of the common people.

During the Renaissance and Reformation periods Martin Luther made use of the Latin translations of the Septuagint, as well as classic Jewish commentators—Rashi, the great twelfth-century French rabbinical scholar, Abraham Ibn Ezra, the twelfth-century Spanish rabbi and suspected rationalist, and Rabbi David Kimhi, a Bible commentator and grammarian who lived in France in the eleventh and twelfth centuries—and produced his own translation of the Bible into German. The Aramaic and original Hebrew texts used in the East were not available to Luther, since no real cultural contact was made with the eastern countries until the conquest of India by Great Britain and the rise of British influence in the Middle East in the eighteenth century.

By 1526 Martin Luther's German translation had appeared for use by Continental Protestants, and William Tyndale's English translation followed. It relied heavily on Luther's version for interpretation. This, after several revisions, became the King James Version of 1611. Most later Bibles were based on King James.

The Tanakh translation was published by the Jewish Publication Society in 1955, and my edition was issued in 1985. I considered it the most reliable and accurate version for my purposes, in which poetry had to rank secondary to historic accuracy. The Tanakh is copiously annotated, which turned out to be very useful in interpreting controversial passages.

II

Tempted by the Canaanites

nce I got my Tanakh I proceeded to look up its version of the pertinent passages concerning Joshua's altar.

> At that time Joshua built an altar to the Lord, the God of Israel on Mount Ebal, as Moses, the servant of the Lord had commanded the Israelites—as is written in the Book of the Teaching of Moses—an altar of unhewn stone on which no iron has been wielded. They offered on it burnt offerings to the Lord and brought sacrifices of well-being. [Joshua 8:30]

This is the last time the name of Mount Ebal is mentioned in the Bible—any Bible. The difference from the King James Version I had read before was slight. King James read "Then" where Tanakh had "At that time" to open the quotation, and what were called "peace offerings" in King James are called "sacrifices of well-being" in Tanakh. In Tanakh it says "as is written in the Book of the Teaching of Moses," where in King James it says "in the book of the law of Moses." As it turned out, the most important difference between the two versions is that the Tanakh Bible says that the altar was built "on" Mount Ebal, whereas the King James says that it was "in" Mount Ebal. The Peshitta Bible, a direct translation from the original Aramaic, also says "in." This turned out to have great significance.

Zvi explained to me that the burnt offerings mentioned are the rites involving sacrificial animals, in which the animal is totally con-

28

sumed in the fire, and none of it is eaten. Sacrifices of well-being ("peace offerings" in King James), on the other hand, were joyous occasions in which the offering was partly eaten by the person who presented it. It implies the idea of a tribute to God to maintain or to establish good relations between him and his worshipers.

The passage in Joshua concerning the altar was fascinating from an archaeological point of view. This archaeological find on Mount Ebal, dealing as it did with the end of the Exodus and the beginning of the occupation or "conquest" of Canaan, involved the history of the entire Western world: Jewish, Christian, and Muslim.

Searching for clues to this epochal event, I read and reread Yahweh's instructions to the people of Israel in Deuteronomy:

> See, this day I set before you blessing and curse: blessing, if you obey the commandments of the Lord, your God, that I enjoin on you this day, and curse, if you do not obey the commandments of the Lord your God, but turn away from the path I enjoin on you this day and follow other gods, whom you have not experienced. When the Lord your God brings you into the land which you are about to enter and possess, you shall pronounce the blessing at Mount Gerizim and the curse at Mount Ebal. [Deuteronomy 11:26–29]

Interesting. The instructions here say neither "in" nor "on" Mount Ebal, but "at." Again, this came to have significance.

I knew from my own research and readings in other sources that Yahweh (the transliteration of the Hebrew letters for the name of God) had reason to be concerned that his people might stray into the more seductive cults of the Canaanites and "follow other gods," those worshiped by the people who then occupied the Promised Land (along with Hebrew tribes that had been there, according to the Bible, for centuries, since Abraham and Sarah first arrived from Mesopotamia).

The Canaanites' religion made use of temple prostitutes (both male and female) and fertility rites that could easily tempt the youth of Israel. In fact, the Canaanites were purposely using their women to lure Israelite men away from the austere worship of Yahweh.

A story in the Book of Numbers makes this vividly clear. When the Israelites were camped in the Plains of Moab, on the east bank of the Jordan opposite Jericho, which was supposed to be their first entry into Canaan, according to Yahweh's instructions, many of them were attracted to the fertility rites practiced at nearby Peor. Possibly as a sign from Yahweh, they at the same time were hit by a deadly plague. Yahweh was extremely angry with the people of Israel. He instructed Moses to find the ringleaders of the defection to the gods of Peor "and have them publicly impaled before the Lord so that the Lord's wrath may turn away from Israel." [Numbers 25:4] So Moses told his people to slay those of their company who were consorting with the Canaanite women.

While Moses was exhorting his flock at the Tent of Meeting, one of the Israelites named Zimri actually came into the camp with a woman, Cozbi, daughter of a Canaanite chieftain. Phinehas, a priest who was the grandson of Aaron and one of Moses' staunchest supporters, saw this and was enraged. He took a spear, followed the pair into the tent where they had presumably already commenced their lovemaking, and pierced the two of them through the groin with one thrust.

The Lord, who observed this of course, told Moses that Phinehas's drastic action had assuaged his wrath to the point that he would not have the Israelites entirely wiped out by the plague as he had planned to do, and in addition would grant Phinehas and his descendants the permanent role of priest "for all time." (This was the second time the Lord had relented to Moses in a decision to wipe out the entire nation of Israel, the first having been following the incident of the worship of the golden calf at Mount Sinai, in which Joshua had been the only Israelite other than Moses not to yield to the temptation of idolatry. [Exodus 32:19–20]) Meanwhile, following the incident on the Plains of Moab, the Lord granted Israel a partial remission from the plague that had been ravaging its ranks: ". . . the plague against the Israelites was checked. Those who died of the plague numbered 24,000" [Numbers 25:8–9]—a deadly lesson to the Israelites of the danger of flouting Yahweh's commands.

All of this took place, incidentally, near the foot of Mount Nebo, from which Moses would ultimately have his last glimpse of the Promised Land, and where, according to the Second Book of Maccabees in the Apocrypha (which is not in the Jewish canon of scripture), the Ark of the Covenant is hidden in a cave. [II Maccabees 2:4–9]

(In the early seventies I took part in a dig in the ancient Phoenician harbor of Tyre in Lebanon, at which were recovered seven statues of Tanit, one of the Canaanite goddesses of fertility, so I was acquainted with the serious difference between the Mosaic religion of monotheism and the much broader, sexually oriented theology of the Phoenicians and Canaanites. The statues I found were considered to be deeply involved with the Phoenician rite of child sacrifice, strictly forbidden by Yahweh. I discovered during my research for this book that they were the easternmost example of this Punic goddess ever found. They are now in the Musée des Antiquités in Beirut, if that is still in existence.)

Having conquered the problems of the plague and the defection of some Israelites into the Canaanite religion, the Israelites began the final step of their entry into Canaan.

Moses and the elders of Israel charged the people, saying, "Observe all of the instruction that I enjoin on you this day. As soon as you have crossed the Jordan into the land that the Lord your God is giving you, you shall set up large stones. Coat them with plaster and inscribe upon them all the words of this Teaching. When you cross over to enter the land that the Lord your God is giving you, a land flowing with milk and honey, as the Lord, the God of your fathers promised you— upon crossing the Jordan, you shall set up these stones about which I charge you this day on Mount Ebal and coat them with plaster. There, too, you shall build an altar to the Lord your God, an altar of stones. Do not wield an iron tool over them, you must build the altar of the Lord your God of unhewn stones. You shall offer on it burnt offerings to the Lord your God, and you shall sacrifice there offerings of well-being, and eat them, rejoicing before the Lord your God. And on the stones you shall inscribe every word of this Teaching most distinctly." [Deuteronomy 27:1–8]

The practice of setting up commemorative stones, or *maseboth*, survives from very ancient times, and is attested by survival of such pillars in many parts of the world. The Israelites erected *maseboth* without ascribing divine qualities to them, so that they could not be considered objects of idolatry.

(The tradition of slabs of stone that are set up in rings to commemorate various ceremonies seems to go back in history in many parts of the world. I personally saw dozens of stone slabs set in rings in Scotland, where a sign dated them to 1500 B.C., and, mysteriously, in the Trobriand Islands off New Guinea. Similar rings exist in Brittany, England, and Ireland. This does not necessarily imply a cultural exchange, but simply suggests that early primitive religions tended to value such constructions.)

But at this point the Bible indicates the significance of this rite of erecting commemorative stones which the Lord had commanded. Now came a crucial moment in the history of Israel. Immediately after the instruction concerning the building of the altar, Moses and the Levitical priests spoke to all Israel, saying:

> "Silence! Hear, O Israel! Today you have become the people of the Lord your God: Heed the Lord your God and observe his commandments and his laws, which I enjoin on you this day." [Deuteronomy 27:9–10]

This actually was the beginning of the concept of Israel as a confederation of tribes, forming a nation devoted to the worship of one God—Yahweh.

(It is interesting to note that the concept of monotheism had arisen earlier in Egypt under Pharaoh Akhenaten, who took the throne in 1367 B.C., during or just preceding Moses' lifetime. Akhenaten decreed the worship of the sun god as the only deity and ordered all other gods destroyed. Akhenaten's wife was the woman whose beauty came to symbolize Egyptian feminine pulchritude, Nefertiti. His religious ideas were abandoned and his memory nearly erased on the succession of his teenaged son-in-law Tutankhamen in 1347 B.C. Some scholars feel that Moses may have derived some of his ideas concerning the worship of a single deity from Akhenaten, whose beliefs would have been at least known to him. This suggestion is strongly opposed in most Judeo-Christian religious circles, which do not accept Akhenaten as a true monotheist.)

III

The Promise of the Land

The instructions concerning the construction of this first altar to Yahweh after the entrance into the Promised Land during the Settlement Period were definite enough, but Moses and the Lord went on to give the assembled twelve tribes of Israel, now committed to a solemn covenant with Yahweh, further explicit instructions: " 'After you have crossed the Jordan, the following shall stand on Mount Gerizim, when the blessing for the people is spoken: Simeon, Levi, Judah, Issachar, Joseph and Benjamin. And for the curse, the following tribes shall stand on Mount Ebal: Reuben, Gad, Asher, Zebulon, Dan and Naphtali.' " [Deuteronomy 27:11–14]

This refers, of course, to the tribes descended from the people named. Deuteronomy, in which these instructions appear, has been believed by most scholars up to now to have been written, or at least assembled, in the time of King Josiah, which was in the seventh century B.C., about six hundred years after the time of Joshua. But many scholars now believe that those passages concerning Ebal were interpolated and possibly adapted from earlier traditional material, either written or oral. (Remember how long the oral tradition had persisted among the Moroccan Jews I met in 1967.)

One seeming anachronism in God's instructions to Joshua is the mention of iron tools, which were not to be used to dress the stones of the altar. Iron was still a rarity until at least two-hundred years after Joshua's time, so this portion of the passage may have been written long after the early Iron Age, but still possibly as early as the

33

tenth century B.C. Nevertheless, iron was certainly known at this time, and it is at least possible that a ruling class such as the priests could have had access to it.

These instructions seem out of place where they are now located in the Bible and probably would have fit better before Chapter 31 of Deuteronomy, when Moses makes his farewell speech to the people of Israel before they enter the Promised Land and announces that it is Joshua who will lead them into Canaan. But wherever placed in the Bible, or whenever written, the location they describe is unmistakable, and the period they deal with is generally accepted as the mid-thirteenth century B.C. (1250–1220 B.C.).

The formula of offering a blessing and a curse on consummating a treaty or a covenant is an old one that traces back to the early Hittite culture in Mesopotamia, preceding the emergence of the Israelites as a people. It remained in the consciousness of students of the Bible long afterward. In a sermon preached to the English House of Commons in 1641, the Puritan minister Stephen Marshall said: "All people are cursed or blessed according as they do or do not join their strength and give their best assistance to The Lord's people against their enemies."

Mark Twain, when he visited the area, was well aware of the traditions concerning Ebal and Gerizim: "At two o'clock," he wrote in *The Innocents Abroad,* "we stopped to lunch and rest at Ancient Shechem, between the historic mounts of Gerizim and Ebal, where in the old times the books of the law, the curses and the blessings, were read from the heights to the Jewish multitudes below."

According to the Bible the curses were recited first, and they were similar at some points to the Ten Commandments, but by no means the same. However, an old Talmudic tradition suggests that each curse was first uttered as a blessing. The curses, as the Talmud sees it, were recorded in the Bible so that they might ring in people's ears as a warning.

The Lord directed that the Levites should deliver these curses "and proclaim loudly to all the Israelites: 'Cursed be anyone who makes a sculptured or molten image, abhorred by the Lord your God, a craftsman's handiwork, and sets it up in secret.—And all the people shall respond, Amen.' " [Deuteronomy 27:15]

This is obviously a paraphrase of the second commandment, but set in the framework of a "curse" rather than a command. There are, in fact, in this series of curses a total of ten that echo the commandments, but sometimes in more detail. For instance, under the commandment against adultery, these curses spell out people with whom one must not have intercourse, including the wife of one's father (in those days of polygamous marriage, this might not be one's mother), one's sister or half sister, one's mother-in-law, or any animal.

There is a curse also on the man who moves his neighbor's landmark, or misdirects a blind man, or who "subverts the rights of the stranger, the fatherless and the widow."

These passages, along with the description of an altar so exactly like the one said to be found by Zertal, impressed me deeply. To find that a message confirming the factual background of these biblical events was reaching me through the millennia filled me with a sense of enormous respect for the historic roots of the Bible—a feeling I knew was shared by all religions that were rooted in the Old Testament. "The West," says philosopher David Hartman, "sees Israel as the modern extension of a 3,000-year-old Jewish connection to this land."

The notion of the Promised Land is peculiar to the Israelite religion, and for the Israelites and later the Jews, it was the single most important element in it, according to Paul Johnson's *A History of the Jews*. "It is significant," Johnson observes, "that the Jews made the five early books of the Bible, the Pentateuch, into the core of their Torah or belief, because they dealt with the Law, the promise of the land, and its fulfillment. The later books . . . never acquired the same central significance. They are not so much revelation as a commentary upon it dominated by the theme of the promise fulfilled. It is the land that matters most."

The Johnson book appeared at just about the same time Zvi came to me in New York with his story of the possible discovery of Joshua's altar. The ancient historic ruin at Ebal, if verified, would be the greatest such find in biblical history, and the most significant. It would be, to date, the *only* religious relic of an Israelite site from the time of Joshua ever discovered.

The Western world has long been fascinated with the question of the Bible's origins and historical roots. It became increasingly evident with the discovery of the Dead Sea scrolls and other artifacts that many incidents recounted in the Bible were based on actual events, dating back to the Flood and the evidence of it discovered on the Euphrates as described in the classic *Ur of the Chaldees*, by C. Leonard Woolley—and the possible mention of Abraham and the Hebrews, and even the biblical cities of Sodom and Gomorrah, whose existence had been doubted by many scholars, in the cuneiform library discovered in recent years at Ebla in Syria. There is also the inscription on the Merneptah stela, an inscription dated about 1220 B.C., in which Merneptah, the son of Rameses II, mentions for the first time in Egyptian literature the people known as "Israel," whom this pharoah says he defeated in battle. This indicates that the people or nation of Israel was already well established by this time.

Naturally, there are a great number of people who feel that the Bible is the revealed word of God and needs no historical interpretation. But to those who are interested in the factual basis of the earliest biblical traditions, most of the events described in the Bible remain mysteries to this day as far as archaeological confirmation is concerned, especially events that took place before the time of David—about 1000 B.C.—250 years or so after Joshua's era. It is believed that many of the biblical traditions were probably based on real events and were transmitted orally from generation to generation, possibly using the mnemonic device of songs, and not written down until centuries after they had presumabaly occurred. Many archaeologists think anything before the time of David is a fable, with no basis in fact. Other scholars feel the stories in the Bible, although not necessarily completely historical, are based on actual events.

To get a perspective on how legends like Bible stories can form around an actual person, think of King Arthur and Camelot—historians are still trying to separate history from legend in that ancient saga. Or think of our own American heritage. In a country only a bit over two hundred years old we have the accretion of legends around George Washington that have him throwing a dollar across the Rappahannock River long before the dollar was invented, and chopping down his father's cherry tree as reported by the unreliable Parson Weems. Did the events at the Round Table described by Malory really take place? Or were stories like these evolved to dramatize the heroic character of people like Washington and King Arthur, and to symbolize their virtues? If there can be such confusion between fact and legend in a mere two hundred years, as in Washington's case, what can we expect from historic traditions going back more than three thousand years? There *was* a Washington, and he *was* an enormously important American leader, but we cannot accept every story told about him as literally true, nor those about Daniel Boone, Davy Crockett, and other such legendary figures in America's early history. So in examining the extraordinary legend of Joshua and matching it to the actual archaeological evidence, we must move with caution and some understanding of how historic events can be transmuted over the course of years or millennia.

Still, as Wendy Doniger O'Flaherty points out in her book *Other People's Myths* (Macmillan, 1988), the persistence of the biblical myth over about three millennia is remarkable. Despite the many translations as the story moved from land to land, there were always apparently great numbers of people who knew the entire Bible, or sizable chunks of it by heart. In the time of Joshua and afterward many passages were told in song, probably so that they could better be remembered in the absence of written records. These songs were later integrated with the prose text in the Bible, so the same story is often repeated several times, sometimes with puzzling variations.

For those who need a refresher course on the story of Joshua, this is what is told in the Bible, augmented by what little factual information exists:

Near the beginning of the thirteenth century B.C., the people of Israel, who had been kept in slavery in the eastern Nile Delta by an Egyptian ruler believed to have been Pharoah Rameses II (1292–1225 B.C.), revolted under the leadership of Moses and demanded freedom. To persuade the Pharoah to free his people, Moses had the Lord send down nine plagues to ravage the Egyptians. The Pharoah remained adamant until the last plague—the slaying of the firstborn. The Hebrew people were able to ward off this disaster by marking their doorposts with the blood of a lamb. The angel of death, flying over Egypt, saw this sign and "passed over" these homes, sparing the Hebrews. (This is the origin of Passover, the oldest Jewish holiday, which was being celebrated by Christ at the Last Supper.)

The Pharoah reluctantly gave the Hebrews their liberty. The Bible says they left the city of Rameses in the Nile Delta (Goshen, biblically) to seek freedom in Canaan, the land that had been promised to Abraham as the homeland of Israel. Moses' chief assistant was Joshua, then a young man. The Israelites—some 600,000 of them, the Tanakh Bible says, or perhaps 600 families, according to certain scholars—fled, guided by a pillar of cloud by day and a pillar of fire by night. They escaped across the dry bed of a place first called the Red Sea, now identified as the Sea of Reeds, whose location is not presently known. Under instruction from Yahweh, Moses miraculously parted the waters to let the Hebrews cross on dry land, leaving the pursuing armies of the Pharaoh in their chariots to founder and drown behind them.

Probably joining the Israelites in their flight were people belonging apparently to related tribes in the surrounding countryside, who had not been in Egypt but had been living in parts of Canaan.

After escaping from the Egyptians the tribes of the Exodus wandered for three months. At one point the Israelites were camped at Rephidim, where Yahweh, through Moses, performed the miracles of providing food in the form of manna and water from a rock. Here the Israelites were attacked for the first time by a group that became a long-standing enemy—the Amalekites—and here Joshua is mentioned for the first time as the leader of Israel's army. At Rephidim Joshua had his first victory over the Amalekites.

At the end of three months, the Israelites were encamped in the wilderness of Sinai at the foot of a mountain called variably Mount Sinai or Mount Horeb, where the Lord communicated his wishes and commands for the people of Israel. He ultimately ordered Moses to ascend the mountain to receive the Ten Commandments, inscribed on two tablets of stone, and other instructions. One of these concerned the construction of an altar: " 'Make for me an altar of earth and sacrifice upon it your burnt offerings and your sacrifices of well-being, your sheep and your oxen; in every place where I cause my name to be mentioned I will come to you and bless you. And if you make for me an altar of stones, do not build it of hewn stones; for by wielding your tool upon them you have profaned them. Do not ascend my altar by steps, that your nakedness may not be exposed on it.' " [Exodus 20:24–26]

IV

Spying Out the Land

After forty days Moses descended from the mountain with the tablets, and they were eventually placed in the Tabernacle in the Ark of the Covenant, which was a wooden chest topped with gold, about as big as a steamer trunk. It was carried on long poles thrust through rings of gold that were attached to it, so the presence of the Lord could be with the Israelites and go before them at all times in their travels.

But Moses was gone so long on the mountain that the Israelites had grown restless. They asked Aaron to make them a god to worship—an idol of gold—and Aaron agreed, saying to them: " 'Take off the gold rings that are on the ears of your wives, your sons and your daughters.' . . . This he took from them and cast in a mold and made it into a molten calf." [Exodus 32:2–4] As Moses approached the camp, Joshua, who had escorted Moses to the mountain and had met him when he descended from the forty-day meeting with the Lord, warned him, " 'There is a cry of war in the camp!' " [Exodus 32:17] Moses saw that it was the sound of the reveling calf-worshipers and was so angry that he smashed the tablets of the Lord at the foot of the mountain. Joshua was the only Israelite other than Moses who had not defected to the calf-worshipers.

Moses and Yahweh were both furious over this backsliding, and Yahweh announced that he would destroy the entire nation of Israel in his anger; but Moses persuaded him to be merciful, and Yahweh acceded, to a certain extent. He did not exterminate them all, but

39

sent a plague to punish Israel for worshiping the golden calf. Moses again ascended the mountain and personally carved two stone tablets, which the Lord again inscribed with his commandments and which Moses again presented to the Israelites. When they had completed the Tabernacle and the Ark to house the new tablets, the people of Israel continued their journey to Canaan, carrying the Ark with them.

Finally, when the tribes had based themselves in the area of Kadesh-barnea for many years, long enough for a new generation to mature, the Lord deemed that it was time to prepare for the conquest of Canaan and he told Moses to send one chieftain from each tribe to "spy out the land." Joshua and Caleb were among the twelve designated spies. When they returned after forty days in the field, all of the spies except Joshua and Caleb decided the chances were very small for conquering Canaan. The Lord, angry over this report, struck each of the other ten chieftains dead on the spot, and had Moses designate Joshua as military leader of the united tribes. Ultimately Joshua, after proving himself in battle against the Amalekites, came to the plains of Moab on the east bank of the Jordan River after forty years of wandering. (The word *Jordan*, incidentally, means "the descender" and refers to the relatively precipitous drop of the river from snow-capped Mount Hermon, where it originates at over 9,000 feet, to the Dead Sea, which is 1,293 feet below sea level, in a distance of only 200 miles.)

This Jordan plain was to be the staging area for the conquest of Canaan. According to the Bible, neither Moses nor any of the adult generation that had left Egypt forty years earlier was allowed by God to enter the Promised Land, only those who had been born during the journey, with the exceptions of Joshua and Caleb, who forty years earlier had spied out the land of Canaan for Moses and reported favorably on plans for occupying it.

Moses had been told by the Lord that he would die on the east bank of the Jordan, and would never actually set foot in the Promised Land. The aging Hebrew leader climbed Mount Nebo, as the Lord had instructed him, from which point he could see all of the land the Lord promised Israel, from: "Gilead as far as Dan, all Naphtali; the land of Ephraim and Manasseh; the whole land of Judah as far as the Western Sea; the Negeb; and the Plain—the valley of Jericho, sometimes called the city of palm trees—as far as Zoar. And the Lord said to him, 'This is the land of which I swore to Abraham, Isaac and Jacob, "I will assign it to your offspring." I have let you see it with your eyes, but you shall not cross there.' " [Deuteronomy 34:1–4]

So, as the Lord had promised, Moses died on Mount Nebo at the age of 120 and was buried in an unknown spot, and Joshua took over the leadership of Israel.

Things moved quickly then. After Moses' death the Lord spoke directly to Joshua: " 'My servant Moses is dead. Prepare to cross the Jordan with all this people into the land that I am giving to the Israelites. Every spot on which your foot treads I give to you as I promised Moses. Your territory shall extend from the wilderness and the Lebanon to the Great River, the River Euphrates [on the east]— the whole Hittite country—and up to the Mediterranean Sea on the west.' " [Joshua 1:2–5]

Joshua led the Israelites at first to Shittim in the plain of Moab on the east bank of the Jordan, where they were to ready themselves for the invasion of Canaan. At Shittim (which can be translated as the "land of the acacia trees") Joshua was told by the Lord to recruit an army from among the able-bodied men of Israel over twenty who had been born since the Exodus from Egypt, and within three days' time, leaving behind their women and flocks, to set up camp with this army at Gilgal, east of Jericho, and from that point to attack Jericho. Joshua first sent two spies to determine the defenses of Jericho. According to the Bible, they were aided by a harlot, Rahab, who wanted to be converted to the religion of Israel. To be fair, some biblical scholars say that the word *zonah*, which is used to describe Rahab's occupation, could also mean "innkeeper." Perhaps she was both. In any event, the information the spies obtained proved extremely valuable. Later Rahab did convert the Judaism, and is credited as being the ancestress of eight prophets, including Jeremiah. Some rabbinical sources say that she even became the wife of Joshua after she was converted, but the Bible does not confirm this. [Megillah Talmud tractate 14b] Actually, there is no record of Joshua's ever marrying, nor of his having children.

After receiving the spies' report, Joshua marched to the Jordan, and the Lord, as though to confirm Joshua's succession to Moses, parted the river's waters so that Joshua's army could cross on the dry stones of the riverbed, as they had crossed the dry bed of the Sea of Reeds earlier, carrying the Ark of the Covenant before them.

(The custom of carrying a portable shrine with holy relics in it was practiced by the Egyptians also. On his military campaigns Pharaoh Thutmoses III [1479 B.C.–1425 B.C.] traveled with a portable shrine that contained an image of the god Amon, "he who is hidden." As with the case of the Hebrews, only the highest priests and Thutmose himself were allowed to approach the shrine. The last two syllables of this pharaoh's name are thought by linguists to be from the same root as Moses' name.)

When the Israelites had crossed over, Joshua had all of the men of his army circumcised (with flint knives) since they had not been circumcised during their forty-year trek to Canaan. They waited and recovered at Gilgal, where they also celebrated the Passover. It is probable that the circumcision immediately before the campaign was intended to emphasize that the land was theirs only by virtue of their covenant with Yahweh, of which circumcision was the outward symbol. At the museum at Ein Shemer, Adam Zertal's kibbutz, there is a circumcised penis in pottery dating to the early Settlement Period, which Zertal found during his survey. The exact date at which the custom of circumcision commenced is a subject scientists have debated for years. Most consider circumcision a relatively recent innovation, but the pottery penis is a provocative clue to its earlier observance.

When the soldiers of Israel had recuperated, according to the Bible, they launched the attack on besieged Jericho, marching around its walls and blowing trumpets for seven days, as the Lord had instructed Joshua, and on the seventh day, with the blowing of the horns and the shouting of the army, the walls of Jericho collapsed. The Israelites then burned the city to the ground.

Now it must be remembered that Canaan was never actually a nation in any sense of the word. The area was populated with clans and tribes often at war with each other. Here and there stood small walled cities, each with its overlord or king, who ruled a tribe or a group of tribes spread out over the surrounding area. Subtribes of the Canaanites were called by many names that have come down to us in the Bible—the Amalekites, the Ammonites, the Horites, the Hivites, the Hittites, the Jebusites, and so on.

Surrounding the fortified towns were settled, cultivated areas, reaching away into open grazing lands and dense forests in the hills, used according to custom by one tribe or another and subject to raids by other tribes that had no fixed areas of their own.

Following their victory at Jericho, the Bible says, Joshua's troops attacked the fortified city of Ai, which they took on a second assault after having failed in their first attempt because they had not all followed the instructions of Yahweh. When he had defeated Ai in a clever military ambush, Joshua and his troops killed all of the people in it and put the city to the torch.

Immediately after this battle, says the Bible, Joshua built the Lord's altar on Ebal and conducted the ceremonies of the blessing and the curse. Later, in that same area, Joshua swore the people to a covenant with Yahweh under a tree on a mountain overlooking Shechem, Ebal, and Gerizim. This, many scholars believe, was the true beginning of the nation of Israel. ". . . the peoplehood of Israel took form only as the Israelites came to power in the land of Canaan," says Norman K. Gottwald in *A History of Israel.*

Following the ceremony on Ebal (no altar in Gerizim is mentioned in the Torah), Joshua, according to the Bible, proceeded to lead the united federation of the tribes of Israel in the bloody military conquest of Canaan, including Samaria and Judea to the south, until his death at the age of 110.

This is the basic background, as told in the Bible, for the archaeological find by Zertal at Mount Ebal.

After poring over the biblical history of Joshua's altar and the archaeological clues that might support its existence, I decided that Zertal's discovery was too important to be ignored. By now Zvi Koenigsberg was back in Israel. I phoned him and told him that I was coming as soon as I could make arrangements, and called El Al Israel airlines to book a flight. Unfortunately, it was their busiest season—Passover week—so it was not until May 1988 that I was able to take off.

V

"The Uncrowned Queen of Palestine"

Zvi had explained to me that one of the complications of the dig was that it was located in Samaria, near Nablus, the largest West Bank Arab city in the territory captured from Jordan by Israel in the 1967 war. In New York everybody acted as though I were headed for the front lines of World War II. The newspapers, almost every day, carried news of what had become known as the Intifada—the organized violent protest against Israeli settlement in Samaria conducted by Arabs living in territories formerly administered by Egypt and Jordan that were now under Israeli control.

Basically the violence consisted of Arab protesters throwing rocks and firebombs or setting up barricades of stones or burning tires to keep Israelis, who had been settling in the area, from traveling on the roads. Israeli troops were sent in to control the demonstrations, and each week at least a half dozen people were hurt or killed. In terms of danger to a visitor from the outside this seemed to me less than a full-fledged war. (However, it later developed that a friend of mine, journalist and author Sidney Zion, was in a car that was heavily stoned en route to one of the West Bank villages.) Anyway, I felt it was essential that I make the trip. I was aware that the publication of the story of an archaeological find tending to support Israel's historic claims to Samaria might touch off further violence from local Arabs, but the story was ultimately going to come out no matter who wrote it.

During my visit to Israel, and up to this writing, there has been an intense dispute over the settlement of Israelis in Samaria, where Mount Ebal is located.

The first area on the West Bank to be settled after the 1967 War was Gush Etzion, in Judea south of Samaria, between Bethlehem and Hebron. The area contained, until about two months before the establishment of the State of Israel in 1948, and the War of Independence that followed, four Jewish settlements. After the women and children were evacuated from these villages during that war, the men remaining in them fought bravely, but were greatly outnumbered and finally conquered by the Jordanian Legion with its British officers, who allowed local Arab villagers to massacre many of the helpless Jews. In 1968, the orphan sons of some of these people who were killed set up a number of settlements in the same places their parents had settled, with the same place names. Though the Labor party which has opposed Israeli settlement in Samaria and Judea, was ruling at the time, there was almost no opposition from Israel's government to these settlements. One of those who settled there then is Hanan Porat, today a member of the Knesset in the National Religious Party, who later became one of the founders of Gush Emunim, a political group formed specifically to encourage settlement in Samaria.

The next stage was the attempt to settle Hebron, also in Judea. On Passover, 1968, a group of Jews rented rooms in the Arab Palace Hotel in Hebron and refused to leave the city. They were allowed to stay, eventually, within the confines of the military center of Hebron. They lived there for close to a year, until the first homes of Kiryat Arba, the new town, were built by the government (again Labor). Some of them eventually moved into the center of the city, where they reside to this day.

Despite its recent attitude of opposition to settlement on the West Bank, Labor always in the past supported settling in the Jordan Valley, according to a plan proposed by the late Yigal Allon, former foreign minister. They set up an entire string of moshavim and kibbutzim there through the early seventies.

But Samaria remained unsettled by Jews until after the Yom Kippur War in 1973, when the movement of Gush Emunim was established for the very purpose of promoting that settlement. The first three towns—Kedumim, Elon Moreh, and Ofra—were settled during the administration of the Labor government. Begin, with his Likud government, came into office in May 1977. Six months later, eleven towns were set up in Samaria in the span of one week in October, during the holiday of Succoth, one of them being Shavei Shomron, where Zvi Koenigsberg settled in 1981.

Today, there are approximately 150 Jewish towns, with a population of over 80,000, in the area much of the world sees as a future Palestinian state. There had been Jewish settlers in Samaria in growing numbers since the Balfour Declaration at the end of World War I; but in 1929 many fled before Arab rioters, who killed some 150 of them. Samaria was not entirely emptied of Jews even after the 1929 massacre. The last Jewish families left Shechem in 1933.

There is no question that the presence of these new Israeli settlers grates on the sensibility of local Arabs, who fear that a population explosion among the settlers could make the Arabs a minority in these ancient lands, and that the historic biblical claim of the Israelites to the land will yield to temporal and actual Israeli government control of all of Samaria and Judea. The settlement has been augmented recently by an infusion of Russian Jews who have immigrated from the newly emancipated Soviet Union. The Arabs seem particularly disturbed by this development and have registered fierce objections.

But the principal Arab objection has been, and despite what Arafat said in Geneva, continues to be, the very existence of a Jewish state in what they consider a center of the Arab world. And the ultimate goal of Arafat and his supporters is still the elimination of Israel entirely from the lands of the Middle East. The matter is still in hot contention. Occupation of these West Bank territories was the chief issue in recent elections in Israel. Critics of Zertal's archaeological work have alleged that he was motivated by politics in his explorations, in which he was given some support by the community of Shavei Shomron, where his field headquarters is located. But my investigation shows the local community involvement to be minimal. Actually the principal support was the advice, work, and encouragement of Zvi Koenigsberg.

The fight over control of the occupied territories still goes on, but I hope that this book will clear up any ambiguities concerning the situation in regard to the Ebal dig in Samaria, or at least shed some light. Certainly it would be regrettable from the viewpoint of Western history to interrupt this research because of political pressures.

Yasir Arafat, speaking for his own faction in the Palestine Liberation Organization, has announced an independent Palestinian state in the territories under question, and has received unanimous United Nations support, except for Israel's own vote and that of the United States. Jordan has renounced its claims to control of the area. Substantive discussions are being talked of, but everything is still in the air. In view of the long history of this conflict, it is unlikely that anything will be resolved by the time this book is published.

Zvi had said not to worry about accommodations—that he would put me up while I was visiting Ebal. But it wasn't until I arrived at Ben Gurion Airport, where Zvi picked me up in his blue Ford Escort, that I quite realized that we were going to be staying in his village, Shavei Shomron, only a few miles from Nablus, an Arab city with a population of some 120,000 people, which has been a rallying point for anti-Israel demonstrations. It is, except for East Jerusalem, the largest city in the West Bank captured in the 1967 war.

Twain gave a description of the physical layout surrounding Shechem which is almost as valid today as it was when he wrote it, more than 120 years ago: "The narrow valley where Shechem is situated is under high cultivation, and the soil is exceedingly black and fertile. It is well-watered and its affluent vegetation gains effect by contrast with the barren hills that tower on either side. One of these hills is the ancient Mount of Blessings and the other is the Mount of Curses; and wise men who seek for fulfillments of prophecy think they find here a wonder of this kind, to wit—, that the Mount of Blessings is strangely fertile and its mate is strangely unproductive. We could not see that there really was much difference between them in that respect, however." Nor could I!

Ebal overlooks the city from the north, and Gerizim from the south. The city was built by Hadrian in A.D. 136, after he had successfully overcome the Jewish revolt led by Simon Bar Kochba, during the years 132 to 135. Hadrian was the Roman emperor who changed the name of Jerusalem to Aelia Capitolina, and Judea to Palestine. He wanted to eradicate the memory of Shechem, an an-

cient Jewish capital, as well, by building a new city nearby with a
different name.

The Romans called it Neapolis—"New City"—but through the
years this has become corrupted into Nablus, since the Arab alphabet had no letter *P*. (Arabs cannot, in fact, pronounce the word
Palestine.) On the outskirts of Nablus, one mile from the center, is
the ancient village of Shechem, which has an extremely important
part in early Bible history. Noted archaeologist G. Ernest Wright
called it "the uncrowned queen of Palestine." Shechem was the
most important city in the northern part of the central hill country
from a least the nineteenth century B.C. to the early Iron Age, around
1200 B.C. It was the first capital of ancient Israel under Jereboam I in
900 B.C., and it remained an important religious center even after
that time.

It was in this vicinity that Abraham was said to have built an altar,
after God had promised this land to his descendants at nearby Elon
Moreh. [Genesis 12:7] Here, too, for 100 silver shekels, Jacob, returning to his homeland after an exile of twenty-two years, bought
land from Shechem, the son of Hamor. (It was this prince for whom
the city was named.) Jacob pitched his tent there, and also built an
altar, which he called "El, God Of Israel." [Genesis 33:18–20]
Nearby, on the southern end of Tel Balata, the ruin of ancient
Shechem, in a small chapel is a hundred-foot-deep well said to have
been dug by Jacob, where Jesus is also said to have met the woman
of Samaria. [John 4:1–42] Jacob's name was later changed by God to
Israel.

Some time after settling near Shechem with his clan, Jacob was
upset by a scandalous incident. [Genesis 34:1–30] Dinah, the daughter of Jacob and Leah, had been out visiting among her women
friends when she was seized and raped by Prince Shechem. Following his assault on Dinah, Shechem apparently fell in love with the
Israelite maiden. He asked his father to suggest to Jacob that
Shechem take Dinah as his wife.

Jacob by now had heard of his daughter's rape, but since his sons
Simeon and Levi were still in the field, he waited for their return
before taking any action. Meanwhile, Shechem and Hamor had arrived in Jacob's camp to apologize. By this time Simeon and Levi
had returned from the fields. They were extremely angry at the

offense Shechem had committed against their sister. But Hamor approached Jacob and his sons and said: " 'My son Shechem longs for your daughter. Please give her to him in marriage. Intermarry with us: give your daughters to us, and take our daughters for yourselves. You will dwell among us and the land will be open before you; settle, move about, and acquire holdings in it.' Then Shechem said to her father and brothers, 'Do me this favor, and I will pay what you tell me, only give me the maiden for a wife.' " [Genesis 34:8–11]

Levi and Simeon conferred on how they would handle this decision and returned to the conference with a suggestion: They said to Shechem and Hamor, " 'We cannot do this thing, to give our sister to a man who is uncircumcised, for that is a disgrace among us. Only on this condition will we agree with you; that you will become like us in that every male among you is circumcised. Then will we give our daughters to you, and take your daughters to ourselves; and we will dwell among you and become as one kindred. But if you will not listen to us and become circumcised, we will take our daughter and go.' "

Their apparently friendly proposal seemed reasonable to Shechem and Hamor, and Shechem lost no time in doing what Simeon and Levi had sugested, because he desperately wanted Dinah. So Hamor and his son Shechem went to the public square of their town and spoke to their fellow townsmen saying: " 'These people are our friends; let them settle in the land, and move about in it, for the land is large enough for them; we will take their daughters to ourselves and give our daughters to them. But only on this condition will the men agree with us to dwell among us and be as one kindred: only on this condition: that all our males become circumcised as they are circumcised. Their cattle and substance and all their beasts will be ours, if only we will agree to their terms, so that they will settle among us.' All who went out of the gate of his town heeded Hamor and his son Shechem, and all those who went out of the gate of his town were circumcised."

To understand why the Shechemites made this offer, and accepted the Israelite terms and had themselves circumcised, it must be realized, as has now been confirmed from ancient Ugaritic texts, that the patriarchs such as Abraham, Isaac, and Jacob were not simple shepherds, although that word is sometimes used in translations of the Bible into English. They could more accurately be described by the Hebrew word *noqued*, which designates somebody in the sheep *business*, responsible for vast herds of sheep and with many employees in their charge, and also involved in cattle breeding and fruit farming. So Abraham almost surely was a man of wealth, substance, and authority, as well as the chief of his clan. He probably would also have been involved in selling wool or mutton throughout the areas near which his herds grazed. With this understanding, Hamor's offer makes more sense. Obviously such an offer would not be made to a mere nomadic herdsman. Hamor and Schechem's own description of Jacob's wealth in their appeal to their countrymen to accept this merger of families clearly indicates it.

On the third day after the circumcision, when Shechem's men were still in pain, recuperating from the primitive ceremonial operation, performed with flint knives, Simeon and Levi, armed with swords, entered the city without opposition and killed all of them. "They put Hamor and his son Shechem to the sword, took Dinah out of Shechem's house and went away. The other sons of Jacob came upon the slain and plundered the town, because their sister had been defiled. They seized their flocks, cattle, and herds and asses, all that was inside the town and outside. All their wealth, all their children and their wives, all that was in the houses, they took as captives and booty." [Genesis 34:26–29]

Jacob was dismayed by the actions of Simeon and Levi. He said to his sons, " 'You have brought trouble on me, making me odious among the inhabitants of the land, the Canaanites, and the Perizzites; my men are few in number, so that if they unite against us and attack me, I and my house will be destroyed.' But they answered: 'Should our sister be treated like a whore?' " [Genesis 34:30–31]

At this point God intervened and told Jacob: " 'Arise, go up to Bethel and remain there; and build an altar there to the God who appeared to you when you were fleeing from your brother Esau.' " [Genesis 35:1]

Many biblical experts believe that Hamor was a Horite rather than a Hivite, and that the matter got mixed up in the minds of biblical scribes. In any event, many scholars feel that the Hivites were descendants of the Horites, who were in control at that time, and the

Horites, not being a Semitic people, would not have been already circumcised. Circumcision was not practiced by the Canaanites, including the Horites or the Assyrians or Babylonians; but it *was* practiced by the other Semitic tribes of the area such as the Edomites, the Moabites, and the Ammonites, as well as by the Egyptians (who reserved the privilege to aristocracy and high priests), so the demand by Simeon and Levi is historically reasonable, although there is no direct evidence of exactly when the rite of circumcision was introduced. In any event, the actions of Simeon and Levi are considered to be personalized reminiscences of the tribes of that name and the Israelite military activities in displacing the Horites. This circumcision rite may tie in to the evident kinship felt later in the time of Joshua between the people of Shechem and Joshua's Israelites.

The city of Shechem had distinctions other than this ancient horror story. It was to Shechem that Joshua brought the bones of Joseph to be buried in the field purchased there by his father, Jacob. This was after completing the ceremony at the altar on Ebal and his victorious campaign in Canaan. The history of the city of Shechem was to play an important part in unraveling the mystery of Joshua's altar.

When I asked Zvi what he thought about the gory proceedings during Joshua's occupation of Canaan, he smiled mysteriously. "Maybe you'll change your opinion when we learn a little more about the history of the conquest."

VI

The Return to Samaria

A group of settlers moved into Judea and Samaria in 1967 immediately after the Six Day War, determined to reestablish the Jewish presence, but the new settlements on the West Bank have become a sore spot in the Arab consciousness. However, Zvi, an alert and sinewy man with the weathered look of a native Israeli, assured me that the Intifada posed no problem. At the same time, I noticed that he had an Uzi submachine gun with a clip in it lying on the floor near the gear shift. I looked at it with some interest.

He waved his hand deprecatingly. "It's just a precaution," he explained. "All of us carry them. The government issues the guns so we can protect ourselves, but they are legal and we must sign for them, and answer for the consequences if we use them illegally or even carelessly. We are not permitted to fire them unless we are in extreme personal danger. All of us are in the reserves, of course, so we know how to handle the weapons."

"Have you had to use it?" I asked.

Zvi shrugged. "I haven't used it, but my wife and I have each been shot once, by a sniper, on our way back from Netanya to Shavei Shomron. Leg wounds. Not too bad. But don't worry, it's very infrequent that anything like that happens."

I sat in silence, and watched the scenery. The villages were small and bucolic. The land was far from barren, with orchards of apricots, oranges, and other fruits, as well as fields of grain, and pastures where mixed herds of goats and sheep grazed peacefully. From time to time we had to swerve to avoid a herd being driven down the road by a shepherd and an occasional dog. Other than that, much of the traffic consisted of donkey carts and peasants riding donkeys to their homes. Every four or five miles we would pass an army patrol of five or six Israeli soldiers carrying both standard weapons and tear-gas launchers, as well as rifles adapted to rubber bullets.

There were five or six small roadblocks before we arrived at Shavei Shomron. They consisted of a row of rocks or iron spikes guarded by a contingent of a half-dozen or so members of the Israel Defense Force (army). Most of the soldiers were young, and from their GI-style haircuts, I judged them to be recent recruits. All Israelis put in three years of compulsory military service, starting at the age of eighteen, and then serve from one to two months in the reserve until they are fifty-five. In wartime, of course, all of the reserves may be mobilized (as Adam Zertal had been in 1973). In recent months reserve call-ups have been extended to as much as sixty-two days because of the Intifada. The presence of an occasional fortyish soldier in the patrols indicated that some of these troops were reserves, putting in their yearly active service.

I asked Zvi the meaning of the name of his settlement—Shavei Shomron.

"Shomron," he said, "means 'Samaria' in Hebrew. Many of the settlements are identified with a biblical or local name and the word *Shomron* after it. *Shavei* means 'the return to.' "

Basically Samaria (the territory, not the city for which it is named) and Judea, the 3,200-square-mile area occupied after the 1967 War, are two D-shaped sectors, hilly and relatively bare of trees, which extend from the border of the thin strip of Israel along the Mediterranean—only nine miles wide in many places—to the Jordan. Samaria is roughly half the size of the state of Connecticut. Some people have described the shape of the two areas as being like a fat man's belly, cinched tightly at the waist, the buckle being Jerusalem. Of the two, Samaria is far larger, about twice the size of Judea. Both areas were settled at least five thousand years ago and fought over by Egyptians, Horites, Hivites, Hyksos, Hittites, the mysterious Sea People, and many other invaders in pre-Israelite times, as well as afterward. Samaria is the northern bulge, lying above Jerusalem and Judea. Between them, on a point of Israel's original land grant, is Jerusalem, whose western half, including the Temple Mount, had been controlled by the Arabs from the 1949 U.N. Truce until the 1967 War.

These divisions are not just present-day geographic conveniences. They have a long, bitter history in Jewish biblical tradition. In ancient times—around 1000 B.C.—there was a long conflict between the Israelite occupants of Israel (Samaria) and the people living in Judah (Judea) to the south, following the death of Solomon.

The victory over the Arabs in 1967 posed a difficult choice for the Israelis. They could hold the newly conquered territories against all opposition, viewing the conquest as a fulfillment of God's promise to Abraham, or they could remember the Exodus command: "You shall not wrong a stranger or oppress him, for you were strangers in the land of Egypt." [Exodus 22:21]

"The Six Day War," writes a contemporary rabbi, O. Hadya (quoted in Tal, *The Land and the State*), "was an astounding divine miracle . . . the end of days has already come . . . it has entered the realm of sanctity."

But opposition comes from one of the great scholars of Jewish messianism, Gershon Sholem: "I absolutely deny that Zionism is a messianic movement. . . . The redemption of the Jewish people, which as a Zionist I desire. . . . If the dream of Zionism is numbers and borders, and if we can't live without them, then Zionism will fall. . . ."

Much of this I was to learn later while reading the Bible and other background material in conjunction with Zertal's find, trying to understand the significance and complications that Ebal and the Israelites living around it have inspired since some time before the Exodus.

At Tulkarm, near the Green Line—the border between Israel and the occupied territory—we had to pass through a cursory check at an army roadblock. We were waved on after a few questions. Arabs are questioned more thoroughly, and sometimes their vehicles are searched for weapons, nationalist propaganda, or the presence of known troublemakers.

"They can tell the settlers from the Arabs by the license plates. The Israelis have yellow plates and the Arabs have blue," Zvi explained. Most of the Arab cars, I noted, were Mercedes-Benzes.

After Tulkarm the beauty of Samaria opens out in all its stilled simplicity. The stillness was partly natural, and partly due to the Intifada. Some villages were on strike, all the stores closed. In others, army barriers closed off streets from access to the road to prevent stoning incidents.

The route leads through rolling, sparsely populated countryside, gray stones scattered on the faces and summits of the hills. The low density of the population surprised me, since the Arabs have protested that the Israeli immigration is crowding them out of their lands.

The road is paved, lined with many olive and citrus groves, as well as lush orchards. The stone buildings of the Arab villages blend harmoniously into the landscape. Where it is not cultivated, the land beside the narrow highway is lined with wild flowers and the ubiquitous thistles that are a feature of the area.

About a mile down the road we came to an Arab refugee camp called Nurshams, which was flanked by a chain-link fence twenty feet high and three quarters of a mile long. At the base of the fence were coils of razor wire.

"What's that?" I asked.

"This was a very tough place. You couldn't get by here for a while without seriously risking a stoning. So they put up the fence. The locals tore it down a few times, so the razor wire was added. Now it's quite safe." (Author's note: It turned out not so safe at all. Zvi later wrote me: "We were stoned at Nurshams, for the umpteenth time, just last week.")

As we passed Nurshams, Zvi said, almost to himself, "That's one bad spot down, now for the next."

Three miles down the road we passed an olive grove bordered by a light-brown hummock, immediately before a hairpin turn in the road. Zvi pointed: "That's the other bad spot. The place where we got shot, my wife, Ofra, and I. It happened on August first of 1983—even before the Intifada—about two hundred yards east of the town of Anabta back there. I had a Motorola portable transmitter in the van and reported the shooting almost instantaneously.

"My wife didn't even realize we were shot at until she heard me say so to the army command at Shechem. I knew we were shot at because I saw the backfire of the rifle, only three yards away. Only

then, after I reported, did we realize we had both been wounded in
the legs. After four hours, we passed by the same spot, returning
from the hospital in our town's ambulance. There were dozens of
security vehicles of all types parked alongside the road, and I realized that they were looking for evidence. I told the driver to stop,
and got out, sending my wife home with him. I located the senior
officer present, identified myself, and asked him what the problem
was. It seems they had been unable to locate the empty shells. I
suggested we re-create the scene. We got into his car, reentered
Anabta, turned around, and started driving east. Not five feet from
where I shouted to the driver to stop, five empty shells were lying
just south of the asphalt road, along with watermelon rinds. It seems
a civilian bus carrying army equipment, and accompanied by a soldier, had been shot at fifteen minutes after we were shot, from the
same place. The soldier mistakenly believed that the shooting took
place about a kilometer away, and the military preferred his version
to the one I gave them on the Motorola, which cost a very dear four
hours. Ironically, units were in Anabta only seven minutes after I
was shot, so had they reacted to my report, they would have caught
the bastards red-handed when they shot at the bus.

"Needless to say, I was furious at their disregard of the report I
made, and expressed that anger by overturning the table of the staff
officer of the military command in Shechem, the next day. Their
disregard of my report cost the life of an Arab taxi driver who had
been an Israeli sympathizer, one year later. The gunmen were ap-
prehended by Israeli security forces only two years later, after some
very daring intelligence work. Their rifle was an old pre–World War
I English Enfield 7.9 1898 model, of a sort that may have been kept
hidden in some local village since that time, or at least the time of
the English campaign against the Turks in World War I. Generally
speaking—so far—the Arabs have not apparently had access to guns.
The roadblocks, of course, are a hindrance to smuggling them in."

We arrived after a half-hour drive at Zvi's village, marked by a
ramshackle overhead sign reading SHALOM in English and in Hebrew
characters. We were waved in by a sleepy-eyed settler-sentry.

In the village Zvi explained that I would be staying in a hostel run
by the settlement for visitors and for groups such as Adam's survey
team, which frequently had used it as a field headquarters. The cost,

he said apologetically, would be six dollars a day. I would eat at his house. There are no restaurants in Shavei Shomron, and only one small convenience store.

The prefab cabin assigned to me was spacious—a bedroom, a dining room/kitchen, and a bathroom with toilet and shower—but sparsely furnished. The beds were narrow as army cots and consisted of a plywood board on legs, topped by a slab of foam rubber about three inches thick and twenty-nine inches wide. All of the furniture had been made at a small woodworking factory in the village. The cabin had been the temporary residence of the first settlers in 1978. I was startled by the rattle of small-arms fire at about 2:00 A.M. and wondered if there was a skirmish going on in the background. Finally, somewhat suddenly, the shooting stopped, and I fell back into a troubled sleep, trusting that somehow my hosts had solved whatever problems existed out in the darkened hills.

The next day Zvi explained to me that there was an army training camp on the hill behind the settlement, and that what I had heard was simply a night skirmishing exercise. Despite the violence of the Intifada, none of the settlements had actually been attacked, probably because each village was virtually an armed camp.

Zvi's home, about a quarter of a mile away from the hostel, was, like most in the village, a spacious four-bedroom villa. It had two stories and a veranda with open space beneath for parking and storage, and a sizable garden planted with flowers and fruit trees. Zvi plans someday to enclose the area under the house as a work space.

"No Arab land has been condemned for these settlements, or confiscated from the owners," Zvi explained. "They are either on government lands, or lands purchased from the government. Or else they are on land bought from the Arabs themselves, many of them absentee landowners, in the same way that the early settlers backed by Baron Edouard de Rothschild had done a hundred or so years earlier. No Arab has been moved out of his house or off his land. Many of the properties were bought long ago from the absentee Arab owners, who frequently didn't even know they held the deeds. Most lived in Syria, Iraq, or other Arab countries, and the deeds go back to the Ottoman Empire and even earlier. Jordan has passed a law that makes it a death-penalty offense to sell land to a Jew. So, you see, the issue isn't simply Palestinian nationalism versus Israeli, but Jew versus Muslim, I'm afraid."

This was Zvi's explanation of the settlers' viewpoint.

"Our responsibility to our grandchildren should also be examined from the security aspect. From most of these Samaritan hills you can see almost all of Israel as if it were spread out on the palm of your hand. Small Arab groups armed with relatively cheap and easily obtainable weapons can strike just about anywhere. A man must ask himself how can we be sure that some extremists will not threaten Tel Aviv from these hills?"

The settlement itself consisted of about eighty families, most living in villas similar to Zvi's, a few living in the old prefab huts like my own hostel. These were the newcomers, who had not had the time or money to build houses yet. Each family had about four children. The adult settlers averaged over thirty in age. There were no old people, and, seemingly, few teenagers. Because there was no high school in the village, many of the youngsters had to stay in Netanya, the nearest large city, about twenty-two miles away, during the week. Netanya was built on the sand dunes of the Sharon Valley in 1928, and now has a population of about 150,000. Until the marshes surrounding it were drained by Jewish settlers in the early thirties, the original settlement could be reached only on horseback or by foot from the railroad station at Tulkarm. Other students from Shavei Shomron attended high schools as far away as Jerusalem.

Two of Zvi's three sons lived with him in Shavei Shomron, but the middle son, who was just past thirteen, would be joining his older brother in Netanya the following term, so both would be home only on alternate weekends.

The little settlement has a peaceful small-town atmosphere. People passing on the streets greet one another with a cheerful "Shalom," and stop to chat or gossip, though they treat strangers like me with some reserve. There was little traffic in Shavei Shomron, mainly because there were practically no cars except those of the occupants and an occasional maintenance person. The town was surrounded by a barbed-wire fence, and on a hill just above it was the army training camp. Inside, the settlement was as placid and domestic as a Swiss hamlet. The only sign of tension I noticed was the occasional pistol, in a side holster or tucked informally into a settler's belt.

As we drove up to Zvi's house I could see dozens of children playing and running in the spacious athletic fields and playgrounds. There was a large swimming pool, scheduled to be filled in a few days—it was still too cold, in May, for swimming. There was a tennis court without a net and a number of basketball courts both regulation and with backboards lowered for the smaller children. Basketball is a most avidly followed sport in Israel. Each basketball team represents one of the many political parties that make up Israel's complicated political picture. Most of the teams have at least one imported American pro playing for them.

These are not the same sort of settlements as the original kibbutzim, which were involved with farming and restoring the land. Some of the new settlements have farms and some have greenhouses, but most of the settlers work either in small local industries, such as factories for electronic components, or in nearby cities like Netanya. Some even work in Jerusalem or Tel Aviv and sometimes spend three hours a day commuting. As far as I could see, all the settlements are built on hilltops, and have stunning views of the ancient and historic mountains around them. In general, they are at a discreet distance from neighboring Arab communities.

Zvi's village is composed mainly of Orthodox Jews belonging to Gush Emunim, a political group composed of Orthodox and non-Orthodox Jews formed for the purpose of settling Samaria and Judea. In Shavei Shomron, most of the Orthodox men wear a knitted *kipa*, or skullcap, bobby-pinned somewhat rakishly to their heads, but not all the people in Shavei Shomron are Orthodox, and other settlements are mixed, or even prefer only nonreligious people. In the West Bank in general, only about one third of the settlers are Orthodox.

"Tomorrow, as a kind of orientation," Zvi said to me over a cup of tea in his living room, "I'd like to go over some of the religious background of Joshua and the altar on Ebal with you in the village library. Then, in a day or so, we'll meet Adam and go out into the field. He's teaching in Haifa University at the moment, but he'll see us as soon as possible. You won't be missing anything, since the digging season at Ebal is over now."

I was anxious to get into the field and to see the altar site, but, as I came to understand, in Israel there are wheels within wheels.

VII

The Ground Which
Jacob Had Bought

While waiting for a meeting with Zertal, who, much to my frustration, now had accepted an assignment guiding an archaeological tour in Turkey to raise further funds for his project, Zvi suggested that we explore the surrounding area, which is rich in ancient remains from the dawn of history through the Crusades and later.

"There are some things you should see in order to understand what we are dealing with here."

We drove east from Shavei Shomron, along a quiet paved road lined with wild flowers, brambles, and thistles, on which the local flocks of sheep and goats grazed peacefully. About a mile northeast of the town of Nablus we came to Tel Balata, which is actually ancient Shechem. To our left was a modest whitewashed domed building guarded by an ancient mulberry tree and a young Israeli sentinel. Zvi took his attaché case and placed his ubiquitous Uzi in it.

"We never leave the gun in the car," he explained.

At the gate to the building, which had been restored late in the nineteenth century, Zvi greeted the friendly guard and showed him the contents of the case. The guard looked at the weapon in it without interest and waved us into the building. A white-and-blue sign outside proclaimed that it was the tomb of Joseph.

Inside the cool, softly lit room was a large sarcophagus draped in blue velvet with a gold fringe. Beside it stood an old Arab guide in a kaffiyah. Zvi gave him a coin and said something in Arabic that indicated that he would handle the guiding honors himself.

"Do you suppose," I asked, pointing to the sarcophagus, "that there is anything actually *in* that box?"

Zvi shrugged. "Nobody will ever know. If it is Joseph's tomb, and he's in there, he might be in pretty good shape, because the Bible says that they embalmed him when he died. But nobody would dare to open it. It is too sacred. It would cause a storm in all of the Western religions."

"Do *you* think Joseph is buried here?"

"There's a chance of it," Zvi said. "Scientifically, it would be foolish to assume that. But the geographic vicinity is certainly legitimate. There are several verses in the Bible relating to the burial of Joseph. The first comes at the end of the book of Genesis. Joseph dies then and is embalmed and placed in a tomb in Egypt, but before he dies, he makes the sons of Israel swear 'When God has taken notice of you, you shall carry my bones from here.' [Genesis 50:25] When the Pharoah let the people of Israel go out of Egypt, it says in Exodus 13:19 that Moses took Joseph's bones with him. The book of Joshua ends with the burial of Joseph in Shechem. 'The bones of Joseph, which the sons of Israel had brought from Egypt, were buried at Shechem in the piece of ground which Jacob had bought from Shechem, the son of Hamor, for a hundred *kesitahs* from the children of Hamor, Shechem's father, and which had become the heritage of the Josephites.' " [Joshua 24:32] (A *kesitah* is a piece of currency of indeterminate value. The *Peshitta* describes this as "100 ewes," a fairly logical medium of exchange for the herdsman Jacob. In actuality, of course, coins were not to be invented until the Persian period, about 500 B.C.)

This purchase, Zvi explained, was made just after Jacob's arrival in the area. It took place before Simeon and Levi destroyed Shechem in the dispute over Dinah's rape, when the pastoral Israelites were still on friendly terms with the city-dwelling Canaanites.

"Rashi, probably the most respected biblical scholar, in the twelfth century says Jacob came here whole in mind and body after wrestling with the angel of God when his name was changed to Israel. [Israel means literally "the man who struggled with God."]

But if Rashi had been a geographer, he would have gone down the road here, about a mile, and seen a little village called Salem, which is the Arabic for Shalem. This is the town for which so many villages in the United States and England are named, including the one which was the site of the notorious witch-hunts in Massachusetts. Rashi would have inspected the remains in Salem at the time of Middle Bronze II, which is the period of the patriarchs, and he would have known that what the Bible was saying was very simple. Jacob came to Salem, which was in the city of Shechem. And now it says, in a place 'facing' the city Jacob bought his land. The word 'facing' has another meaning in the Bible as well. It has a directional meaning: 'east of.' Where did Jacob buy the ground? East of the city of Shechem.

"We are now thirty yards away from the eastern gate of the ancient city of Shechem. So if there *was* a Jacob, and if there *was* a Joseph, it certainly makes sense that the grave site of this Joseph is somewhere in this vicinity. Now what about the very place that we are in now? This same place has been considered the grave site of Joseph by the Samaritans, who have been a continuous presence here for the past twenty-seven hundred years. So as long ago as that, it's been considered his grave site, and one of the first Christian pilgrims from Bordeaux, in France, wrote a chronicle of his pilgrimage to the Holy Land in the years 333 to 334 describing this site exactly where it is.

"Now, one very important thing. There's a Breita (which is, according to tradition, one of the sacred texts available to the compiler of the oral history of Judaism), by Judah the Prince, which he did not deem important enough to include in the Mishnah, one of the texts on the oral law written in A.D. 200, where it is written that, if the Gentiles come and say, 'This isn't your land, we've been living here before you,' and so forth, you should know that there are three places that you actually purchased for good money.

"One is the site at Hebron, where the burial places of Abraham and his wife, Sarah, were bought [the Cave of Machpelah]. The second site was Mount Moriah, where David, despite the fact that he had conquered the Jebusites, took the trouble to buy the land to prove ownership, which became the site of the temple, and the third site, of course, was the land Jacob bought, where we are standing right now. It is also of interest that when Jacob was dying he said to Joseph: 'I am about to die; but God will be with you and will bring you back to the land of your fathers.' That's in Genesis 48:21. Now he says: 'I assign to you one portion more than to your brothers.' But there is a possible pun here, because in Hebrew the word translated as 'portion' is *shechem*, which also can mean 'mountain slope.'

"All three sites are considered by the Arabs today to be a vital part of the future Palestinian state," Zvi added.

We left the tomb of Joseph, and from our right there came the subdued murmur of group classroom recitation.

"Come look," Zvi said. We walked around the corner of the tomb building and were faced with an annex with high, wide windows, behind which were a group of about twenty rabbinical scholars in sidelocks, yarmulkes, white shirts, and fringed vests reading Hebrew texts aloud, swaying rhythmically in the time-honored traditional fashion to the internal rhythms of their recital.

"They have a Rabbinical Academy here for some of the very devout Orthodox Jews. There is also a small army detachment stationed here, in case of any anti-Jewish activity. After all, this city is the center of West Bank Arab nationalism. This site is holy to the Muslims as well as the Jews and Christians, so it had been thought that there would not be any incidents here. But in fact there have been a number of attacks by Arabs, including the use of firebombs."

When we left the tomb, Zvi opened his attaché case and took out the Uzi, then returned the case to the car. "It's been a little tense around here, so it's a good precaution to take this," he said, "though it's doubtful anything will happen." We crossed the road and followed a narrow, overgrown path down to a large open area.

"Now this," Zvi said, gesturing to the field before us, which contained a large group of partially excavated ruins, "is Tel Balata— ancient Shechem, predating the Israelite occupation of Canaan by at least two thousand years.

"Ernest Sellin, a German, conducted the dig here for two short seasons during World War One. The dig was continued after the war by the British, who now had the mandate for Palestine, between 1926 and 1928. In 1934 the dig continued again. It has been established that this site goes back to the Chalcolithic period, around 4000 B.C. There is no evidence that life in Shechem was interrupted between the thirteenth and twelfth centuries B.C., when the Israelites arrived, nor is there any sign of destruction after their arrival. The city was not conquered at that time. We know that a people called the *habiru* were established there at the time of Labaya, one of its kings in early biblical days, probably in the fourteenth century B.C. Labaya was ultimately killed in the reign of the monotheist Pharaoh Akhenaten.

"There are some who think the *habiru*, who are mentioned in a number of Egyptian documents such as the famous El Amarna letters, are actually the Hebrews, but this is by no means established. It is possible that the word *habiru* described a certain group in terms of their actions, and meant something like 'raider' or 'mercenary,' so a tribe could be described as *habiru* and not necessarily be Israelite. [The El Amarna letters are a valuable Egyptian archive of cuneiform tablets dating from 1379 to 1362 B.C., which is the most important source of written information on early Israel. The letters were inscribed during the reign of Akhenaten.] There is confirmation of the relationship of Labaya to the *habiru* in the El Amarna letters, where it says: 'Shall we do like Labaya who gave the land of Shechem to the *habiru?*' In another segment of El Amarna it is alleged that the king of Shechem is not only working with the *habiru*, but that a son of his has joined them. Could this have reference to the story of Jacob, Simeon, and Levi? Nobody knows, but the timing is about right."

Zvi continued his exposition, which was so detailed and erudite, I learned, because he had been giving lectures at various historic sites to students of Israel's archaeological field schools for several years. He has been reading everything on the subject of the early history of Israel avidly for over two decades. "This is the first place where the nation of Israel is defined as consisting of the twelve tribes," he continued.

"There is no mention in the Bible of the capture of Shechem by the Israelites under Joshua. Possibly some Hebrews were there already, never having left for Egypt, and kept a religion with a Yahwistic concept. Deuteronomy says that the Israelites were to break the pillars of the nonbelievers. Yet the pillars in Shechem were allowed to remain. They're still right here. You can see some lying over there to our left, and one *maseba* right in front of us, only partly broken, and probably at a later date." He pointed to a monumental slab a bit farther down the path in front of the ruin. It was in the shape of a broken molar.

"The Israelites probably were not anxious to antagonize the local people, with whom they seemed to have a friendly and probably mutually dependent relationship. It is likely that at least some of the natives were themselves related to the newly arrived Israelites, but since they had not immigrated to Egypt, they had not adopted the monotheism introduced by Moses. Joseph, in Genesis, tells Pharaoh, 'I was stolen out of the land of the Hebrews,' indicating that the Shechem area and Israel were regarded as home by Israelites before Moses and Joshua, dating back to the time of the Lord's promise to Abraham at Elon Moreh."

As we left Tel Balata we passed a Palestinian refugee camp also named Balata. This was the town, I knew, that in 1987 had launched one of the first of the disturbances that was to develop into the Intifada. After some five thousand years the area of Shechem still held the seeds of violence. And the verification of a supremely important Jewish holy site on the outskirts of this city could only add to the intensity of the conflict.

VIII

The Frightened Samaritans

We said "Shalom" to the young guards at Joseph's tomb and got back into Zvi's car.

"We might as well take a look at Mount Gerizim, so you'll have some perspective on it," he said, making a frightening U-turn in the dirt road leading past the tomb. "It's only a short distance from here."

We headed south of Shechem, through the unnatural quiet of the streets, caused by the on-and-off protest strikes of storekeepers and the frequent road patrols of the army, and drove up the narrow, tarred road leading to the steep, bare mountain of Gerizim, which loomed over the southern part of Nablus. The road climbed past a row of two-story houses near the base toward the summit, which was 2,891 feet in altitude, somewhat lower than Ebal's 3,085 feet. The top of the mountain was fringed unexpectedly with a cool-looking grove of evergreen Tabor oaks, perched on a steep hill overlooking the valley. From the crest there was a magnificent view of the city and to the north, historic Ebal, crowned with radar antennae. The road finally narrowed to an unpaved one-lane trail and became impassable, even for our small car, near an old stone churchlike structure, just above a field of partially excavated ruins. From the top of the building, which apparently was still in use, several men in white turbans waved at us in a friendly fashion. We waved back.

"Those are Samaritans," Zvi explained. "There are about five hundred and fifty of them left, all living in Israel. Most of them, about three hundred, live here on the mountain at least part of the time; a lot spend only their summers here—to keep the franchise, you might say. The rest, about another two hundred, live in Holon, near Tel Aviv. Most of them usually live in their own neighborhood at the foot of Mount Gerizim toward the western exit from the city.

"Until the Intifada, they lived in their homes on the top of Gerizim only three times a year: the entire month of Nisan, which is the month in which Passover is celebrated, one day of Shavuot (Pentecost), and one day of Succoth (Tabernacles). They're staying full time on the top of the mountain now because they are afraid to return to their homes, having been threatened by Arab extremists and accused of collaboration with Israel.

"That building we're looking at is a synagogue they use today. It was built sometime after the Arab conquest of this area following the Crusades, in the fourteenth century or so. Inside their other synagogue down in town, the Samaritans keep their Torah, which they date to the early years of the Israelite occupation of Canaan under Joshua. Most scholars, however, place it around the third or second century B.C., about the time when the rift with the Jews became permanent."

Near where we were standing, there was a large stone, surrounded by a low fence.

"That's the place the Samaritans say Abraham nearly sacrificed Isaac, but the Bible indicates that it was Mount Moriah, in Jerusalem. Except for the authority of the Bible, of course, nobody knows where it happened—or *if* it did.

"And that," he said, pointing to another fenced-off stone area near the top of the mountain, "is where the Samaritans say Joshua built his altar. But there are no archaeological remains confirming this claim, nor are there any Iron Age sites on Gerizim. The earliest pottery archaeologists have found is from the Greek period—around 700 B.C."

Also near the synagogue was the ruin of a fifth-century octagonal stone Byzantine church. A tower near the church is believed to contain the remains of Sheikh Ghanem, an Islamic holy man.

During the Dark Ages the Byzantine rulers of Palestine launched ferocious pogroms against the Jews, and even against those Christians who did not accept their special interpretations of Christianity. In the fourth century the Samaritans had a bit of a revival. At least eight new synagogues were built at that time. But this renewal of Samaritan belief drew the hostile attention of Byzantine authorities. In 438 Emperor Theodosius II applied the existing anti-Jewish statutes to them. Forty-five years later, the Samaritans rebelled. They massacred Christian communities and burned Byzantine churches. But the Byzantine armies put them down and in the repression they lost their ancient sanctuary on Gerizim, which became a basilica of the Blessed Virgin. Then came Emperor Justinian in 527. He was even stricter than Theodosius II, and the Samaritans rose again. The ensuing vengeance from Justinian was so bloody that the Samaritans were virtually destroyed as a religious sect and as a people. The Jews, who still did not see the Samaritans as members of their own faith, certainly did not come to their aid at this time, and thus probably avoided being destroyed as well.

"The church," Zvi explained, "is said to be built over one of the outposts where the Samaritans watched for enemies, announcing their approach by building bonfires that could be seen from mountaintop to mountaintop. This was a frequent method of signaling in those days, and as you can see from the many mountaintops visible around here, it could be a very quick and useful means of communication.

"Somewhere near here, historians estimate, the Samaritans erected their first sanctuary, in about 350 B.C. It was destroyed in 168 B.C. by the Seleucid King Antiochus IV, and converted into a shrine, first to Zeus and later to the Roman Jupiter. The shrine was built at Tel A-Ras, in the grove of trees just beneath and north of the peak of Gerizim, as part of the process of Helenization under the Greeks. In 128 B.C. it was destroyed again, this time by the Hasmonean John Hyrcanos, who wanted to incorporate the Samaritans into his kingdom. Actually, the Samaritans were persecuted as much as the Jews by various conquerors, including Pontius Pilate, Vespasian, and Roman and Byzantine emperors from Hadrian to Justinian II. Emperor Zeno had the temple on Mount Gerizim destroyed again and replaced by that Byzantine Christian church.

"There are remains of an old stairway that extends from the base of the mountain to the top, dating to about the third century A.D., that confirms the age and continuity of the settlement here."

Hostility toward the Samaritans by the Jews supposedly dates to the time when the Jews returned from the Babylonian exile. There were people in the Shechem area practicing Judaism who said they were Jews who had never left during the earlier exile of the northern kingdom. But the returning Jews maintained that these were actually Assyrians who had been brought in by the conquerors and had absorbed the Jewish religion. According to Jewish tradition, the Samaritans had been transported from five different cities in Mesopotamia by the Assyrians, after the conquest of Samaria and the destruction of the northern Israelite kingdom, circa 700 B.C. (Iron Age III). Zertal discovered Cuthite pottery in sites of this period, with designs that match exactly pottery found in Iraq. Adam came upon a paper published in Baghdad that described this very pottery and cuneiform design.

The Iraqi pottery was discovered in three of the five cities mentioned in II Kings 17 as the origin of the Samaritans. "The king of Assyria brought [people] from Babylon, Cutha, Avva, Hamath and Sepharvaim, and he settled them in the towns of Samaria in place of the Israelites; they took possession of Samaria and dwelt in its towns." [II Kings 17:24] According to II Kings these people did not worship the Lord of the Israelites, so the Lord sent lions, which killed some of them. The Samaritans complained to the king of Assyria: "The nations which you deported and resettled in the towns of Samaria do not know the rules of the God of the land, therefore he has let loose lions against them which are killing them. . . ." [II Kings 17:26] Hearing of this, the king of Assyria sent for one of the Israelite priests whom he had exiled and had him settle in Bethel to teach the locals "how to worship the Lord." But they worshiped the Israelite Lord will still serving their own gods, and so were never accepted.

Sanbalat, governor of Samaria during the Persian period when the Jews returned from Babylon, was not respected by the Jews. As a result, he was the one to make the changes in the biblical texts that set the Samaritans apart from the Jews finally and absolutely.

Ultimately the importance of the argument over whether the altar in Samaria was on Gerizim or Ebal has more to do with a concept called the centralization of the cult. That is, the designation of one place "that God shall choose" as the only official center of Judaism. According to Jewish tradition, the rites of sacrifice could be observed only "in the place that God has chosen" and no other place. This, before the fall of the temple, was where the Ark of the Covenant would be located.

Zvi, after a careful reading of the Bible, believes the first altar built as a centralized place of worship for the nation of Israel could well have been Ebal (or Gerizim, according to the Samaritans). But after designating the mountains of the blessing and the curse, the Bible never says that an altar was built on Gerizim, but only on Ebal.

Ebal makes geographical sense as the mountain the altar was built on. It is the highest ground in the area, with a commanding view. From the summit one can see for many miles in all directions. In the words of the nineteenth-century geographer George Adam Smith, from Mount Ebal "we feel the size of the Holy Land.—Hermon and the heights of Judah both within sight, while Jordan is not twenty nor the seacoast thirty miles away. . . ." On the other hand, from Mount Gerizim it is not possible to see very far to the north because the view is blockaded by the taller Mount Ebal.

Then why did the Samaritans choose Gerizim for the site of their holy temple? And why, in the traditional text, was it Mount Gerizim rather than Mount Ebal that was selected for the direction of the blessings? There are at least two theories. One is that in the ceremony of the blessing and the curse, the Levites, who guarded the Ark of the Covenant, may have faced initially toward the east—the primary direction in biblical tradition, the direction of the rising sun. If so, then the position of honor, for the blessing, would likely be on their right—toward the south, toward Mount Gerizim. Mount Ebal would then be on their left, to which they would turn for the curses. (The Samaritan version substitutes Gerizim for Ebal in Deuteronomy 27.)

Another theory suggests that the physical appearance of the mountains was the decisive factor. The southern flank of Ebal, facing Shechem, is parched—virtually barren. It receives the harsh direct rays of the noonday sun, and as a result of underlying rock formations, no springs gush forth to water these slopes. In contrast, the north face of Gerizim, opposite Shechem, appears green and fertile. This slope is partially shaded, so moisture is retained longer by the soil. Furthermore, numerous springs issue along the dip of its rock formations, helping to support vegetation, possibly making it appear a more felicitous place for the blessing to the authors of the Bible.

As the center of Israelite power shifted southward—archaeological finds indicate a great increase in Israelite sites in the south after the Early Iron Age I of Ebal—Shiloh seems to have become the central place, and the Ark was said to have been moved there.

The Samaritans, however, insist that Gerizim is the place God chose as described in Deuteronomy. They even claim that somewhere on this mountain are the twelve stones Joshua brought from the Jordan and placed near the altar. The temple built by Solomon in Jerusalem had been destroyed by the Babylonians in 586 B.C. [2 Kings 25:8–17] The Jews refused the Samaritan offer of help in rebulding the Temple in Jerusalem in 517 B.C., probably because they suspected the Samaritans' real motive was to ensure that the Jerusalem temple was not properly restored and so would not eclipse their own holy sites in Shechem.

Nehemiah, who was the leader of the returning exiles, was particularly vehement against the Samaritans, and asked God to invalidate any marriages between Jews and Samaritan women, for God to put away from him any children born of such marriages. The biblical description of this feud is believed to have been written very near to the time it occurred.

Although there is controversy over when the Samaritan temple was first built, there is general agreement that it must still have been in existence at the time of Christ's encounter with the woman of Samaria in Shechem. Remember that at that time the Jews and Romans both despised the Samaritans, not only as religious renegades in the Jews' eyes, but as a generally despicable people to whom all sorts of evil practices were attributed.

Jesus, according to John, wanted his message to reach all people, not just Jews. The woman of Samaria first says to Jesus: " 'How is it that thou, being a Jew, askest drink of me, which am a woman of Samaria? for the Jews have no dealings with the Samaritans.' " [John 4:9]

After some discussion, Jesus establishes that the site of this colloquy is indeed at the foot of Gerizim, at Jacob's well (where we had been earlier in the afternoon).

" 'Art thou greater than our father Jacob, which gave us this well and drank thereof himself, and his children, and his cattle?' " [John 4:12]

Then, after some further conversation about the water, the woman of Samaria touches on the heart of the Jewish-Samaritan feud: " 'Our fathers worshipped in this mountain [Gerizim] and ye say that in Jerusalem is the place where men ought to worship.' "

Jesus answered her in this way, referring to the dispute over the centrality of the cult: " 'Woman, believe me, the hour cometh when ye shall neither on this mountain [Gerizim], nor yet at Jerusalem, worship the Father. . . .' " [John 4:21]

This passage appears only in John, who was concerned with converting the Gentiles. Matthew, on the other hand, says that Jesus commanded him: " 'Go not into the way of the Gentiles, and into any city of the Samaritans enter ye not. But rather go to the lost sheep of the house of Israel.' " [Matthew 10:5–6] Despite this, John says that Jesus spent two days preaching to the Samaritans after his encounter with the Samaritan woman. And in the end they were convinced that he was the Messiah, not only to the Jews but to all people.

The woman of Samaria clearly thought of worship in terms of external features, such as the temple and the altar. But Jesus replied: " 'Woman, believe me, the hour cometh when the true worshippers will worship the Father in spirit and in truth, for the father is seeking all such to worship Him.' " [John 4:21,23]

In the parable of the Good Samaritan, an unfortunate traveler, presumably a Jew, who has been assaulted and robbed "and left half dead," is ignored by both a priest and a Levite. But he is assisted by a Samaritan, supposedly his blood enemy. This story appears in Luke 10:25–37. Its implication seems to be that *even* among the lowly Samaritans a charitable heart could be found.

As we drove back to the little settlement down the mountain from the Samaritan synagogue, Zvi pulled to the side of the road. "This is something you should see," he said, leading me toward a flat paved area, about the size of a tennis court. At one end of the pavement was a grandstand with room for about seventy-five people. Around it were several large concrete pits with iron grills across them. It was the site of the Samaritan Passover sacrifice.

IX

The Samaritans Today

Every year at Passover," Zvi explained, "the Samaritans slaughter about a hundred sheep and roast them on those grills—one to a family, according to the instructions in the book of Exodus. This is their interpretation of strict adherence to the law as set down by the Pentateuch—*their* Pentateuch, that is. The Samaritan version of the Torah says that Joshua's ceremony and altar were on Gerizim and not on Ebal. Altogether, the Samaritan text differs in six thousand instances from the generally accepted Jewish version based on the Masoretic text."

As he was talking to me, a tall man, tieless but in a black suit, approached us. He had olive-toned skin and a long aquiline nose. His eyes burned with what I thought was a peculiar intensity. He approached us and spoke briefly to Zvi in Hebrew. Zvi interpreted: "He wants to know if we want him to explain all this." My first reaction was to say no. We had almost no money between us, as I had not had a chance to get back to Netanya to exchange my travelers' checks, and there was no bank in Shavei Shomron. I was sure the tall man was a professional guide or a dragoman such as one finds near the pyramids in Egypt, but before I could decline his offer he was deep in conversation with Zvi, who nodded agreeably and asked a few questions.

"He just told me about the Passover ceremony. He said that hundreds of people come every year to watch it, and that it was on Israeli TV last year. Every year for about the past two thousand two hundred and fifty years they celebrate the ceremony here. Paschal

73

lambs are ritually slaughtered and skinned before nightfall, while the high priest conducts hymns and prayers. The lambs are roasted whole on the grill over there on fires of brush. Then they are eaten by every member of the community and any guests present. After that, the ceremony, with more singing and prayers, continues until late in the night."

The man spoke again to Zvi and smiled at me engagingly. He had big shiny white leporid teeth.

"He asks," Zvi explained, "if we want to come to his house. It's just about fifty feet away—over there." I figured whatever the deal was, we were involved in it now, so I nodded my agreement, and the man led us to his home, a typical Arab house with an open area underneath that served as a storage shed or possibly a garage, and a set of steps leading to the living quarters on the second level.

Inside, the house was spotlessly clean and decorated with plastic-covered furniture that looked as though it had come from Sears. There was a long low sofa, and in front of it a stainless-steel and Formica coffee table, covered with books and papers.

"I make you welcome," he said, obviously pleased with his English. Most Samaritans, I learned, speak perfect Arabic and Hebrew, and as a result are in demand by the Israeli government for jobs requiring fluency in both languages. Few, however, speak much English, due to their isolated living situation and life-style.

In reply to his greeting I said, *"Toda raba,"* thank you, which were among the few Hebrew words I had yet learned.

"My name," he said, again in English, "Moise Kahane—I am a *kohen.*" The *kohenim* are a hereditary priestly class in the Jewish tradition, supposedly descended from Moses' brother, Aaron. Until the destruction of the temple in the first century, it had been their function to supervise sacrificial rites, among other things. But sacrifices were abandoned by the Jews once the altar at the temple of Solomon was destroyed. Without an altar, there could be no sacrifices. The *kohenim* in Judaism now serve a more or less honorary position during certain synagogue rites. People with names like Cohen, Kahn, or Kahane are probably members of this clan.

I had run out of Hebrew words, so I raised my eyebrows in appreciation of his distinction, and said, "Shalom," which, after all, could do no harm.

A pleasant-looking, dark-skinned woman of about thirty came out to be introduced as his wife. She nodded shyly, but did not offer to shake our hands. There was a serious, dark-eyed four-year-old boy clinging to her skirt, peeking cautiously at the strangers. Our new friend Kahane explained through Zvi that this was the youngest of his five children—four of them boys.

After settling on the sofa at his invitation and accepting a cool glass of cola (I had learned that in Israel an invitation for a drink probably did not mean anything alcoholic), I nudged Zvi and asked him if he had mentioned to our host what our mission was. Zvi smiled sardonically and shook his head. "I don't really think that is the best idea."

The man was talking to him again about the Samaritan religion. "He says," Zvi translated, "that the Samaritans do not believe in the Ten Commandments in the exact form that we do. They contend that the First Commandment, 'I am the Lord, et cetera,' is not a commandment at all, but rather an opening sentence. They inserted into the Ten Commandments their version of a Tenth Commandment, which is a corruption of a verse in Deuteronomy: 'Three times a year shall all your males appear before the Lord in the place that he will choose: On Passover, Shavuot, and Succoth.' " [Deuteronomy 16:16] Kahane listened to Zvi's translation, trying to understand some of the English words, and smiled in agreement.

Now he took his notebook from his pocket and explained to Zvi in Hebrew what he had written in it. He indicated some figures written in ancient Hebrew in the book. Zvi took the book to study what Kahane had inscribed. As they talked I glanced at the table in front of me and noticed a large tabloid with a logo reading in English *The Samaritan*.

Kahane, following my glance, smiled encouragingly. "You look," he said, indicating the photo on the cover. "Is me!"

He riffled through the pages and spoke in Hebrew. Zvi explained to me that Kahane was the son of the late former high priest of the Samaritans, and that an interview with him was featured for some eight pages in the most recent issue of *The Samaritan*. The magazine, Zvi explained, circulates to schools and universities that are interested in this unique vanishing sect, as well as to Samaritans. It is printed mainly in ancient Hebrew, the Samaritan language, plus modern Hebrew, English, Arabic, and sometimes German and French since most articles seem to be photocopied pickups from other publications.

As I leafed through the back issues of *The Samaritan* in front of me, Kahane returned to the schoolboy's copybook in which, he explained to Zvi, he had inscribed the age of each biblical figure and added them up to get the exact age of the earth, which he calculated to be 6,201 years old. The Samaritan calculation says that there were 1,307 years between Adam and the Flood. The Septuagint says it was 2,242. Kahane asked me through Zvi if I could get his theory printed somewhere. Apparently Zvi had told him I was a writer. I suggested he try one of the universities. Oddly enough, this was a possibility, since there is a great academic interest in this tiny ancient cult.

As Zvi and I were glancing through the magazine we were startled to come upon a photocopy of an article by Adam Zertal, which he had published in an American magazine, *The Biblical Archaeology Review*. On a facing page was a rebuttal to Adam's evaluation of the Mount Ebal site by one of Zertal's college instructors, Aharon Kempinski. Luckily we hadn't mentioned our mission. Gerizim is the whole base of Samaritanism, and if Ebal were confirmed as the site of Joshua's altar, it would just about invalidate Samaritan beliefs of some twenty-two hundred years. Kahane did not notice our interest in the article, so when our colas were finished we thanked him and prepared to leave; but not before he had taken out his Polaroid camera and gotten a photo of each of us posed with him.

We were now dramatically aware of at least one group with a vested interest in denying Zertal's find on Mount Ebal—a group whose entire religious history would be negated if that find proved authentic. I suspected, though, that even if Ebal contained a contemporary written account, signed by Joshua himself, the Samaritans would not accept it. Their creed, like that of most Christians, Jews, and Muslims, is based on faith, not on artifacts—nor on facts, for that matter.

X

Searching for the Evidence

Finally, more than two weeks after my arrival in Israel, I was able to make plans to meet Adam Zertal. Zvi had made an appointment to rendezvous with him at an army camp near a site on the road linking Wadi Farah and Wadi Malich. This I later learned was the last place Adam had been able to work on his survey, during the early days of the Intifada. Today it is considered a risky area. Zertal can only estimate that the survey will be completed two years from whenever the Intifada ends. At present it is very hard for him to raise money, since no one wants to risk the confrontations that may be involved in further exploration of this area.

Adam had not yet arrived when Zvi and I pulled up to the Israeli Army base. The guard on sentry duty at the base was a Falasha—one of the ten thousand black Ethiopian Jews from the provinces of Gondar and Tigre who were secretly rescued by Israel in 1984 and 1985. He smiled and showed us a shady place to park near the entrance to the base.

Within a few minutes after we parked, Zvi spotted Adam's dilapidated blue jeep bumping along the highway in the distance; a few minutes later the battered army-surplus four-wheel-drive vehicle pulled into the camp. "He painted the jeep blue," Zvi told me, "because according to Arab belief the color blue wards off the evil eye."

Zvi introduced me to Zertal, a broad-shouldered man in his early forties with a serious expression occasionally illuminated by a sudden brilliant smile. He was dressed, like the other two men in the jeep, in blue jeans and a plaid shirt, and wore the crushed-straw farmer-type hat that I later realized was his trademark. Behind him on top of some canvas-wrapped bundles of equipment, I could see a pair of aluminum crutches. He shook my hand and introduced me to Nivi Markam, his chief assistant and factotum.

"Nivi knows as much about identifying Canaanite pottery as anyone in the business," Zertal explained with a laugh, "and he is the only man in the world who can keep this heap of junk running."

Markam was in fact a farmer on Zertal's kibbutz, who had volunteered to work with Adam on the survey and resultant dig. He was a pleasant, shy man with wire-rimmed sunglasses and the weathered skin of an outdoorsman. In back of the jeep was a young volunteer, Shlomo, a student of Adam's at Haifa University. (At Haifa, Zertal's chief is the distinguished archaeologist Moshe Dothan, who had dug an important ancient site at Afulah, in the Jordan Valley, and had worked with Yigael Yadin on the ruin of Hazor.)

"Today," Adam explained, "we will be going on a follow-up to the survey, which has already been through here. We are looking especially for Mycenean ware, but if you see anything that looks interesting, just let me know. Do you have any questions?"

"Plenty," I said. "First, explain exactly how you conduct a survey."

"An archaeological survey," Zertal explained, "is conducted by surveyors, who systematically walk over a defined area, which is marked off square by square, so that trained eyes examine the surface of every square meter of the land, slope after slope, ridge after ridge, field after field, searching for evidence of human occupation. All such evidence is carefully mapped, examined, recorded, and in the case of our survey, programmed into a computer. We were the first to use the computer in this way. Each segment is stored in a plastic bag, and ultimately in a box, marked with the coordinates of the area in which it was found. A limited excavation may then be undertaken at key sites. A survey is a slow and tedious process and yet, paradoxically, exciting.

"Almost all of the evidence consists of broken sherds of pottery. Pottery was cheap, easy to make, and did not easily deteriorate, though it could be broken. Therefore, in ancient times, broken pottery tended to be left where it was."

The forces of nature, Zertal explained, such as wind, rain, cold weather, and heat, and the activities of man, such as plowing, digging, building, and so forth, accomplish for archaeological researchers the task of uncovering sherds from the various periods. They need only search patiently and scrupulously on the top and slopes of the land. The slopes are especially convenient for finding sherds. Sometimes the survey must be repeated in different seasons of the year. In this way it is possible to assemble a sufficient quantity of sherds from each phase of the site's occupation to establish the periods in which settlement existed there and when it was most extensive.

Until about fifty years ago, Zertal added, archaeology consisted mostly of the excavation of tells—mounds left by the accumulation of layers of debris as one city built upon the ruins of another.

"From years of archaeological studies we are now able to identify most sherds easily both as to origin and date. We can do this both from the design of the pottery and from the materials of which it is made, as well as through certain scientific dating methods, such as thermoluminescence and spectographic analysis. But these techniques have a margin of error that tends to cover too great a span of years. Dating by types of pottery and decoration is still our best tool. In our case, since we were lucky enough to get the donation of a computer by IBM, we are logging all of our finds into a data base, to keep track of them and make them more accessible for study."

We squeezed into the backseat of the jeep, which was a tight fit, and started up a barely defined, potholed trail that quickly dwindled into rolling, hilly, open country, with dramatic vistas in all directions. Around us, in addition to the huge number of boulders and smaller rocks, were many rounds of expended ammunition and burned patches of ground.

"This section we're passing over now is part of an army target range," Adam told us. "But it's not in use at the moment."

As we bumped along, Adam began to talk to the others in Hebrew. Although he is fluent in English, I could sense it was still something of an effort for him to speak it, and the others on his team spoke it with much less ease. Occasionally Zvi would translate their conversation for my benefit.

We skirted the army base, easing over alarmingly deep holes and large rocks. Adam had bought the surplus military vehicle for three hundred dollars and Nivi had reconditioned it and kept it running with baling wire and whatever parts were available. After twenty minutes of jarring progress, we came to the area Adam was surveying. Nivi parked the jeep on the crest of a hill and we began to walk through the brambled fields, picking our way carefully over the ubiquitous limestone rocks and patches of grass charred by artillery fire. It was the hottest day they had seen there in forty years—about 100 degrees Fahrenheit. Adam made sure I had brought my canteen, and urged me to drink plenty of water. "The air is so dry and evaporates so much body water you will find that you don't sweat, but you can easily become dehydrated."

Conditions in the field are so grueling, with loose rocks, steep cliffs, and endless inclines, that it is hard to see how Adam has been able to cover this territory, maneuvering on his two aluminum crutches, when I could hardly cover it in my newly purchased heavy-duty Rockport walking shoes.

There is no square foot without a loose rock you could break your leg on. The rocks are not anchored in soil, so each is unstable and wobbly. Surrounding them are foot-tangling vines and thistles everywhere that penetrated my thin tropic-weight khakis. I saw now why the others wore jeans, whose rugged thickness repelled the thorns. The exploration of the hillsides was heavy going, but Adam, Zvi, and Nivi were considerate. At the top of each hill they would point through the haze in the distance to some area that was our apparent target. To me the goals they set seemed unachievable. At every opportunity to look for sherds I peered about me and stalled for time to catch my breath. Meanwhile Adam was bounding over this terrain on his crutches like an eager gazelle.

In the distance we actually did see a few gazelles bounding through the fields. Nivi pointed out the neat little piles of scat pellets, some still warm, that they had left behind.

We spread out in a skirmish line, about fifty feet from one another, and began slowly and methodically to march over the hilly terrain looking for bits of pottery. Adam, his injured leg still heavily bandaged around the ankles, moved so nimbly over the difficult ground that I actually envied him the support of those crutches. I felt in my own case that there was an excellent chance I would break my ankle with every step I took. I soon was yearning desperately for a single stretch of level unrocky ground.

I peered about avidly, hoping to make my mark by finding a particularly marvelous piece of pottery, or an even more striking artifact. There were a number of flat claylike fragments that looked tantalizingly like potsherds and turned out to be only rocks. Finally I spied one, and it was real. I held it up excitedly. Adam glanced over.

"Very good!" he said encouragingly. "That's Byzantine. Put it in your sack." He had provided us each with a plastic bag to contain our finds. I felt as though I had picked up a diamond, although I knew he was looking for earlier stuff. Byzantine, from the fifth or sixth century A.D., was almost modern from Adam's point of view. Later I asked Adam how he could identify a sherd from such a distance, and he explained that much of it was simply experience based on the color, thickness, decoration, or shape of the piece, as well as the material of which it was made.

What we were mainly looking for, Adam said, was bits of black volanic rock such as was usually found in the Jordan Valley, but not up here in the hills.

A half hour later, after a number of lackluster finds of mainly undistinguished Iron Age I Israelite sherds, which had been found in abundance in this area, I made my big find of the afternoon—a Middle Bronze sherd with a twisted rope design to identify it. Adam seemed pleased, and I was ecstatic with joy at this small contribution. It was as Adam had said: painful and boring, but still exciting. I was even more pleased later on when Adam let me take the little piece of clay, almost four thousand years old, home with me as a souvenir.

But actually, the undramatic, prevalent Israelite Iron Age pottery was the exciting thing; it proved the presence of Israelites on this route at the time of the Canaanite occupation. At that moment I felt I was actually walking in the footsteps of Joshua and the Israelites.

After the first hour I was running out of steam. My city-conditioned legs were shaking with fatigue and my lightweight tropical clothes were constantly penetrated by the pervasive thistles and brambles. Finally, with the sun almost directly overhead, we reached a ruin from the Crusades era that looked as though it had recently been occupied by local shepherds. Running along the base of its rough stone wall, I could make out a six-inch strip of shade. Sheepishly I asked for permission to rest, promising that I would soon catch up with the rest.

Adam smiled sympathetically. "I'm afraid it is a bit difficult for a new man, especially in this heat. Why don't you rest here and we'll pick you up on the way back?" I acquiesced with almost pathetic gratitude.

I tried to arrange myself on the rocks in the shadow of the wall, but could not get comfortable. Finally I spotted a fig tree about fifty yards away that seemed to offer more comfort and shade, and settled down under it in relative contentment, watching Adam and his team move down into the valley before me and up the hill on the other side. The hillsides were unobstructed by major vegetation, and it was possible to see for miles. I nodded in the soporific sun and drowsed briefly, half dreaming of Joshua leading his troops over the Jordan (whose plain I could see, hazy in the distance) and these once-forested hills to Shechem. From time to time I sipped tepid water from my canteen or munched on one of the oranges Zvi had given me that morning.

After two hours Adam, Zvi, Nivi, and Shlomo returned, and we retraced our steps to the jeep and back to the army camp for our midday break. We lunched in a shed-garage just outside the army base, sitting on wooden skids. Zvi and I had brought hard-boiled eggs, olives, oranges, and home-baked bread. Adam unpacked the lunch he had brought from his kibbutz, Ein Shemer, which specialized in farm products: oranges, olives, cucumbers, scallions, radishes, bread, hard-boiled eggs, and an excellent kosher-style salami. Also a refreshing mint tea, which Nivi brewed up from leaves he had gathered in the field.

The other men talked cheerfully in Hebrew about the work they had done that day. I asked Adam about the results of the earlier part of his survey in the nearby valley of Dothan, where Joseph had been sold into slavery by his brothers. According to the historian Eusebius, Dothan was located twenty miles north of Shechem. A tell there had been excavated in 1935 and later between 1955 and 1960. The city of Dothan dated back to the Chalcolithic times (about 4,500 B.C.). In the early Bronze Age it was already a large well-fortified city, but most of the finds there were dated to Iron Age II, at least fifty years after Joshua's time. Excavation showed that it was destroyed by fire around 800 B.C. This may have been in connection with the fall of the Israelite Kingdom to the Assyrians in 720 B.C. Dothan was actually, aside from its historic situation, the most practical area for Adam to start with, as it was the nearest of the new territories to Ein Shemer.

"What did you find at Dothan?" I asked Adam.

He answered between crunching bites of crisp radish and scallion. "At Dothan we had a special goal. It was not just a regular survey. The problem was the location of the city of Aruboth, which was the capital of the Third Solomonic District mentioned in First Kings 4:10. There the Bible says: 'Ben-hesed in Aruboth—he governed Socho and all the Hepher area.' In First Kings 4:7 to 25 we have a description of the division of Israel into twelve districts by King Solomon. 'Solomon had twelve prefects governing all Israel, who provided food for the king and his household. . . .' They were set up for tax collecting purposes because each district had to provide the palace and the military with necessary funds for one month a year. The Third District was a mystery. Nobody really knew where Aruboth was located. Yohanon Aharoni, in *The Lands of the Bible*, says that the Third District, according to his theories, extended from the Yarkon River to the border of the Fourth District, which cannot be well defined but was in the area of ancient Dor, to the north.

"There were two theories: one that it was located on the coast, and the other that it was located in the mountains of Manasseh. The problem was to find the main cities of this district. There are three cities mentioned, one of which, Socho, is the suburb of Tulkarm called Shweika—a notorious center of rioting lately. Another was called Aruboth, and the last was called Hepher. We felt somehow that the place where it should be located is around the valley of Dothan. We had some hints in the Bible. And we started our survey."

XI

The Entrance into Canaan?

T here," continued Adam, "we found Aruboth. It is on the site called Khirbet el-Hammam by the Arabs today. It is a city that was founded, according to the pottery on the site, in the time of King Solomon, in the tenth century B.C.—between Iron I and Iron II—the time of the United Kingdom, which ended with the death of Solomon in 926 B.C. when the kingdom became divided between Israel and Judah. The site of Aruboth continued as a city until at least Roman times.

"The most obvious feature on the tell, noticeable even before the digs began, was a rampart, and a line of siege camps two kilometers in diameter surrounding the site, similar to those at Masada. The two seasons we worked there verified the dating, and we were able to identify the site as Narbata, which probably was the Zealot city. This assumption is based upon its similarity to Masada, to which the Jews of Caesarea fled after the synagogue had been burned down. This is mentioned by the noted Jewish historian Flavius Josephus. There is no mention of Narbata elsewhere in Josephus, just one single reference. The striking similarity to Masada led us to the logical conclusion that the Roman fortifications and siege systems common to both sites were an indication of how much the Romans feared and respected the common enemy in both cases—the Zealots. In the end, hopelessly surrounded and cut off, the people of Masada committed mass suicide rather than surrender to the Romans. (The site is now a major tourist attraction.) Edward Gibbon, in *The Rise and Fall of the Roman Empire*, also agrees that the only revolt that stood a reasonable chance of success against the mighty Roman Empire was the Jewish Revolt of A.D. 66 to 70. Beneath the Jewish Zealot city of the Roman period, we found a thousand years of continuous civilization, at the bottom of which was a Solomonic city. The retention of the letter of Aruboth in the name Narbata led us to conclude that this was indeed one of the capital cities of the Third Solomonic District.

"One problem with finding Narbata was confusion over the name. The name was actually preserved in a nearby Arab village called Araba. The N is an Aramaic prefix. With names, prefixes and suffixes come and go. We felt that the name of the local village was a good sign. Historical references placed the biblical city somewhere in the vicinity, and the pottery dates we found in the survey made it seem a likely spot to investigate further. We had been proceeding in the survey square by square, but now we had a defined target for a preliminary dig in Narbata as Aruboth."

Zertal made an important friend in an odd way as a result of his exploration of Aruboth. Aruboth and Hepher were identified in the 1920s by Professor Benjamin Mazar, one of Israel's leading archaeologists, as being in the Sharon Valley. As a result, the regional council, which is the local administration for all the small kibbutzim and moshavim in the area, is called to this day the Hepher Regional Council. Adam presented his idea that Hepher and Aruboth were in the Dothan Valley in a lecture at a meeting of the Israel Exploration Society in 1977. When the novice archaeologist concluded his presentation, Mazar, who was in the audience, and was acting president of the International Organization for the Study of the Old Testament, applauded. He had never exchanged a word with Adam until that day, but Mazar got up in the midst of the attending scientists and said: "That young man is right, and I've been wrong for fifty years!" Since then, they have become very friendly, and Mazar has become one of Zertal's most influential supporters.

"We started out with only two people in our crew, Nivi and myself. And then we had three and sometimes we had four, mostly students in my classes or other university colleagues, and sometimes again two. Now, we don't work there in the summer. It is too hot, which is too bad, because that is when we have the most volunteers: teachers and students on vacation. But in those times, about ten

years ago, we worked in a concept that was first developed by a
British archaeologist named W. M. Flinders Petrie, in 1890, while
digging at Tel El Hesi, which he at the time thought was biblical
Lachish, whose king, according to the book of Joshua, was vanquished by Joshua during the Settlement Period. Actually, it turned
out to be the biblical city of Eglon, whose king was also said to be
vanquished by Joshua in the same campaign. In any event, Petrie,
now regarded as one of the pioneers of modern archaeology, realized
the value of what has come to be called *stratification*.

"Cities in ruin sites," Adam explained, "tend to be built on top
of other cities, and by carefully identifying each layer with the type
of artifacts—mainly pottery—found in them, according to the techniques devised by Petrie, it is possible to get a very good picture of
the sequence of events on a site, and the dates on which they
occurred."

Ultimately, I learned, these layers of piled-up civilizations form a
mound, which is called a *tell*—or sometimes a *tel*. The word, of
Semitic origin, describes a man-made mound that is an accumulation
of the various layers of civilization that have occupied the site. Such
mounds are found in many regions of the Middle East. Some reach
a height of seventy feet or so.

The problem was that not enough was known in Petrie's time
about the different types of pottery and the people they represented.
So, until about fifty years ago, archaeology restricted itself mainly to
the digging up of tells. The introduction of the survey concept,
learning the history of a piece of ground by searching it foot by foot,
was really developed by William Foxwell Albright, who brought the
science a long way toward being able to date pots by referring to
finds in classic digs at Jericho, Sebastia, Megiddo, Shechem, and so
forth.

Once identification of pottery became commonplace, it was possible for scientists to scan particular geographic and historical areas
systematically. They are able to identify the various cultures that
inhabited that particular area, thereby creating a "mapping" of each
area during each particular period. Of course, if Adam had not set
out to survey Manasseh, the likelihood of a discovery like Ebal
would have been almost impossible, because of its out-of-the-way
location. An example of how such a survey helped Zertal understand

hitherto unknown history: The defeat of Samaria (now known as the city of Sebastia) by the Assyrians in 720 B.C. is mentioned in II Kings 17. What is not mentioned is that the city first underwent a long siege. This was indicated when it was discovered that the Assyrians built extensive siege camps around the city, seven of which Zertal's team discovered in the survey. The earlier excavators of Samaria never had an inkling of that, though they worked the site extensively and intensively for six years (1929 to 1935).

Another important element in the survey is the ecological factor. An examination of the ecology of the particular periods explains much about why people lived where they did, how they lived, the agriculture and so forth, and gives a much clearer picture to the historian studying that period. In a sense, archaeology is an auxiliary tool of the historian and the Bible scholar, one that in time will focus much more sharply the hazy periods of the past.

After a dessert of apples, grapes, and oranges from Adam's kibbutz, and more mint tea, we went to another site a few miles away. This was one of the offshoots of the Wadi Malich, one of the valleys draining into the Jordan, where we combed the surface for signs of volcanic-rock artifacts. In the dig at Ebal, Zertal had turned up in the earliest level an almost perfect chalice carved from a porous black volcanic stone. What interested Zertal in this piece was that there were no sources in the Manasseh hills for this type of stone. It was found only in the Transjordan, that is, on the east side of the river up which the Israelites may have come, or in the Golan, far to the north. The chalice itself resembled in its shape cultic stone vessels discovered in the Egyptian temple at Sarabit-el-Hadam by Petrie in 1906.

It was in the relatively unexplored Wadi Malich that Zertal had found a site with numerous sherds of the Middle Bronze era; to his surprise, he had also found some early sherds of the Israelites. This was unusual in that almost all early Israelite relics have been found in areas long abandoned by earlier civilizations. The early sites were to the east and the south, moving gradually into the west bank in a westerly direction.

"I believe," Adam told me after lunch, as we trudged over the rocky terrain, "that the location of the Israelite cultic center followed the direction of their settlement. So the earliest cultic center was Ebal, and that was the national cultic center when they were only a nucleus of the tribes who were wandering and settling in the hill country of Manasseh. There are six big valleys here, including Dothan, Samwil, and Tubas, that gave it its fertile character. When the Israelites overpopulated the east bank, they began to leave it and go to the only place they could find empty country. Then, as they were prospering and growing, they needed more land, so they moved south to the forests of Ephraim and ultimately to Judah and Jerusalem.

"The cultic center of the Israelites moved from Ebal, after much less than a century, probably, to Shiloh, which is in the middle of the territory of Ephraim, and has been thoroughly excavated as far back as 1922, though few remains have been found as yet of early Iron Age I. There were, however, remains dating back to the Middle Bronze Age and earlier, and a Late Bronze stratum following destruction of Middle Bronze II fortifications, as has frequently been the case in the settlement sites. The area was excavated again as recently as 1984 by Finklestein under the auspices of Bar-Ilan University. He found many Iron Age I artifacts, but they are dated about a century after Ebal. For the cultic nature of the site we have only the Bible's say-so, but it seems logical in view of the trail of artifacts and their dates.

"The movement of Israel did not stop. It went more and more southward in search of land, exactly like America, with its Manifest Destiny in the West. Shiloh was destroyed by the Philistines in 1050 B.C., a little before the time of Saul and the beginning of the monarchy, and then the center of the cult was moved by David to Jerusalem. So within two hundred and fifty years you have Ebal, then Shiloh, and finally Jerusalem as the centers of Israelite religious life.

"A sacred center was necessary for keeping this loose-knit federation together as a nation. The idea of national unity required a central place, like the Vatican for the Roman Catholics. In ancient times, after the monarchy of Solomon, it was always the temple in Jerusalem, until that was destroyed by the Romans. Today Jerusalem is still the national center, even though the temple no longer exists. This is exactly what went on in Greece three hundred years later. A treaty among twelve Greek tribes established the amphic-

tyonic league. Martin Noth (a prominent postwar German biblical
scholar) was the first to notice and make this comparison. I don't
think it's coincidental that Israel and Greece are the most important
influences of Western civilization. They were both organized in the
same way, with twelve tribes. Why the number twelve is another
intriguing question. This organization of twelve tribes was kept, it
seems, from the very beginning; but the cultic center before the
final establishment of the Temple of Solomon followed the direction
of settlement.

"Israel Finkelstein, who conducted an important survey of
Ephraim, south of here, states that the sites in the north, near
Shechem, have much more early Israelite pottery than the sites in
the south. This makes sense. In Judah, only a maximum of twenty
sites had early Israelite pottery. The real settlement in Judah was
not until the time of David, two hundred and fifty years after Joshua
first came into the land—the end of Iron Age I, the beginning of Iron
Age II. Incidentally, iron didn't really reach Israel until about David's time.

"The only way to actually understand the settlement process is by
making a survey, because if you dig in only one site, or one city, you
get only the local picture. Only when you do a foot-scan search,
which takes years and years and years, can you start to get a full idea
of what is going on in the whole country. This also helps in planning
sites for digs, since we are limited in funds, and possibly time, in the
number of sites we can explore.

"This is a crucial point. Seventy percent of our sites were on
virgin ground, newly founded settlements. This is the situation even
today. The land is underpopulated and underdeveloped, not
crowded as was once believed. The area was originally surveyed by
looking at a map, and on the map every little village, even those that
were practically abandoned, looked like a big town. So they didn't
actually go and examine these sites, and that's why long ago the
Jewish National Fund did not go to the trouble of purchasing land in
areas they assumed from the maps were densely populated. If not
for this quirk during the 1930s, there might never have been any
political problem today about identifying the area as Israel proper."

Even today, I noted in the course of my own research, the new
Israeli settlers in the West Bank were able to occupy completely

undeveloped sites, usually far from other villages, and generally, as in ancient times, on mountaintops.

When I parted from Zertal that Monday afternoon, I made an appointment to see him at Haifa University on Wednesday for a long interview. Meanwhile, Zvi said he had something to show me that he felt was important as background and impressive as a personal experience.

XII

Where the Land Was Promised

The next day, Tuesday, Zvi and I started out in the car and took the road through Nablus, past Joseph's tomb and Balata, and headed east, toward the Jordan. A few miles outside of town the road began to climb in long sinuous curves.

"This is Mount Kebir," Zvi explained. We passed a neighborhood of neat small villas clinging to the mountainside with numerous children playing in the courtyards and fields between them. "We are at an elevation of two thousand feet here. This is the town of Elon Moreh, which is the regional headquarters for the territory of Samaria. It is named for an important site from patriarchal times mentioned in the Bible."

Now the road curved northward as we rounded the crest of Mount Kebir and finally pulled into a small barren parking lot. About five hundred yards above us toward the top of the mountain stood a domed Arab tomb acting as a finial to the peak, like the nipple on a breast. This was supposedly the tomb of Sheikh Bel'al, the muezzin of the prophet Mohammed. Arabs in the vicinity considered it a very holy place until a century ago, when Arab historians began to contend that Bel'al died and was buried in Iraq.

"We are now on top of Mount Kebir, or Jebel Kheibir, which means 'the great mountain' in Arabic," Zvi told me.

As we climbed out of the car and started up the steep sandy path that spiraled toward the top, Zvi began a lecture, which, he told me, he was accustomed to deliver to various groups of hikers and students who came to visit the site. "I promise you," he said, "when we reach the top you will see one of the most impressive sights of your life."

We finally reached a small setback with a stone railing and a bronze plaque describing the scene before us—a breathtaking panorama that included almost all of the sites mentioned in the Pentateuch and Joshua. There was a narrow green tree line far below in the valley tracing the route of the stream Wadi Farah down to the Jordan. On the right of the setback was a huge spreading oak that looked to be at least five hundred years old, about eight feet in diameter, and behind it some small caves with more plaques identifying them. This, some believe, could be the place known in the Bible as Elon Moreh—the oak of Moreh. There are those who believe that this is where God promised the land to Abraham on his first journey through Canaan, showing him the territory he had promised to Israel. Although this has not been proven archaeologically by artifacts, the site certainly fits the biblical description. The town below took its name from the biblical references to the historic site, but this was only symbolic, and in any event, the town itself was not on the supposed site of the biblical oak, but a mile or so down the road. Now we were standing in the place where the ancient oak might have grown.

Below me in the shimmering bluish haze I could see nothing to remind me that it was now at least thirty-five hundred years after that time, and though I knew the oak I was looking at could not be the original Elon Moreh, I felt a heart-stopping awe to be standing, it seemed, in the very spot where Abraham made his covenant with the Lord.

"From here you can see Ebal five kilometers across the valley. If you take a look at the way the top slope leads up to the second level, Shechem is between the two mountains and Gerizim is on the other side. Now you see the road in the valley leading south, and there is the valley of Michmethah named in Joshua 17 as being one of the areas within the bounds of the tribe of Manasseh. The allotment of the half tribe of Manasseh was the biggest of any tribal share. On a clear night you can see all of that land, plus the lights of Jerusalem, from here. Tirzah, across the valley almost straight ahead, was the name of the city near the source of Wadi Farah, which is the green line of trees growing near the creek that is flowing there in the canyon below us. Tirzah was one of the first capitals of Israel; its site has been located in the valley beneath Jebel Kheibir, where we now stand.

"When areas to be assigned to the various tribes of Israel were announced by Moses in the plain of Moab, just before the occupation of Canaan, the daughters of a man called Zelophehad, who was a descendant of Joseph's son Manasseh, appealed to Moses that since their father had died, and had not had any sons, they had been denied their fair allocation of territory in the Promised Land. Moses conferred with the Lord Himself on this complaint, and the Lord said: " 'The plea of Zelophehad's daughters is just: you should give them a hereditary holding among their father's kinsmen; transfer their father's share to them.' " [Numbers 27:7]

"Adam has been able to identify the areas the daughters inherited, which correspond to five of the valleys of Samaria, one of them being Tirzah. The valley is mentioned in Song of Songs 6:4. 'You are beautiful, my darling, as Tirzah.' "

Zvi explained to me the significance of this mountain to the Ebal legend: "In Deuteronomy 11:30 the Bible explains how to get to the site where Joshua must carry out this ceremony of the blessing and the curse in five easy steps. 'Are they [Ebal and Gerizim] not across the Jordan? In the direction that the sun sets across the Aravah plain inhabited by the Canaanites opposite the Gilgal next to Elon Moreh?'

"We're going to take this step by step and try to understand it in terms of where we are standing right now, which is the best place to see it. First of all, the Jews were on the other side of the Jordan—the east bank. Naturally, step one makes sense. They have to cross over the Jordan. Second, they have to go in the direction of the setting sun. Now the Aravah plain: 'You have to cross over it where the Canaanites sit.' The biblical Aravah is everything in the Jordan Valley from the lake of Tiberias down to Eilat. Now we get to step number four, which is *the* greatest problem in the biblical historiography of the land of Israel. Because it says 'opposite the Gilgal.' Since the Gilgal to date has been identified as a site near Jericho, sixty kilometers to the southeast, how could it be opposite Ebal?

The discovery of an egg-shaped Israelite camp down in the valley, made of piles of stones, in Hebrew *gal*, solves the problem, as this camp lies directly opposite Ebal in a place where there is still an ancient oak." In other words, according to Koenigsberg (and Zertal), this *gal* could be the Gilgal described in this part of the Bible.

French archaeologist Roland de Vaux, who excavated Tirzah, discusses the landmark tree on Mount Kebir: "It is . . . certain that the oak near Shechem where Jacob buried his family's idols [Genesis 35:4] belonged to a place of worship.

"This apparently refers to the tree that stood in the 'sanctuary of Yahweh' at Shechem, beneath which Josue [Joshua] set up a big stone [Joshua 24:26]; hence we may identify it with the 'terebinth of the stele which stands at Shechem' . . . which marked the place where Abimelech was proclaimed king in the middle of the twelfth century B.C. The same tree is also called the Oak of Moreh." The word *terebinth* is interpreted both as an oak and a cashew tree and is considered sacred. There is a long tradition in many cultures of regarding large oaks as sacred. At one time in Germany a person who damaged an oak could be executed.

"You know," Zvi said, "that wherever an oak has grown, another is likely to arise in the same place." I admitted that I had never known that, but would check it, as he suggested, with a paleobotanist at the earliest opportunity. Back in New York I contacted the information department of the Brooklyn Botanical Garden, which confirms that this statement is substantially true. They sent me a clipping from *Forest Ecology* by Stephen Spurr and Burton Barnes, which states: "When the bole [of an oak] is killed, the root system remains alive almost indefinitely, sending up generation after generation of shoots . . . that perpetuate both the individual tree and the dominance of oaks in the forest."

"If you trust the Bible," Zvi suggested, "you can find something suggesting this in Job 14:7–9 where it is talking of the relative shortness of a man's life compared to a tree's possible immortality:

> There is hope for a tree:
> If it is cut down, it will renew itself;
> its shoots will not cease.
> If its roots are old in the earth,

and its stump dies in the ground,
at the scent of water, it will bud,
and produce branches like a sapling.

Benjamin Mazar, in his book *The Early Biblical Period*, comments on the "ever-recurring motif that the Patriarchs pitched their tents near sacred terebinths in the proximity of cities, erecting altars and *maseboth*, and binding themselves by treaty and protective arrangements to the inhabitants of the cities. . . ."

Zvi pointed out the factors that made Elon Moreh a vital biblical landmark: "The mention of Elon Moreh as guidepost to Ebal in Deuteronomy 11:30 means that it was already a geographically identifiable site at that time. The site was known, and because it is the only place that contains pottery from the Settlement Period from which you see both Ebal and Gerizim, it substantiates the idea that I talked to you about earlier. When you connect this with the version of the blessing and the curse from Joshua, it stands to reason they may have stood here on this hill and the entire ceremony of the covenant takes place right there. But the sacrifice had to be at the altar 'in the place where God had chosen.' "

After that ceremony, Joshua 24:25–27 comments: "On that day at Shechem Joshua made a covenant for the people and he made a fixed rule for them. Joshua recorded all this in a book of divine instruction. He took a great stone and set it up at the foot of the oak in the sacred precinct of the Lord; and Joshua said to all the people, 'See this very stone shall be a witness against you, lest you break the faith with your God.' " In the very next line it says: "After these events, Joshua, son of Nun, servant of the Lord, died at the age of one hundred and ten years." This is the last page of the Book of Joshua.

There are provocative things in these passages, I found when I later examined them and discussed them with Koenigsberg. Most important is the presence of the Ark of the Covenant, without which this could not be a central cultic location. Another is the instruction to call "in a loud voice" [Deuteronomy 27:14] the words of the Lord—as though those listening were at a great distance. Another is the mention of a "sacred enclosure," which would be what is called a "temenos wall," also necessary for a central cultic site. All of this fits very well with the possible location of the original Elon Moreh on Jebel Kheibir, though this location has never been offically identified, and would offer enormous difficulties to excavation, principally because of opposition by the Arabs, who would argue that we would be disturbing one of their holy sites.

But if we ever *do* dig there, we could, for the first time, find archaeological relics from the time of Abraham. The survey covered this area and it showed signs of the site's having been visited from the Middle Bronze Age, which is the patriarchal era—Abraham's time. Among the Israelites the temenos delineated the area sacred to Levites and priests, to which the general public was not admitted. The survey showed a temenos wall, which denotes a holy place, around the peak from that same period. The Arabs built a holy site there, which is in accord with their building on top of sites that were holy to previous cultures. It has oak trees—*elon* means "oak" in Hebrew. In the progression of Wadi Farah from the Jordan to Shechem, the site stands out geographically as the only significant landmark en route to Ebal.

"You can see well past the Jordan River," Koenigsberg pointed out, as he peered into the haze shrouding the distant valleys, "and perhaps right down there is the place where Joshua and the Israelites crossed the Jordan, dry-shod, carrying the Ark of the Covenant before them."

In the Bible, Elon Moreh was the exact site where Yahweh gave Abraham the Promised Land:

"Abram passed through the land as far as the site of Shechem, at the terebinth of Moreh. The Canaanites were then in the land.

"The Lord appeared to Abram and said, 'I will assign this land to your offspring.' And he built an altar there to the Lord who had appeared to him." [Genesis 12:6–7]

So it can be seen that the entrance into Canaan was not simply the settlement of a land promised to Moses, but actually a return to the Israelites' ancestral home, out of which they had been taken in bondage centuries earlier.

XIII

Adam's Dream of Blue Mountains

On Wednesday we made the two-hour drive from Shavei Shomron to Haifa, along the coast highway, for our meeting with Zertal at the university. Haifa itself is considered by many the most beautiful city in Israel, also the cleanest and the greenest. It curves in a semicircle around the sandy beaches at its foot. The modern port at the base of the mountain is the busiest in Israel, yet with its spotless streets and lush parks, there is no feeling of being in the midst of an industrial metropolis. The route to the university ascends via spectacular spiraling roads up three slopes to the top of Mount Carmel, which is about one thousand feet above sea level. From the peak there is an astounding view of all of northern Israel.

The university itself is in a high-rise building soaring some thirty stories above the already lofty mountaintop. It was built in 1963 and existed for several years under the protective aegis of Hebrew University, before declaring itself an independent educational institution. It now has almost ten thousand students, including Arabs and Druze as well as Jews.

Archaeologically, the area in which the city of Haifa is located postdates Joshua's time by several hundred years, although the region, but not the city, is mentioned in Joshua's allocation of land to the tribes as the territory of Issachar.

We were to meet Adam at a student cafeteria in one of the vast

97

downstairs rooms of the university. On our way to the meeting we passed the Reuben and Edith Hecht Museum, a part of the university that contains many exhibits of biblical archaeology. Zvi pointed to a wall-size photo-mural that showed a heap of piled-up stones with a straw-hatted figure astride the topmost rocks.

"Recognize him?" Zvi asked. "It's Adam at Ebal!"

We found Adam waiting and, after fortifying ourselves with coffee, sat down to tape the first of many interviews.

"I grew up," Adam told me, "in the kibbutz called Ein Shemer in the Sharon plain—the central part of the coast. I was born six kilometers from the place where the mountains rise from the plain."

Ein Shemer, Adam explained to me, is a community of some 350 adults—1,000 in all including children. It grows cotton, avocados, apples, and various other crops, keeps cows for milk, has a well-developed plastics factory, and makes parts that go into tires for export. (Nivi is in charge of the cultivation of avocados.)

Adam is the son of one of the early leaders of the Mapam, a party aligned with Labor for many years (until the last election, when they went independent again), whose philosophy ruled the kibbutz. Mapam is the political offshoot of the Hashomer Hatzair ("the young watchman") Movement, which began in Poland and Russia in the early 1920s, and set up kibbutzim in Israel. Their movement was not the largest, but was certainly very active in settling areas that were densely populated by Arabs. Their original philosophy called for a dual-nationality state of Jews and Arabs. They were and are the farthest left-wing movement (aside from the Communists) in Israel, and their political wing, Mapam, is in opposition to the Likud ruling bloc as of this writing. They are staunchly in favor of a Palestinian state on the West Bank, and as a group are against West Bank settlement by Israelis. Their philosophy, to this day, includes an almost total rejection of Jewish traditions. For example, only their kibbutzim will raise pigs, and Yom Kippur is more or less just another working day. The movement as a whole idealized Russia, and underwent a very serious crisis ideologically when Stalin's crimes came to light. (What effect the current collapse of Soviet Marxism will have on their views remains to be seen.)

Adam's father, Moshe, was a prominent force in the Mapam movement for many years. His sister, Idit, is a far-left journalist, today writing for the daily newspaper *Hadashot.* In view of this upbringing it is ironic that Zertal was later accused of right-wing political motivations in his Ebal dig. It was alleged by some that he had established the Ebal dig at the prompting of the Israeli settlers of Samaria to give added historical justification to their movement. But Adam is completely apolitical in regard to his work. He has, however, from his earliest memories, felt a fascination with the area that was biblical Canaan.

"When I was a child, many years ago," he recalls, "I remember seeing those mountains of Manasseh. In the afternoon they looked blue, and we called them 'the blue mountains.' But we could never go into them. As children, and even when I was a boy a bit older, say fifteen or sixteen, we could never explore those mountains, because that area was Jordanian territory. It was in charge of the British under the mandate first, and then the Jordanians, who forbade any Jew at any time to enter there, or to own property. To sell property in Samaria to a Jew was declared by Jordan to be a death-penalty offense. So, though the hills of Samaria were quite close, we could never explore them.

"It was a dream of my childhood, one day to go into those mountains. I felt like Moses standing on the other side of the Jordan and not being able to enter the Promised Land. Especially since I was on a kibbutz named Ein Shemer. The name Ein Shemer means 'the stream of Shemer'—Samaria."

Omri, who was king of Israel in 876 B.C., Zertal explained, bought the mountain of Samaria: "For two talents of silver he bought a hill from Shemer and on it built a town which he named Samaria after Shemer who had owned the hill." [I Kings 16:24–26]

The city of Samaria was named capital of Israel by Omri, who was the father of the infamous Ahab. The Arabs today call that city Sebastia. It's just outside the settlement of Shavei Shomron where I was staying. It has been the site of many archaeological digs, but no ruins have been found until now that date back as far as Joshua's time. A few sherds of Middle Bronze pottery were found from some earlier occupants, but basically it's a post-Solomonic site. It can be said, however, that it is the first Israelite or Jewish city to be built from the ground up, and not on the ruins of previous sites.

Adam continued his story: "Archaeology is my second career. My first career was in economy of agriculture, at the university. Before that, like the rest of the kibbutz members, I was a farmer, milking and herding cows, helping to plant and bring in crops. I loved that work, and when I am at home I still take my turn at milking the cows. But I would say that like so many other Israelis, one part of my mind was always taken up with dreams of finding the secrets of history hidden under our feet."

At the kibbutz, Adam studied his economics texts from the university, and fulfilled his farm duties. After earning his undergraduate degree he was sent to the Central African Republic to serve for several years as an adviser.

After serving in the Six Day War in 1967 Adam turned to writing fiction. Several of his short stories were published in a book called *Wilderness Table.*

In 1973 Adam was recalled to active duty to serve in the Yom Kippur War. He was thirty-two years old, married, and the father of three children.

Zertal was severely wounded during that conflict. As a captain in the Engineer Corps, he had been in command of a group defending the bridgehead at the Suez Canal against heavy artillery attack by the Egyptians. An artillery shell landed only yards from his outpost. His second in command was killed, and his principal assistant had both legs blown off. Zertal himself was riddled with shrapnel but managed to cling to life. "I was the lucky one," he comments ironically. Half of his left foot had been shot away, and his legs and hips had been riddled with shell fragments. He also suffered severe injury to one of his eyes and his right hand.

"They thought for a while I might die," Adam recalls. "I was in the hospital for more than a year. The worst damage was in my hips and legs." He was in a cast for two years.

During the Six Day War, Israel had finally regained control of the hills of Samaria after a lapse of more than 3,200 years. But it was not until he was wounded in 1973 that Zertal had the chance to fulfill his early ambition. At first, in the hospital, he was aware only of the pain and the foggy perceptions of his mind under the influence of the pain-killers. But as he gradually came out of his immediate agony, he wondered what his future held. What would happen to his wife of fifteen years and his two sons and daughter? How would he support them? Could he continue to work a farm, or travel as an agricultural consultant? Would he, in fact, *ever* walk again or be able to use his injured hand? Confined to the hospital for over a year, recuperating from his severe wounds, Zertal was ultimately interviewed by a committee of the Ministry of Defence, who asked what sort of work he would like to do after he was released.

What sort of work *could* he do, he wondered, without the use of his feet or one hand? His mind wandered over the possibilities, but he could concentrate only on the fact that this was the first time he had actually been given a *choice* in what he wanted to do. The farm and kibbutz life were simply part of the heritage with which he had grown up, unquestioning. Now they were asking him what he *chose* to do. His lifelong ambition leaped to mind, despite its seeming impossibility.

"I told them," Adam says, "that it had always been my dream to be an archaeologist."

His counselors reacted with smiles of disbelief. How could he in any way be capable of the strenuous demands of this occupation? They were skeptical that he could ever handle such a job with his severe injuries. But Zertal got support from a visiting archaeologist named Yoram Tsfarir, who had himself sustained serious leg injuries.

"Never mind what they say," Tsfarir counseled him. "You can be whatever you want. This is your chance." He offered Zertal encouragement. Despite the severity of his injuries, Tsfarir told him, he could fight back and someday become a full-fledged field archaeologist.

Tsfarir's enthusiasm for Zertal's ambitious proposal persuaded him to insist on being allowed to pursue an archaeological education, and the Ministry of Defence, though its advisors had serious reservations, finally agreed to finance Adam's dream.

"You must remember that Israel's first Chief of Staff, Yigael Yadin, was originally an archaeologist, and went back to that work as soon as the war was over. He was instrumental in discovering the Dead Sea Scrolls, excavated Masada, and excavated the huge ruin at Hazor, among other things. I mention this because Hazor is one of the cities supposedly conquered by Joshua. [Joshua 11:10–13] The ruler of Hazor was one of the thirty-one kings the Bible says were

conquered by Joshua. [Joshua 12:19] Yadin found signs of burning
and destruction that dated to the time of Joshua's conquest, and that
the next inhabitants were a seminomadic people with few permanent buildings but many sunken stone-lined silos or storage pits.
Yadin felt that these were signs of an early Iron Age Israelite settlement, though his finds were basically only pottery. There were no
ruins to confirm his theory."

The Defence committee finally said to Adam: "Okay, you can
take that course if you like; but your work, naturally, will have to be
purely theoretical since you can no longer really walk."

"In that moment," Adam remembers, "I thought, 'Even if they
put me in a wheelchair I'll somehow find a way to do the work.' My
real rehabilitation came when I decided to take the hardest way
instead of the easiest way. But that was later."

XIV

Learning to Walk

At first," Zertal told me, "I did my work in the hospital. Some of the professors came from Jerusalem and Tel Aviv and read me the lessons. In a way it was excellent, because it was private instruction and I could proceed at my own pace and ask all the questions I wanted to. The first three or four years I was in a wheelchair. Part of my left foot had been shot off, and it took some time for the other wounds to my eye and hand to heal; but finally I was liberated. They gave me two aluminum crutches, and I could move again over rough ground on the outside where the wheelchair could not go. I was on the two crutches for several years, and then they graduated me to one crutch—sometimes two, if I was in the field.

"I started my master's on the survey of Manasseh hill country in the winter of '77. I wanted to test myself on a real job in the field. We started in the valley of Dothan, which was nearest to Ein Shemer."

What Adam learned is that the profession of the archaeologist is much like that of the detective. Like a detective, the archaeologist attempts to reconstruct events that he was not present to observe. He may have the reports of witnesses, such as the Old Testament, if he is studying the history of ancient Israel, but he must question their credibility. He may have other clues, bits of pottery, bones, burned debris, writings from other countries such as Egypt or Ugarit, or written clues from Mesopotamia. He can be helped to evaulate this information nowadays by various modern tools. One can now

103

locate objects with ground-probing radar or sonar. What has come to
be called "the new archaeology" includes such devices as flotation to
recover minute remnants like pollen granules, neutron-activation
analysis to establish the provenance of clays used in pottery, carbon-
14 tests to date organic substances. Human bones (rare in Israel) are
studied when found to determine ancient diseases and disease patterns.

The archaeologist-detective has to assemble the testimony of the
witnesses (who unfortunately cannot be cross-examined except by
comparing their written testimony to that of other witnesses, or to
other physical evidence) and then apply his deductive powers to
piece together what happened on the site he is investigating—"the
scene of the crime."

To call oneself a biblical archaeologist is a complicated matter,
and not many in the profession are willing to use that terminology.
If you stress the word *biblical,* you have one group of partisans on
your back; but if, as many archaeologists do, you say that you are not
interested in the Bible, only in what the physical archaeological
evidence shows, you will be attacked from another direction, by the
upholders of the literal truth of the Bible. Adam describes himself
simply as an archaeologist.

"Personally," Zertal says, "I am not very religious, and I do not
think that every word of the Bible was dictated by God. But I think
the Bible is a valuable tool, and I would certainly not have found the
site of Dothan, or Solomon's Third District, without it as a guide."

The "dig" or excavation, Adam learned in his classes, is basically
the most important tool of the archaeologist, since without it he
would recover only a fraction of the information available to him
about man's past. "Excavation," William Foxwell Albright, one of
the fathers of modern archaeology, has said, "is both an art and a
science."

"There is no correct method of excavation, but many wrong
ones," said pioneer archaeologist Sir Mortimer Wheeler. The words
of these two great archaeologists underline the main feature of archaeological technique—a continuous striving for perfection in excavation and in the publication of the results. Digging up any site,
whether small or large, involves the destruction of the primary evidence. You move one rock or artifact, and the evidence of where it

had been is no longer there. So, Adam learned, excavation should never be undertaken without serious consideration. There are many processes involved in excavations and many decisions to make. First: Should the site be excavated at all? This decision may be affected by the amount of time available before the site is disrupted by the building of new roads, expansion of towns, farming or natural erosion, and, frequently of extreme importance, by political considerations. Sometimes the archaeologist is forced to undertake what is called a "rescue mission."

If he does decide to dig, he must decide how big an area he will dig, and what sort of dig it will be. If time or money is short, a sampling may be all that is possible, such as digging a vertical trench to the bedrock to try to determine the different levels of civilization that have existed on the site. But sometimes this is misleading, as a similar trench a few yards away may reveal different information from the first one.

If a large-scale excavation is attempted, the technique that is best suited must be considered: whether to excavate the whole area inch by inch, or to set up grids with walls between them (balks) and dig in a checkerboard pattern.

How will the soil be removed? By hand or by machine? If only an inch or so of soil lies above the bedrock, or the ground has never been plowed, then the topsoil could contain valuable information and should be hand-dug. But if it has been deeply plowed, removing it by machinery would probably be practical, and much quicker.

Perhaps it was his early success in making informed guesses based on passages in the Bible, or perhaps the virtually virgin nature of this deeply historic terrain contributed. Certainly from the beginning Zertal showed that sixth sense that makes an art out of the science of archaeology. I have seen it in operation myself on marine archaeological digs where nothing was visible on the sea bottom to the untrained eye, yet my mentor, the pioneering marine archaeologist Robert Marx, could lead me straight to a two-inch bronze rudder pin, sunk in the mud, or a coral-encrusted silver ingot invisible to any eye but his. Certainly this sort of instinct comes from training and experience, but beyond a certain point it becomes an inspired art.

Zertal continued sketching in his background, as we sat in the sunny university cafeteria. After testing himself in the field that

winter, and making numerous interesting finds, a great many of
which pointed to a strong Israelite presence in Manasseh from the
mid-thirteenth century B.C. on, Adam convinced himself that he
could confute the prophecy that he would have to remain a wheelchair explorer and decided that, despite the fact that he had been
told he would never walk again, he was determined he *would* walk
and work in the field someday and become a serious archaeologist.
After he was liberated from his wheelchair, he took long walks on his
crutches along isolated roads around Arab villages in Samaria to train
himself for the arduous cross-country treks to come. He felt a great
kinship to these barren, rolling hills.

"Actually we were not such strangers there," Adam later wrote in
his notebook. "Maybe even less strange than anyone else. Maybe
belonging there much more."

Very little work had ever been done in Samaria. In terms of
archaeology, it was virtually *terra incognita*. In 1967, just at the Six
Day War's end, an emergency survey was made, but it was hurried
and incomplete. Some two hundred sites of all periods were
discovered—less than 15 percent of what Adam's team later
discovered—and Adam's survey is only 75 percent completed. Furthermore, the sites in the emergency survey were examined only in
a perfunctory way.

XV

Where His Brothers
Sold Joseph

dam, after painful years of physiotherapy, finally learned to walk on crutches over even the most challenging terrain, and in 1978, under the auspices of Tel Aviv University, launched his physically challenging master's project.

Zertal later extended his master's thesis to a doctorate on the Settlement Period in Manasseh. He expanded his survey to include the entire tribal area of the hill country of Manasseh. This was the territory assigned by Joshua, shortly before he died, to the tribe of Manasseh following the entry of the Israelites into the Promised Land. [Joshua 17:1–11] The tribe of Manasseh, descended from one of Joseph's two sons by his wife, Asenath, was the largest, and as a result was given an additional share of territory east of the Jordan. Ironically, the original Manasseh, who was the older son of Joseph, did not receive his proper inheritance as the oldest son. It was awarded, over Joseph's wishes, to his younger brother, Ephraim, by their grandfather, Israel, on his deathbed.

It is interesting that Israel, born Jacob, had managed to appropriate *his* older brother Esau's inheritance "for a mess of pottage," just as Ephraim had ultimately taken Manasseh's inheritance. Curiously enough, Moses was also the younger brother of Aaron.

According to biblical law, the firstborn was entitled to twice the inheritance of his younger brothers, but the Bible seems to have a prejudice against older brothers. Later, Solomon also usurped his

older brother Adonijah's right to the throne. [I Kings 2:15] The fact
that the tribes of Ephraim and Manasseh were from the north might
have had something to do with the deadly rift that developed from
the time of the kings onward between Judea and Samaria.

Although, according to the Bible and archaeological research, the
Israelites never actually conquered the inhabitants of Shechem, it
was the most historic of all areas in the Manasseh hill country to the
people of Israel at the time of the Israelite settlement. Indications
are that there was a peaceful coexistence between the Canaanite and
the Israelite cultures, with the Canaanites already worshiping El, a
Yahweh-like God who was their principal deity, while retaining their
older gods. Certainly there were implications of this possibility in
the discussions between Hamor and Jacob, following the rape of
Dinah.

It was in the vicinity of the mountain near Shechem, which I had
visited earlier, that Yahweh may have made his first covenant with
Abraham, telling him that this was the Promised Land of his people.
" 'It is to your descendants that I will give this land. . . .' " [Gen-
esis 12:7]

"Abram (Abraham) passed through the land as far as the site of
Shechem, at the terebinth of Moreh. The Canaanites were then in
the land.

"The Lord appeared to Abram and said, 'I will assign this land to
your offspring.' And he built an altar there to the Lord who had
appeared to him. . . . [Genesis 12:6]

The oak tree near Shechem that I saw on the mountain is possibly
descended from the one mentioned in Genesis 35:4. "They gave
Jacob all the foreign gods in their possession and the earrings that
they were wearing. Jacob buried them under the oak near
Shechem." In Joshua 24:26 Joshua makes a covenant and sets a
memorial stone under the oak "near Shechem." These show a relationship between Genesis and Joshua. It is an exciting thought
that these relics of Abraham might be buried somewhere under the
roots of that giant oak. But in light of the continuing conflict in the
area, will anyone ever dare to dig on this site?

Shechem is mentioned in ancient Egyptian documents going back
before 2000 B.C. Its ruler in the nineteenth century B.C. was Labaya,
one of the strongest of the pre-Israelite Canaanite rulers. He an-

nexed a great number of cities in the area and established a strong kingdom, with Shechem as its center.

By the time Joshua arrived, the city had been conquered many times by Egyptians from the south, and Hittite warriors from the north. What had once been a massive fortified city—or rather a series of fortified cities—had become a small unfortified town, exhausted by years of conflict, resting on top of the ancient ruins. It was at this point that the Israelites arrived and began to blend in with the local Canaanites, and possibly other Israelite tribesmen who were already there from the time of the patriarchs.

Shechem ultimately was razed by Abimelech, who was deposed after a brief but bloody attempt to take over the throne. In the next two hundred years, after the arrival of the Israelites, a city grew upon the site of the small town, and it became the capital for the northern Israelite tribes, who were then warring with the Judean tribes to the south in a dispute that arose following the death of Solomon and the succession of his son, Rehoboam. Ultimately, Omri, the fifth king of the northern empire, bought the mountain of Samaria and moved the capital to that city, today called Sebastia. He was succeeded by Jeroboam II, who rebuilt the city as his own capital. [I Kings 12:25]

In 1927 there was an earthquake on Ebal. Local people felt this was the fulfillment of "the curse" mentioned in the Bible. Few had read the actual text, so did not know that it was not the mountain that was cursed, but that it was from Ebal that the curses were to be pronounced, according to an idea presented by Mazar. They were satisfied that the earthquake had erased God's curse, and that the mountain was now free of it. A few Arabs have settled there since, but it is still relatively bare.

The postwar emergency survey, for all its importance, was selective. Some areas were thoroughly explored, while others were hardly touched. Also, the ecological and environmental aspects were not dealt with.

As a result, many of the evaluations that resulted from this early survey were incomplete, or incorrect. Zertal's survey, which was designed to cover the area thoroughly, would be the first true examination of the historic territory.

"In the beginning it was a small survey," Adam recalls. "Around the valley of Dothan, many times mentioned in the Bible. It was the valley where his brothers took Joseph and put him into the cistern.

"At that time I wanted to test myself. To see whether I was capable of doing the job or not. While working on it I used the two aluminum crutches most of the time. I think that was how I really rehabilitated myself. I became very enthusiastic. I liked it so much that the project went on and on and on. The results of the Dothan survey in the years '78 to '79 were so good, such a success, that with Nivi Markam, my friend and chief assistant, we decided to expand the territory to about one hundred square kilometers. That was the beginning, then to fifteen hundred square kilometers. And then we went on and on, and in '81, when we met Zvi Koenigsberg, we went down to Dothan and Shechem and east to the Jordan. The results also were so promising and successful that we simply expanded our plans again, and decided to survey all three-thousand-odd square kilometers of the Manasseh hill country.

"We were working where no one else had thoroughly explored before. This was very exciting and rewarding, too. The Manasseh hills were the first foothold of Israel in the land of Canaan, and the place in which the occupation of the Promised Land under Joshua's leadership had started."

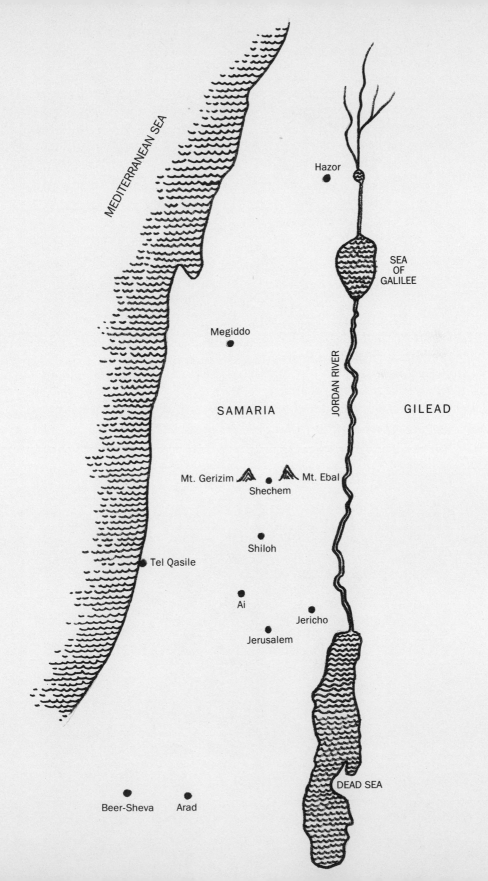

MEDITERRANEAN SEA

Hazor

SEA
OF
GALILEE

Megiddo

SAMARIA

JORDAN RIVER

GILEAD

Mt. Gerizim ⛰ ⛰ Mt. Ebal
Shechem

Shiloh

Tel Qasile

Ai

Jericho

Jerusalem

DEAD SEA

Beer-Sheva   Arad

An artist's rendering of the Ebal altar shows the ramp, with its ledge, the two courtyards, and other features: the retaining wall around the sacred precinct and the temenos wall, with its wide three-step processional entrance.
Drawing by Jock Stockwell

Artist's sketch of the altar on Mount Ebal showing ramps and temenos wall
Drawing by Jock Stockwell

Zertal and his assistants evaluate finds. Note Uzi on the table. *J. R. Ensey*

A golden earring of Egyptian origin found in an installation on the site. This is one of several finds tying the altar to Egypt. *J. R. Ensey*

Adam and his assistants compare pottery finds to an album enabling them to identify the sherd as to date and origins. *Victoria Nixon*

Adam and an associate chat with Abu Fathi, owner of the altar site. Adam's jeep is in the background. *Sharon R. Beisley*

Author at the site of the altar, south of ramps

Adam identifies pottery sherds to volunteers. *Richard Dameshek*

The oak tree at Elon Moreh, possibly descended from the oak under which Abraham buried his fetishes

Author near the summit of the altar site

Author near one of the installations surrounding the altar

Author at the temenos wall, the fence that traditionally surrounds a holy area

Author at a wall that extends to the center of the altar. This may have served the priests as a path to the sacrifice area. Stone would preserve the purity of the site.

Adam with a ritual piece
found on site. *Gail Merian*

Adam with a small incense altar found on site. His son Naboth is at left.
Ruth Whither

A tomb said to be that of Sheikh Belal, the Muezzin to Mohammed, on Elon Moreh, at the summit

Zertal on the dig with volunteers in the background. *Eugene Sucov*

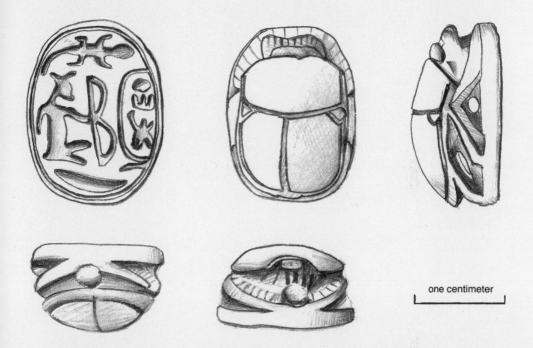

one centimeter

Artist's sketch of a scarab found buried in place in the altar area

Egyptian scarab dated to the time of Rameses II, commonly believed to be the pharaoh of the Exodus (1190–1224 B.C.). It was found just north of the altar. The incised image that looks like the letter "B" in the center of the scarab is a complex double bow held by a kneeling archer. The cartouche of the emperor Thutmoses III, in whose honor the scarab was issued, appears at the far right. At the top is a salamander, the Egyptian symbol for abundance. Surrounding sketches show side and top views. The scarab is modeled on the dung beetle, believed by Egyptians to be a symbol of immortality. This scarab and the other found on the site positively tie the altar to the time of the Exodus and indicate that the builders were of Egyptian origin. *Sketch by Jock Stockwell*

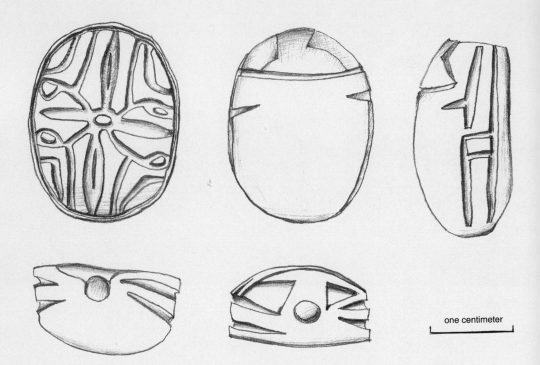

one centimeter

This scarab, like the other found on the site, is very rare. Only five like it have ever been found. It is dated to the time of Rameses II and Rameses III—the time commonly accepted as the date of the Exodus. This scarab (with side and back views) fixes the earliest date for construction of the altar as the thirteenth century B.C., and since it was found buried deep within the site, it certainly could not have been placed there at a later date. *Sketch by Jock Stockwell*

Artist's reconstruction of the Mount Ebal altar from above, indicating the ramp and ledges, plus the surrounding installations. The large square section is the sacrificial area. *Sketch by Jock Stockwell*

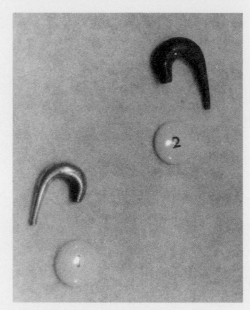

Silver and gold Egyptian earrings recovered on site, along with a bronze spearhead

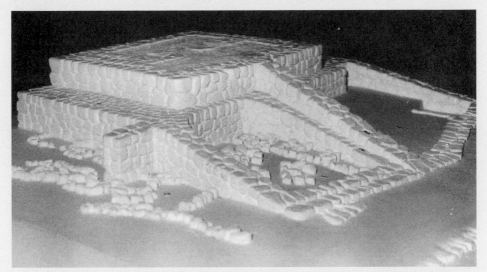

Reconstruction of the altar on display at the museum on Zertal's kibbutz, Ein Shemer

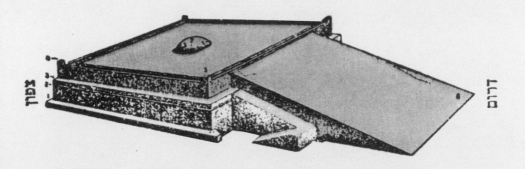

Sketch of the Second Temple altar from the Mishnah that gave Zertal his first insight into the exact function of the altar at Ebal

An aerial view of the altar. Ramp is to the left. Biblical Archaelogy Review

XVI

Who Was Joshua?: The Bible View

At this point it is worthwhile to ponder who Joshua really was. According to on-the-spot translations made for me by Zvi in the library of Shavei Shomron from the *Biblical Encyclopedia* (Hebrew edition, Volume 3, page 542), these are the facts:

Joshua's original name in Hebrew was Hoshea. It was changed to Yehoshua—Joshua in English—by Moses. Yehoshua is the Hebrew name of Jesus also. In Hebrew it means "God is salvation." *Jesus* is the Latin interpretation of the same name, from the Greek *Iesous*.

Joshua is first mentioned as the servant of Moses in Exodus when Moses is commanded by Yahweh to accept the stone tablets containing the commandments: "So Moses and his attendant, Joshua, arose, and Moses ascended the mountain of God." [Exodus 24:13]

Joshua is next mentioned after Moses erects what he calls the Tent Of Meeting, where he converses with Yahweh, who appears as a pillar of cloud at the entrance to the tent: "The Lord would speak with Moses face to face, as one man speaks to another. And he would then return to the camp; but his attendant, Joshua, son of Nun, a youth, would not stir out of the tent." [Exodus 33:11]

He next appears in Numbers when he, with Moses, hears a report about two of the Israelites who had begun to set themselves up as prophets in the camp: "And Joshua, son of Nun, Moses' attendant from his youth, spoke up and said, 'My Lord Moses, restrain them!' But Moses said to him, 'Are you wrought up on my account? Would

127

that all the Lord's people were prophets, that the Lord put His spirit upon them!' " [Numbers 11:28–30]

The following mention is apparently Joshua's initiation as a battle leader, with the spiritual support of Moses:

"Amalek came and fought with Israel at Rephidim. Moses said to Joshua, 'Pick some men for us, and go out and do battle with Amalek. Tomorrow, I will station myself on the top of the hill, with the rod of God in my hand.' Joshua did as Moses told him and fought with Amalek while Moses and Aaron and Hur went up to the top of the hill. Then, whenever Moses held up his hand, Israel prevailed; but whenever he let down his hand, Amalek prevailed. But Moses' arms grew heavy, so they took a stone and put it under him, and he sat on it, while Aaron and Hur, one on each side, supported his hands; thus his hands remained steady until the sun set. And Joshua overwhelmed the people of Amalek with the sword.

"Then the Lord said to Moses, 'Inscribe this in a document, as a reminder and read it aloud to Joshua: I will utterly blot out the memory of Amalek from under heaven!' " [Exodus 17:8–14]

According to Genesis 36:16, Amalek was the grandson of Esau. In the time of Judges, which was either contemporaneous or just after Joshua's time, the Amalekites were in alliance with Midianite bandits. They were still formidable in David's day, so apparently in spite of Yahweh's promise, Amalek's memory was not wiped out from under heaven for at least two hundred years, when David finally overwhelmed that tribe.

Joshua next appears in Numbers as one of the twelve spies, one from each tribe, who were sent by Yahweh's own orders: " 'Send men to scout the land of Canaan, which I am giving to the Israelite people; send one man from each of their ancestral tribes, each one a chieftain among them.'

"Moses, by the Lord's command, sent them out from the wilderness of Paran [in the Sinai Desert]. All of the men being leaders of the Israelites." And these were the names of the tribes he mentions: Reuben, Simeon, Judah, Issachar, Ephraim, Benjamin, Zebulon, Joseph (Manasseh), Dan, Asher, Naphtali, and Gad.

Those were the names of the tribes whose leaders Moses sent to scout out the land; but Moses changed the name of the leader of the tribe of Ephraim, Hoshea, the son of Nun, to Joshua. [Numbers 13:1–16]

This list is interesting as an indication of which tribes may have joined the covenant with Yahweh to become the nation of Israel. (It is believed by many that only the Josephite tribes of Manasseh and Ephraim, as well as Moses' own tribe of Levi, actually were in Egypt, the rest being already settled in various parts of Canaan.)

When Moses sent the spies out to scout the land of Canaan he said to them: " 'Go up into the Negeb on into the hill country and see what kind of country it is. Are the people who dwell in it strong or weak, few or many? Is the country in which they dwell good or bad? Are the towns they live in open or fortified? Is the soil rich or poor? Is it wooded or not? And take pains to bring back some of the fruit of the land.' " [Numbers 13:17–20]

At the end of forty days the twelve spies returned to the Israelite camp at Kadesh-barnea in the Sinai, from which they had departed. They carried produce of the country they had visited as Moses instructed them to; but they seemed very dispirited as they made their report to Moses, Aaron, and the assembled community. They told him: " 'We went to the land you sent us to; it does indeed flow with milk and honey; and this is its fruit. [They deposited a bunch of grapes so large that it took two men to carry it on a pole between them.] However, the people who inhabit the country are powerful, and the cities are fortified and very large; moreover we saw Anakites there. [A legendary race of giants.] Amalekites dwell in the Negeb region; Hittites, Jebusites, and Amorites inhabit the hill country and the Canaanites dwell by the sea and along the Jordan.' " [Numbers 13:27–29]

Caleb, leader of the tribe of Judah, argued with this pessimistic viewpoint: " 'Let us by all means go up, and we shall gain possession of it, for we shall surely overcome it.'

"But the men who had gone up with him said, 'We cannot attack that people, for it is stronger than we.' Thus they spread calumnies among the Israelites about the land they had scouted, saying 'The country we traversed and scouted is one that devours its settlers. All the people that we saw in it are men of great size, we saw the Nephilim there—the Anakites are part of the Nephilim—and we looked like grasshoppers to ourselves, and so we must have looked to them.' " [Numbers 13:30–33]

Only Joshua and Caleb differed from this view.

The distressing report of the other ten spies threw the people of Israel into a panic. They wept and wailed all night and complained to their leaders: " 'If only we had died in the land of Egypt,' the whole community shouted at them, 'or if only we might die in the wilderness! Why is the Lord taking us to that land to fall by the sword? Our wives and young children will be carried off! It would be better for us to go back to Egypt!' And they said to one another, 'Let us head back for Egypt.' " [Numbers 14:2–4]

Moses and Aaron were so appalled by this response, they threw themselves facedown on the ground in humiliation. Joshua and Caleb tore their clothes in grief and disgrace. Joshua spoke to the dispirited crowd:

" 'The country that we traversed and scouted is an exceedingly good land. If the Lord is pleased with us, he will bring us into that land, a land that flows with milk and honey, and give it to us. Only you must not rebel against the Lord. Have no fear of the people of the country, for they are our prey; their protection has departed from them, but the Lord is with us. Have no fear of them!' " [Numbers 14:7–9]

At this point the angry people even talked of stoning Caleb and Joshua; but at the crucial moment Yahweh appeared in a pillar of cloud at the Tent of Meeting. He was extremely angry with the people of Israel: " 'How long will this people spurn me? And how long will they have no faith in me despite all the signs that I have performed in their midst? I will strike them with pestilence and disown them. And I will make of you [Moses] a nation far more numerous than they!' " [Numbers 14:11–12]

But Moses argued desperately with Yahweh and asked him to give Israel another chance. He pointed out that it would look very bad to the people who had been conquered, who had already witnessed Yahweh's support of Israel, if he did not deliver his chosen people to the Promised Land, but instead slaughtered them.

Yahweh finally relented, but ruled that none of those who had left in the exodus from Egypt, except for Caleb and Joshua, would be able to enter the Promised Land, only the children and grandchildren born in the wilderness after the flight from Egypt. (For emphasis this is repeated at least twice elsewhere in the Bible.) To further show his wrath, Yahweh struck dead on the spot the ten remaining spies who had disparaged Israel's chances of winning Canaan. This explains the forty years spent by the people of Israel in the desert before entering Canaan, since it would take that long to raise another generation of Israelites capable of conquering Canaan.

As Moses was approaching his final days, he expressed concern to Yahweh about who would succeed him as leader of the people of Israel, and asked the Lord to appoint a new leader. Rabbinical scholars say, according to the book *Joshua and Judges*, that Moses had in mind one of his own sons; but Joshua had earned the distinction by a lifetime of service, whereas Moses' sons had not. Nevertheless, naturally, he left the choice to the Lord.

" 'Let the Lord, source of the breath of all flesh, appoint someone over the community who shall go out before them and come in before them, and who shall take them out and bring them in, so that the Lord's community may not be like sheep that have no shepherd.' And the Lord answered Moses, 'Single out Joshua son of Nun, an inspired man, and lay your hand upon him. Have him stand before Eleazar the priest and before the whole community, and commission him in their sight. Invest him with some of your authority, so that the whole Israelite community might obey. But he shall present himself to Eleazar the priest, who shall on his behalf seek the decision of the Urim before the Lord. . . . Moses did as the Lord commanded. He took Joshua and had him stand before Eleazar the priest and before the whole community. He laid his hands upon him, and commissioned him—as the Lord had spoken through Moses. [Numbers 27:16–23]

Eleazar was the third oldest son of Aaron. His two older brothers, Nadib and Abiyahu, had been destroyed with fire by the Lord at Mount Sinai when they mishandled an incense sacrifice. Eleazar succeeded as high priest after Aaron's death at Mount Hor, in the presence of Moses, just before the Israelites arrived at the Promised Land, and Eleazar became more or less a spiritual co-leader to Joshua.

In one of his last speeches to the people of Israel, Moses reaffirms

Joshua's ascendancy to leadership. He tells the men to gather together for the assault on Canaan, leaving their women and flocks behind. Moses says: " 'I also charged Joshua at this time, saying, you can see with your own eyes all that the Lord, your God has done to these two kings: So shall the Lord do to all the kingdoms into which you shall cross over. Do not fear them, for it is the Lord your God who will battle for you.' " [Deuteronomy 3:21–22]

The Bible says in Deuteronomy 27:4–5 that Moses then told the Israelites when they arrived at their destination to set up plastered stones with the words of his teachings written on them and to build an altar on Ebal. " 'When you cross over to enter the land that the Lord your God is giving you, a land flowing with milk and honey, as the Lord, the God of your fathers, promised you—upon crossing the Jordan, you shall set up these stones, about which I charge you this day, on Mount Ebal, and coat them with plaster. There, too, you shall build an altar to the Lord your God, an altar of stones. Do not wield an iron tool over them. You must build the altar of the Lord your God of unhewn stones. . . .' " And after this the Bible describes the curses that shall be offered on the mountain. In Deuteronomy 28:1–15 there is a short recitation of the blessings to be delivered on Mount Gerizim; but then from Deuteronomy 28:16 to the end of that chapter is another litany of curses.

Moses died, according to tradition, on the seventh of Adar, the twelfth month of the Israelite year. It was the beginning of Joshua's leadership.

XVII

Who Was Joshua?:
Modern Views

Much of the discussion about Joshua centers around concepts of who wrote the Bible and when. Students of the Bible text who are not fundamentalists, and who do not accept that every word in it is the word of God, have many theories, and these theories have importance in interpreting the meaning of stories and statements in the Bible. For instance, it was traditionally believed until the seventeenth century that Moses himself had written the Pentateuch (the first five books of the Bible). But the British philosopher Thomas Hobbes, in addition to many earlier rabbinical scholars who did not receive serious attention at that time, collected numerous cases of facts and statements through the Pentateuch that were inconsistent with Moses' authorship. For instance, the text frequently states that a certain situation is the case "to this day." This is not the phrase of someone describing a contemporaneous event. In fact, it suggests that many years have passed between the event and the Bible narrative. Hobbes was one of the first Western thinkers to raise the question, and it stirred strong negative feelings in most religious quarters, both Christian and Jewish.

But all of the questions raised by Hobbes, and by scientists who study the Bible today, were considered by traditional Jewish commentators such as Rashi, Ibn Ezra, Nachmanides, and Maimonides, among others, centuries before. The difference, of course, is that

133

these earlier scholars approached the subject from a theological position rather than a rationalistic one.

Four years after Hobbes's analysis, Isaac de la Peyrere, a French Calvinist, also wrote that Moses was not the author of the first books of the Bible. His book was banned and burned, and he himself was forcibly converted to Catholicism and imprisoned until he recanted to the pope.

Baruch Spinoza, the seventeenth-century Dutch-Jewish philosopher and rationalist, was among the first nonrabbinical Europeans to point out that the phrase at the end of Deuteronomy, "Never again did there arise in Israel a prophet like Moses" [Deuteronomy 34:10], did not make sense if Moses was considered the author of that book. Spinoza did not believe the Bible was divinely inspired. His theory essentially was that God is nature, and he introduced a concept of pantheism that is both rationalistic and mystical. Spinoza had already been excommunicated from Judaism. Now he was condemned by the Catholics and the Protestants as well.

However, it is important to note that these two were among the first Western philosophers to question the historical authenticity of the Torah, and each of them felt the necessity to develop an alternate philosophy, as a result of their having "lost" their original beliefs: Hobbes became one of the fathers of capitalism, and Spinoza was one of the first to make the equation of God-equals-Nature.

As years went by, into the nineteenth century, speculation about who wrote the Bible began to crystallize around certain perceptions.

A German scholar named Julius Wellhausen, born in 1844, became the most influential interpreter of the Bible of his time. In 1875 he published *Prolegomena zur Geschichte Israels*, in which he brought together all of the arguments then current. In 1880 and subsequently, he added research and opinions of his own to form an organized, if controversial, synthesis.

The presumed sources were divided up by Wellhausen into four groups, designated by the initials J, E, P, and D. The author of the document associated with the parts of the Torah that referred to God as Yahweh, or Jehovah, was identified with the letter J. The parts of the Bible that referred to God as Elohim were assigned to author E. The author of the third and by far the largest document, having much to do with biblical law and priestly matters, was designated by the letter P. And the source that seemed involved only with the book of Deuteronomy was named D. Later this reference was expanded to include D-1, D-2, and D-3. It is generally believed that D—called the Deuteronomist—wrote the book of Joshua, or most of it, also.

There was much speculation in succeeding years as to who had written what and when, based on both textual arguments and the archaeological evidence, extremely scarce for that era.

What has this all to do with Joshua's altar? A great deal, as we shall see as we look further into the ramifications of the subject.

XVIII

Finding Solomon's Lost City

Adam Zertal, as noted, had been fascinated by the "blue hills" of Manasseh since his childhood. But there were more important reasons for him to choose this area for his survey—mainly the fact that it had been almost untouched since the development of modern scientific methods of archaeological exploration. It was a perfect area in which to win his spurs in his chosen field, and his hunch soon proved spectacularly correct.

Adam had already told me that in this early portion of his survey, he soon discovered two important biblical sites: Khirbet el Hammam, which has now been definitely identified as Narbata, the site of the first Jewish revolt against Rome in A.D. 66, and the stratum beneath it, which has been identified as Aruboth, the Third District capital of King Solomon. This indicated that the site had been occupied by Israelites for about one thousand years. In 1981 he received his master's degree for his thesis entitled *Aruboth, Hefer, and Solomon's Third District*.

But more important, he discovered 160 Israelite sites from the early Iron Age—Joshua's time—tending to confirm the Bible's statement that this was the area where the nation of Israel first started. At least it tended to confirm that *some* Israelites had arrived via this route.

Zertal's research indicated that two thirds of the estimated population of Canaan in the eleventh century B.C. during the Settlement Period—25,000 out of 40,000—were in the Manasseh hill country and one third of the total sites located were Israelite. The pottery

136

trail led northward up the east bank of the Jordan, which, according
to Exodus, was the route of entry of the Israelites into the Promised
land.

Zertal was well aware that, according to the Bible, his survey was in
the area conquered by Joshua, but he also knew there was confusion
over biblical military history and a total lack of archaeological support. Jericho, for example, had been excavated years before by British archaeologist Dame Kathleen Kenyon. Kenyon decided there
had been no substantial settlement on the site at the time of Joshua,
and that the city had been sacked hundreds of years before his
arrival there. Fact: To this date almost no archaeological confirmation of *any* events in the Bible has been found prior to the time of
David—around 1000 B.C.

But as this is being written, a new theory has evolved concerning Jericho. Dr. Bryant Wood of the University of Toronto re-
opened the case of Joshua, long thought to have been settled.
Marshaling masses of evidence from pottery types, stratigraphic
data, Egyptian royal scarabs, carbon-14 dating, seismic activity,
and the actual tumbled walls of Jericho, he announced in an article
in the *Biblical Archaeology Review* [March–April 1990] that Jericho
was a fortified city that was destroyed by military action in 1400
B.C. This puts the event only two hundred or so years before the
presumed time of Joshua, and makes it more likely that the biblical story may have been based in folk history—or that Joshua's
time must be backdated.

Wood says that previous diggers were misled because they had
been excavating the wrong section of town. He based his new dating
of the destruction of Jericho on several pieces of evidence. A three-
foot layer of ash, containing many pottery fragments and mud bricks
from the city's wall, was found at the site, well preserved because it
was sealed by sediments that had accumulated atop it during the
years the city lay unoccupied. The charred fragments on the ash
layer have been carbon-dated to 1410 B.C. with an error variation of
forty years. In addition, several Egyptian scarabs or amulets have
been found in tombs near Jericho with inscriptions that date them to
the same period.

While Dr. Wood could not definitely establish that the crumbling of the wall had been the result of battle rather than normal decay, the crumbled walls seemed to date to the same time as the destructive fire that left the three-foot layer of ash.

Other evidence examined by Wood seemed to support the Joshua connection. The Bible says that Joshua's attack on Jericho took place during the spring harvest, and that after conquering the city Joshua burned it. Excavations uncovered large stores of grain buried in the pits under the houses, indicating that the city indeed fell after the spring harvest.

"The presence of these grain stores in the destroyed city is entirely consistent with the biblical account," Dr. Wood stated. "The city did not fall as a result of a starvation siege, as was common in ancient times. Instead, the Bible tells us, Jericho was destroyed after but seven days."

Wood also cites the record of seismic activity in the area as the possible reason that "the walls came tumbling down," as well as the basis for the stopping of the Jordan's waters so Joshua's troops could cross the riverbed dry-shod, as the Bible states. This temporary stoppage has happened at least four times over the years.

Adam continued his detailed survey of the Manasseh area, but troubles were on the horizon. He had originally been promised funding for the Narbata excavation by the Israeli archaeological officer for Samaria and Judea, who was the local representative for the Department of Antiquities in that area. On the basis of that support (which never came through), Adam went ahead and got permission from the owner of the Ebal site, an Arab named Abu Fathi, a farmer who lived in the nearby village of Asireh-E-Shemaliya, to dig in the area of Mount Ebal, in return for a job as caretaker. He obtained a permit from the Department of Antiquities to go ahead with the dig, but no funding. (The title of "watchman" applied to Abu Fathi is ironic to say the least as he is half blind, over eighty, lame, and rather timid.)

Once he got the go-ahead from Israeli authorities, Adam hired four Arab workers to clear away stones at the site. It was a grueling job, especially in July. But bureaucracy being what it is, and political sensitivities being what they are, money to pay the workers never arrived, and Zertal and Nivi had to spend July and August dodging the angry laborers. At one point Nivi was pursued on a four-hour chase into the avocado fields of the kibbutz, where the workmen finally gave up and went home peacefully.

Adam, who gets only a small allowance for personal expenses from the kibbutz itself, finally managed to scrape up some money by giving lectures in the evening in far-off cities and by guiding archaeological tours. He finally succeeded in paying the workers, but funding continued to be the most serious problem for the dig. To work properly at even a minimum level Adam had to raise from fifteen to twenty thousand dollars per season, an enormous sum for a kibbutznik.

Ebal, by Israeli standards, is a huge mountain—heart-shaped, about six and a half square miles, in the southern part of the Manasseh hills. It is, at three thousand feet, the tallest in that part of the country, and seems still taller since the Jordan Valley, which it overlooks, is about at sea level; in fact, the river itself is more than six hundred feet *below* sea level at that point.

From its peak, on a clear day, one can see the snows of Mount Hermon in Lebanon to the north, the mountains of Gilead across the Jordan to the east, the Mediterranean to the west, and the hills surrounding Jerusalem to the south. Below is the deep narrow valley of Shechem. Straight ahead in the valley is the green line marking the regularly flowing stream of Wadi Farah and, above it, the ancient city of Tirzah, a Canaanite settlement conquered by Joshua, according to the Bible. [Joshua 12:24]

"On a cool spring afternoon early in April of 1980," Adam recalls, "when we had nearly completed our survey of the mountain, we came upon a large heap of stones on Ebal, which was not very different from the thousands of stone heaps we had already found, collected by farmers who were clearing their fields for planting. True, this heap of stones was somewhat larger than the typical one; but what really distinguished it was the great quantity of pottery sherds lying around it."

The mound he was looking at, Adam found, was called El Burnat by the local fellahin, for its shape. In Arabic this means "the hat." It was in a field on the eastern slope of Mount Ebal, on a low stony ridge. The eastern slope of Ebal consists of four large steps, and the mound site was on the third level from the top. The site was enclosed on three sides by beautiful little valleys, producing an amphitheaterlike setting.

Adam was aware of the biblical significance of Ebal, but at first didn't dwell on the possibility that this was the site of Joshua's altar. Four expeditions had already looked for that altar and had failed. This seemed to be on the wrong side of the mountain. So what *was* this large mound? A house? A tower? A temple?

The sherds that covered the field in which the mound was located, Adam could quickly determine, were from the early part of Iron Age I—the period of the Israelite occupation of Canaan at the end of Exodus. But what made the site on Ebal unusual was that the field in which the mound was located contained almost entirely sherds from the Israelite Settlement Period. And, as it turned out, this was the only early Iron Age I settlement on the mountain. Eleven other sites were discovered but all were dated at least seven hundred years later than those found near the mound on Ebal.

Adam was now definitely interested, but it took nearly two years to raise money for the dig. His original grant had been for a survey only. It turned out that one of the reasons he had problems raising the money was the fact that the site was in Samaria, which many considered "occupied territory." American universities and most other foreign institutions would not finance it as long as it fell under the rule of the U.N. Resolution forbidding digs in the occupied lands. Feelings in Israel were even stronger, with the left, or Labor party bloc, violently opposed to any development of the West Bank, and the right, or Likud bloc, favoring settlement in and exploration of the West Bank, in which Samaria is located.

"We weren't really in a rush," Adam says, "because I had no idea that there was any profound importance to the site. It was simply the one I felt was most worth investigating more thoroughly."

At one point a group of wealthy English Zionists offered to provide all the funds needed for the project. Adam was elated, but ultimately the offer was withdrawn when the regional archaeological officer would not confirm Ebal as an official archaeological site within a reasonable amount of time, despite repeated requests, by which time the Englishmen were disgusted and lost interest.

Finally, partly under the auspices of Tel Aviv University and partly through private sources, Adam was able to raise seed money to start digging. A considerable part of the help came from the regional council. In addition, many of Zertal's personal friends helped him as volunteer experts.

XIX

Blisters, Sun, Thorns, and Thirst

The first season, in the spring of '82, was devoted almost entirely to building the road to get down to the site. This consisted basically of the murderous work of moving huge boulders off the site of the dig, after they had first been identified as not being part of the ancient context.

Step one for Adam's expedition was trying to define just where to start working. It was only after he started to plan in 1981 that the logistics of the whole project were mapped out. He received much free help from a lanky, bearded young archaeological architect named Zvi Lederman, now studying for his doctorate at Harvard.

In a way, a part of funding is the enlistment of volunteers—the foot soldiers who do what is essentially drudge work in return for the adventure of working the dig and the educational and spiritual benefits that may accrue from such work. The majority of the volunteers are recruited from among students and biblical scholars. Most come from Israeli schools, but others are recruited principally by announcements in popular publications such as the *Biblical Archaeology Review*. In general, volunteers must pay a minimal sum of one hundred dollars a week for food and lodging at Ebal during their stay at the base camp near the dig. Usually the work is augmented by lectures and tours of other sites. Often course credit is given to those students who are matriculating, especially in Israeli universities. The idea of the credits was something Koenigsberg suggested to

Adam back in 1983, for the purpose of increasing the number of American volunteers, primarily for financial reasons. It made the idea of joining the dig much more attractive, since the cost of a credit was considerably less than the much larger sums charged by U.S. schools. The work is grueling, usually starting before sunrise and continuing through the hot Israeli summer days. Unfortunately, the bulk of the work must be done in the summer, because that is the time when volunteers are generally more available. In Adam's case, many of the volunteers were from his own classes at Haifa University.

Also there was Nivi Markam, who became Adam's chief assistant. It was Nivi's practical expertise that kept Adam's ancient blue jeep and other machinery functioning through the years. But, though first used as a technical assistant, Markam soon became a top expert on identification of pottery, as knowledgeable as most trained professionals in the sherds that were likely to turn up in the terrain of Manasseh.

But there were other sorts of volunteers too: experienced specialists such as Zvi Lederman, who served many seasons as an architectural adviser and draftsman, archaeological sketchers and photographers, members of university staffs who without pay lent their expertise on carbon-dating, thermoluminescence, paleobotany, ecology, and other highly specialized fields, whose work would cost a fortune if not offered gratis by interested scientists. One of the services volunteered early in the expedition, through the efforts of Zvi Koenigsberg, was the use of vacant buildings at Shavei Shomron for field headquarters and residences for the volunteers at a modest sum. Adam's kibbutz contributed by allowing him to earn his allowance while working on the project, and by assigning Nivi Markam and sometimes others to assist him. In addition to his mechanical ability, Markam was knowledgeable about natural phenomena and first aid.

"He treated the blisters on my hands the first day," one volunteer recalls, "and convinced me to wear the gloves he had given me. It didn't take much to persuade me after that first day. I had a multitude of splinters and thorns from the dried-up bushes, and the blisters I already had acquired were proof enough that I needed the gloves."

Only after preliminary work had started in 1982 did the edifice begin to take form. Aside from the structure, one of the earliest finds was fieldstone-lined pits with an average diameter of one meter near the north wall that might be offering installations for religious rites. These gave the first clues as to what the function of the site might be. But by that time the season was over and the dig had to be covered to protect it for the following year.

XX

"The Perfect Crime"

In 1983 there were two seasons, one in the spring and one in the fall. The former was almost a catastrophe because the first volunteers were still inexperienced. They really didn't have any practice at working on a dig, which requires extreme care in disposing of any finds, being sure exactly where they came from. This includes rocks and bits of unidentifiable material as well as pottery sherds. Every ounce of earth exhumed from a site must be passed through a sieve to catch any tiny bit of evidence it might contain. Later the sherds, which are put into marked containers to show exactly where they originated, are carefully washed to bring out any markings that may lie under the millennia of dirt and dust coating them. If no inscription appears, they are gently brushed to see if something may lie under the next layer of dirt. This technique was developed about twenty years ago by the noted Israeli archaeologist Yohanon Aharoni while excavating the ruins of the town of Arad. The technique requires extraordinary effort; any Near Eastern dig will uncover thousands of sherds, but the results are often worth the effort. At Arad, for example, thanks to this technique, a rich collection of epigraphic materials was uncovered, some of which clearly identified the dig as an Israelite religious site. Later an entire archive of more than two hundred inscribed potsherds, called *ostraca*, were unearthed, dating to the sixth century B.C. and written both in Hebrew and Aramaic. Included in this material was the first and only reference to the temple in Jerusalem ever found in a Hebrew inscription.

The techniques and information involving archaeology are evolving so fast that a textbook written today would be out of date by the time it was published. Yigael Yadin, excavator of Hazor and Masada, was attempting such a text when he died in 1984. But archaeologists have found at least a stopgap answer to keeping the ceramic record up to date. They have compiled what they call an album, which includes the latest additions of pottery found on various sites. This album is a summary of finds from ten or fifteen sites, and it is used to make it possible for the finds to be typed and dated. The album specifies the color, shape and size, and decorations of each type of vessel. Israelite Iron Age pottery, for instance, is fairly thick-walled and almost devoid of paint or decoration.

Two basic types of jars were found at the Ebal site. The first is thick and symmetrical, the other a bit thinner and smaller. It is not symmetrical, and a part of the rim is pinched into a spout for pouring. The description of the color of the clay reads "light pink" for both types. But though all Israelite pots of this era are light pink in color, some are not actually pink all the way through. If a piece is "sandwiched" so that it is darker in the middle, or "twinned" so that it is darker on one side than the other, that pottery was either fired at a low temperature or for a short period of time. When a piece has been fired at a high temperature it tends to be light pink all the way through.

During the reading of the pottery finds of any given day, the album is in constant use to identify each piece. After the pottery is read, it is tagged in one of three ways: with a minus, a plus, or a "W." A minus indicates that the piece is worthless and can be thrown away. Plus-marked pottery is saved and sent to the lab for restoration, if at all possible. A piece marked "W" indicates that the sherd may be significant at a later time, and so should be held to await future developments.

All pottery not sent to the lab is returned to the site to avoid confusion. If an archaeologist a generation later discovers piles of pottery out of place for the site, misconceptions could develop.

For the final publication a photo is taken, and each piece is drawn, given a number, and recorded. A copy of the drawing is entered into the computer and compared with finds at other sites to give it an accurate approximate dating. This is one of the newer processes; but even this method is still evolving so that soon it should be possible to give the computer the job of making complete drawings and giving the margins of time for dating. This should save archaeologists much valuable time, and tend to eliminate guesswork.

Adam had to sit over his volunteers like a mother hen to make sure the young enthusiasts didn't misplace any of the things they dug up. They could move one stone and break up installations, or they might otherwise disturb the delicate factors that indicated the origins of the artifact or piece of stone involved. Lederman, who worked three seasons on the site and continued as a part-time consultant when he was called away by other work, observed: "In archaeology we constantly commit the perfect crime. A rock or an artifact in its proper place can tell us a dramatic story, but move it a few feet from the site, and the evidence no longer exists. It has disappeared."

Lederman told me that a volunteer had once moved a stone, and it had been two years before they realized it was a vital part of the stairway that led to the northern courtyard, adjoining the ramp.

The life of a volunteer on an archaeological site like Ebal can be inspiring but it is not easy. Barbara Lo Bianco, a volunteer on the Ebal site in the 1986 season, kept a diary of her experiences, part of which was published in the *Biblical Archaeology Review* in January 1987.

A forty-nine-year-old housewife from the Pittsburgh area and the mother of five, she decided to fulfill a dream by becoming a volunteer on Adam's dig on Mount Ebal.

Barbara, who had never participated in a dig before, chose Mount Ebal after reading Zertal's 1986 story. She is a religious teacher at her church and had often read in Deuteronomy about Moses' command to Joshua to build an altar to God on Ebal. She kept a daily journal while on the site. Here are some of the entries:

June 23, 2:50 P.M.: We were awakened at 3:30 this morning by Nivi knocking softly on our doors, and saying "BO-ker tov," which is "good morning" in Hebrew. We had coffee in the dining room, and piled into the vans by 4:30 A.M. for the forty-minute ride up the mountain. Out of the vans and then a twenty-minute walk down a steep slope and up an adjoining hill to the site of the dig.

At sunrise, the scenery is breathtaking. The mists lifted as we walked past groves of olive trees and rocky fields. I heard the tinkle of a bell before I saw its source, a young goat. A herd appeared a second later, followed by sleepy young goatherds.

We continued our walk up the hill; here the rocks are larger, the path is all but gone and the rocks and thistles are everywhere. Soon the sun was up, and the stones of the excavation site gleamed back, blindingly white. Adam, who walked with us, pointed out the main structure, its inner and outer walls, the entrance to the main enclosure, and the step area where we Americans ended up working today.

Our first instructions were to pull the weeds that have grown around the site since last season. We were given heavy gloves and small picks to loosen the dirt and a bucket to put the weeds in. We pulled weeds for about three hours and were so busy that we failed to notice that a tent had been set up about 100 yards from the altar site. When Nivi called us for breakfast in the tent, we gladly stopped work. Breakfast consisted of a hard-boiled egg, a cucumber, a tomato, humus (chick-pea paste laden with garlic), bread, olives, sour cream, chocolate spread (an Israeli specialty we became accustomed to), watermelon and coffee or tea.

By breakfast's end the sun had cleared the air—a promise of the day's coming heat. Adam took us up to the high point of the site from which you can see for miles. He pointed out the Jordan Valley and Tirzah. I felt as though I could see Joshua and his troop marching through the valley up to Mount Ebal. Soon I was back pulling thistles.

June 24, 3:15 P.M.: We were up again this morning at 3:45. At the dig we were each issued a bucket, a brush, a pick and a trowel used to gently remove dirt. When we found pottery sherds we put them in a separate bucket marked with a number indicating the precise area in which we were working. After an individual's bucket was full of dirt, it was carried to a screening area and the dirt sifted for sherds, bones and tiny artifacts.

XXI

Mysterious Stone Circles

Every inch of soil covering the bottom of the locus being dug by the volunteers could represent one hundred years. In six seasons only eighteen inches of covering were removed. None of the earth—not "dirt," they were told—was thrown away. Everything went into the bucket, and they later took it to a big wire-mesh sieve.

I got the feeling, talking to some of the volunteers after their work on the dig, that the experience could be boring and exciting at the same time. One of the volunteers in the '83 season, John Delph, a theatrical technician and organ player in a New Jersey church, described a typical day's work to me: "We found hundreds of sherds, which we later washed and gave to the archaeologists for evaluation. Most of them were discarded as having no valuable information. The archaeologists were interested mainly in the rims, the handles, and the bases, as well as the neck. Pottery changed as often as every fifteen years, we were told, and so it was a very valuable tool for dating sites. We used fingernail brushes to wash pottery. There was a backlog, so sometimes we washed the previous weeks' finds as well. There was a huge pile of discarded sherds from which we were allowed to select souvenirs—a pile four to five feet high. But before throwing the sherds into the pile we kept a computer count of identity of pieces.

"You can't move a stone until you have cleared the terrain all around it and swept around it," Delph observed. "It is slow, meticulous work. I knew that digging took a lot of patience, and I was

149

wondering if I could handle it; I did. I was amazed, because Adam was wonderful, he made it so inspiring and he was so excited and it was infectious. He made the whole experience come alive. . . . In the evenings he would give us lectures explaining the significance of what we were doing. Sometimes also in the daytime on the dig.

"On the final day they brought a big ladder to get photographic angles in shooting the site and recording how it looked at that time. When they closed the site up they would cover exposed artifacts with sand to protect them from thieves and vandals.

"We saw the Arab owner occasionally, Abu Fathi, striding around the property with his shepherd's staff, inspecting his land. We were told that in biblical times it was forested and they had to clear the land to use it for pasture and agriculture."

Generally Abu Fathi had no problems with the work going on at the site, but one day there was an apparent dispute between Abu Fathi and Zertal: "A hush fell over the whole site," a volunteer recalls, "And everyone stopped working. Apparently the owner was upset because we were putting rocks where he didn't like them to be. He and Adam spoke for a long time, and while they were doing so one of the young volunteers went over and took a trial ride on Abu Fathi's donkey. After a small dispute the discussion was ended with no apparent ill will."

During that season the diggers uncovered some stone enclosures that were believed to be holding pens for animals to be sacrificed in the area. There was much discussion among volunteers, especially Christians, about their religious beliefs. One even saw an analog to resurrection in Adam's return from near-death in the Yom Kippur War to his present achievements on Ebal.

Most of the walls were found intact and did not have to be reconstructed. Zvi Lederman was on site sometimes, or other professionals observing the work. The wall between loci, called the "balk," retains stratification so that the time reference is not destroyed by the digging. Idan, a professional, sketched and mapped all the sites before they were closed.

The same year, 1984, excavators discovered a collar-rim jar in a circular stone installation in the altar's courtyard. There were no ashes in the vessel, but it was in a cultic location, so Zertal assumed it had contained a nonburnt offering—perhaps some liquid that had evaporated, perhaps a libation of oil. There is still no information on what this liquid was.

The structure itself was the main area of operations in both the spring and the fall seasons of 1983. In any event, in 1983 the edifice really began to take shape. In the beginning you were able to make out this mound of rocks. You could discern the wall going around the large enclosure, which was very interesting in itself.

The central structure turned out to be almost square, measuring 24.5 feet by 29.5 feet with walls 5 feet thick. The stones, untrimmed, are laid on top of one another with no mortar or cement to hold them. Its height is almost 9 feet, which, because the structure is so well-preserved, Zertal assumes to be close to its original height.

But one of the most interesting things about the structure was the fill that lay between the walls. It was not the normal debris that might have accumulated from some building above that had collapsed. There were no signs of fire or deliberate destruction anywhere.

Instead, the fill seemed to have been laid down from above in deliberate layers until the whole structure formed a sort of stage. It took several seasons to excavate this fill. Half of it was left in place to serve as reference or proof. There were four distinct layers found by the diggers; they were labeled A to D, from bottom to top.

Zertal concluded in his preliminary report of the dig: "It seems that the filling of the structure was the result of one single activity and not of accumulation. There are no signs of fire or other uses on the inner sides of the walls, which might have indicated activity *after* the building stage, and *before* the fill was put into place. The composition of the fill and the direction of the layers support this claim. The layers are identical throughout the structure, and their direction indicates their being spilled from above the dividing walls. The pottery types inside the fill are identical, and it is almost impossible to assume a long period of accumulation." Additionally, Zertal noted, there were no parallels to this type of fill discovered to this date. Most others were of stones or pebbles, or simply earth.

In addition to this, Zertal found that all the pottery in the fill, which dated from 1250 B.C., was from separate vessels, so that no complete pot could be assembled as is the case where a building has collapsed, even if all the ceramics are shattered. The broken pottery had obviously been assembled from different sources and dumped in the structure.

The four layers of the fill consisted, from bottom to top, of:

Layer A: a relatively thin layer of pure black ash evenly laid, composed of many animal bones and sherds. About sixteen inches thick. It lies on a "paving" of Level II just above the bedrock.

Layer B: Composed of a sizable quantity of stones and earth with few animal bones and sherds, between twenty-one and thirty inches in depth.

Layer C: The majority of the bones and sherds are found at this level. Here, too, the southern and eastern sides were highest, indicating that the fill was poured from this direction. Its thickness is from eighteen to twenty-one inches and contains ash, ash mixed with earth, and many bones and sherds. The quantity of stone is small. Zertal calculated that this fill had been assembled elsewhere and brought to the site.

Layer D: Made of earth and stones. Being at the highest level it was most exposed to the elements. Apparently it formed a base for the top paving of the structure, but this top level is missing.

The large structure (Level I) was divided by two cross walls. If these walls had been extended farther, they would have met in the middle of the structure. They were too short to meet, however.

Under the fill, on Level II, the digging team found some curious stone-built installations. One of them consisted of a circle of medium-sized fieldstones. The outside diameter of the circle of stones was 6.5 feet. Inside the circle was a thin layer of yellowish burned-looking material, which has not yet been identified. On top of this yellowish layer was a thin layer of ash and animal bones. The round stone installation lay on the bedrock, exactly under the center of the main structure on Level I. Near the circle were small groupings of stones with signs of burning that might have served as the site of local cook fires. A similar circle of stones has been found in an earlier dig near the Yarkon River in the Tel Aviv area, at a place called Tel Qasile, by noted archaeologist Amihai Mazar, and had been interpreted by the excavators in 1980 as a sacrificial altar.

(In my own reading I found another curious parallel in a dig in Egypt, the results of which have not yet been published. In 1979 at a site called Tel el-Daba, near the biblical city of Rameses in the

eastern Nile Delta, Austrian archaeologist Manfred Bietak, of the
Austrian Archaeological Institute in Cairo, found a temple or cultic
site far more primitive in artistry and execution than the Egyptian
work surrounding it, which he dates to the time of the Hyksos
occupation of Egypt, three hundred years before the reign of
Rameses II. Bietak identifies this site as the Hyksos colonial capital
of Avaris. The Hyksos at the time were in control of the area, having
conquered the Egyptian forces. According to recent research reported in *The Archaeological Encyclopedia of the Holy Land,* the Hyksos
ruled Egypt, Syria, and Palestine during the years 1650–1542 B.C.
On the outskirts of the city, Bietak found a large sacred area, together with a nine-foot-long rectangular altar, the surface of which
was covered with ash and charred bones. All around this altar were
pits filled with ashes and more charred bones, obviously from animal
sacrifices. Analysis of the bones showed them to be principally of
cattle and a few sheep with, it is interesting to note, not a single pig
bone among them. Bietak estimates that the people who built the
site were Canaanites of the patriarchal era or earlier, who worked for
the Hyksos and were allowed to pasture their flocks in the area. The
site is not on a "high place," probably because the land in this area
is as flat as a pool table.)

A Beetle Emerges
from the Past

One of the dividing walls of the upper structure that Zertal found was built directly over the center of the circular structure, passing over the circle of stones on the lower, earlier, level.

"It is quite obvious," Zertal concluded, "that the installations at the bottom of the structure represent an earlier phase, and the large structure itself represents a later phase—both from Iron Age I." The ash in the fill of the main structure consisted of burned wood and animal bones, which Adam also sent for analysis to Liora Kolska-Horowitz at the zoology department of Hebrew University in Jerusalem. There were some three thousand pieces of bone in the fill.

Including the second, more primitive level, laid on bedrock, there was no sign that any people but the Israelites had ever occupied this site from the time it was built.

Because of the ash in the lower installation, Adam tended to believe that the installation was used in some fire-related activity before the larger structure was built.

It is likely that the lower level was used for religious purposes when it was dedicated in anticipation of the building of the upper structure. A similar thing occurred just after the exile when the Israelites returned from Babylon and were invited by King Cyrus to rebuild their temple: "When the builders had laid the foundation of the Temple of the Lord, priests in their vestments with trumpets, and Levites and sons of Asaph with cymbals were stationed to give praise to the Lord. . . ." [Ezra 3:10] This passage gives at least a precedent for ceremonies at the foundation site.

Zertal continued to sketch in the earlier background for me. "In 1983 the structure really began to take shape. In the beginning you were able to identify a large mound of rocks. You could make out the wall going around the large enclosure, which is very interesting in itself. The structure itself was the main area of operations in both the spring and the fall seasons of 1983.

"Probably the most exciting single find during that third season of the dig was the scarab we found on Level II, dating to the period of Rameses II. It is an oval object in the shape of an Egyptian dung beetle. It was only about three quarters of an inch long, and would have been easy to miss. These little carved figures were regarded as important talismans by the ancient Egyptians. The dung beetle ate dead meat and in so doing, in a sense, gave it new life. The Egyptians thought of this as a symbol of the resurrection of the body with which they were so involved. This scarab had a rare design. Within its elliptical frame the scarab had a motif embodying a geometrical pattern consisting of a four-petal rosette and, between the petals, four branches. From each branch comes an Egyptian cobra, called a uraeus.

"We sent it for identification to Baruch Brandl, a noted Egyptologist at Hebrew University, and the expert on such scarabs, but we were already very excited because this scarab, which was clearly Egyptian in design, being found stratigraphically located in the site, would give us an unchallengeable date for when the structure was built. Also it tied the Israelites of Ebal to an Egyptian heritage, giving some support for the Exodus version of the origins of the nation of Israel," Adam told me.

When Brandl's report came back, Zertal was very happy with it. Brandl said that the scarab was very rare; only five like it are known to exist—one from Egypt, three from Israel, and one from Cyprus. By means of these parallel finds the scarab can be dated as somewhere between the period of Rameses II—the nineteenth dynasty, which was in the thirteenth century B.C.—and the period of Rameses III—the twentieth dynasty, beginning at the twelfth century B.C. This is exactly the period generally agreed upon as the beginning of the Israelite settlement (or conquest, depending on your view of Israelite history).

This scarab fixed the earliest date for the construction of the Mount Ebal altar; it could not have been built before the thirteenth century B.C. Of course in theory it could have been built later. The scarab could have belonged to someone for any amount of time before being deposited in the place where it was found, but the fact that it was found in a stratigraphic situation associated with pottery of the same era as the scarab made this all but impossible. Most important was that the scarab had been found in an undisturbed stratum on the bedrock of the earliest level. It was almost impossible that it could have been placed where it was at a later date.

According to Adam, "Scarabs have not been considered by some to be absolutely reliable as dating clues. Because they were rare and precious, they tended to survive a long time, so it seemed at first that it could be possible that a scarab found on a site had been dropped or deposited there many years after the time of Rameses. But the Ebal scarab—with a stone seal found at the same time—was the *only* scarab ever found in a stratigraphic location in a small isolated site which almost certainly was not visited after its period of usefulness had ended. It is not possible to conceive that someone dug up the site without disturbing the stratification and placed these objects in different parts of the ruin without disturbing the site, nor is it possible to conceive of a reason that anyone would do such a thing. Therefore the altar could not have been built at any time earlier than the manufacture of the scarabs, and from the stratigraphic evidence, not much later."

Finkelstein, the explorer of the adjacent highlands of Ephraim, said when he learned of the scarab's discovery: "Unless later parallels to these scarabs will be found they constitute the single, direct, definite piece of archaeological evidence for the existence of an Israelite Settlement site as early as the Thirteenth Century BCE."

This buttressed Adam's other finds, including collar-rimmed storage vessels, called pithoi, commonly used by Israelites during the Settlement Period to store water and other liquids, and dated by almost all archaeologists to the thirteenth through the twelfth centuries B.C. These large jars are similar to jars found at the cultic center in Shiloh—the only place they were found in this area. In

Shiloh they were the only artifacts found of this period. Similar jars of a later design were found near the altar at the Temple Mount in Jerusalem, indicating that this was a prototype of a vessel connected with religious ceremonies. No Israelite pithoi are earlier than those at Ebal.

In the midst of the excitement about these key finds, there was an unexpected staff problem. The bulk of the volunteers that year were from an Orthodox yeshiva school; but there were others from various kibbutzim in Israel, as well as foreign volunteers—and some of these volunteers were *girls*. The yeshiva boys had been kept from contact with girls their own age throughout their upbringing, and these girls were mainly dressed in revealing shorts or tight-fitting jeans. But the rabbi who accompanied the boys was sympathetic and managed to defuse the situation in the interests of biblical research. He explained to his students that sometimes, in these modern days, you had to "suffer such things." By the time the dig was over, the boys, probably for the first time, had a fair idea of the human female anatomy. For them, the dig was doubly educational.

Some months after the closing of that dig season, the osteological report came from Liora Kolska-Horowitz. The analysis of the bones Zertal had found on the site contained interesting news. The bones turned out to be from young male bulls, sheep, goats, and fallow deer. Most of the bones had been burned in open-flame fires at a low temperature of between 390 and 1,200 degrees Fahrenheit. Some of the bones had been cut near the joints.

It would appear that these were the usual sacrificial animals, with one exception—the fallow deer.

A sacrificial animal is described in Leviticus as an animal "without blemish" [Leviticus 1:3]. It may be a bull [Leviticus 1:5], or a sheep or a goat [Leviticus 1:10]. It is interesting that a sizable proportion—about 20 percent—of the bones were from domestic cattle, indicating that the Israelites were already well settled in the area, as cattle are not suited to nomadic existence.

"The close match of the bones found in the fill with Leviticus 1:3 was a strong hint to the nature of the site we were excavating," Zertal noted. "Although fallow deer were not included in the biblical description, they are a kosher animal that may be slaughtered and eaten, so it is possible, some biblical scholars feel, that during the early stages of the Israelite religion, a fallow deer could also have been used as a sacrifice." The fallow deer today is considered extinct, or nearly so in this area. According to the Kolska-Horowitz faunal report: "The high frequency of *Dama* (fallow deer) suggests that there was genuine forest parkland in this region, since such an environment is necessary to support a large fallow deer population." The deer may actually have died off because the early Israelites cleared off the forest park on the hilltops that were its natural habitat. But there were then and are now pigs, mules, horses, dogs, and burros on the mountain. No bones of these animals appeared on the Ebal site. Nor did fowl, rabbits, or other presumably available animals, except for a few modern accidental intrusions. In other Iron Age sites, according to the osteological report, at least one of these species appears at each site, usually more than one. "The species represented and their frequencies," says the report, "suggest that only edible animals are present at Mount Ebal, while at other sites animals possibly used for various purposes (such as equids) are present."

In regard to fallow deer, it must be noted that Leviticus is generally believed to have been written long after the time of the Ebal altar, at least 250 years later, possibly at a time when the fallow deer was not so common, or extinct in that part of the world, following the destruction by the Israelite settlers of the forest park in which they dwelled. Also, since the deer bones were found on Level II, the earlier level, it is possible that the deer were eaten as part of the ordinary kosher meals and not sacrificed by those involved with the later site, and were then incorporated with the fill. From another angle, there is an opinion in the Talmud in the tractate of Pesahim (Passover sacrifice) that fallow deer are acceptable as sacrifices, but this idea was rejected by the majority of the Talmud scholars at that time. The Ebal find may change thinking on this subject. The function of the underlying circle of stones and ashes was probably to sanctify the site before going on to construct the larger structure and surrounding installations.

XXIII

The Question of "A Man's Face"

In the third season the site revealed further mysteries. One discovery, for instance, was that two corners of the structure, within an error factor of less than one degree, point north and south. Since the structure is rectangular, the other two corners point approximately, though not as exactly, east and west.

Attached to the structure on the southwestern side were two adjacent stone-paved courtyards. In each courtyard were stone-built installations—basically holes in the ground lined with stones and surrounded with stone circles like the ones found in the beginning outside the northeast wall. There were three in one courtyard and four in the other, and they contained either ashes and animal bones or complete pottery vessels—jars, jugs, juglets, and containers of various shapes of apparent religious significance. Some of the installations were paved with crushed chalk or plaster.

What at first glance appeared to be a wall separating the two courtyards outside the large rectangular structure actually rises from the far side of them and approaches the main structure, at an incline of 22 degrees. This turned out to be a ramp leading up to the stage on top of the main edifice. This ramp is a bit over three feet wide and twenty-three feet long. It is made of medium-size fieldstones. The highest point of the ramp indicates that the main structure was one layer of stones higher than its present elevation, rising to a height of approximately ten feet. So both the ramp and the excellent

state of preservation of the main structure indicate it has been preserved to nearly its full original height.

Not everyone on the team was as certain as Adam that it definitely
was a ramp and not simply a collapsed wall. Zvi Lederman, the
architectural consultant on the project, agreed, but with reservations: "As a ramp, as it was found during the dig, it's not a good
ramp, that's for sure," he told me when I interviewed him later at
Harvard. "It's a problem. But the other explanations are no better.
When a stone wall collapses, it doesn't collapse only to one side. It
collapses on all sides, unless there's an earthquake."

About three feet below the top of the main structure is a thin wall
that encircles three sides of it, in effect creating a ledge attached to
the outer wall on the three sides that do not include the ramp. As
this wedge goes from the northwest side to the southwest side it
gradually widens from about 2 feet until it reaches a width of 7.5
feet. Remember that the upper corner, as you face the structure,
faces due north. This ledge also curves around the corner formed by
the intersection of the ramp and continues down one side of the
ramp.

There is absolutely no functional explanation for this thin wall or
ledge, says Zertal. "Obviously it wasn't built to strengthen the main
structure whose walls are made of large stones. These walls of large
stones certainly would not be supported by a thin wall on the outside. Moreover, the archaeological evidence indicates that the thin
surrounding wall was built at the same time as the thick inner wall
against which it leans; the thin wall was not a later addition."

The structure, together with its ramp and courtyards and adjacent
area, is surrounded by a thin elliptical wall enclosing about 37,650
square feet—somewhat less than an acre. This Zertal identified as a
temenos wall. This is a term used frequently in archaeology, which
means in Greek "an enclosed sacred place." When Moses made his
covenant with Yahweh on Mount Sinai, the Lord warned him: "Set
bounds about the mountain and sanctify it." [Exodus 19:23] According to Benjamin Mazar in his paper *The Middle Bronze Age in Canaan*,
"It seems likely that the tradition of a temenos, containing a chapel
or small temple and an unroofed 'high place' surrounded by an
enclosure wall, was generally preserved from the middle of the
Bronze Age down to the end of Middle Bronze IIB, except that

during this particular period—in the second half of the 19th century B.C.E.—attention was already being paid to the erection of an elaborate entryway and service quarters."

The temenos wall stands about one and a half feet high, and is made of small fieldstones. It encloses an area of almost an acre, as noted. The wall is built on the edge of a slope. About seven feet west and down the slope from this wall is a containing or revetment wall, which might possibly have been an earlier temenos, made of large boulders. The space between is filled with fieldstones that support the later temenos wall. There is no way that these walls could be regarded as protective perimeters, so the site can be regarded as having no military defenses.

Surrounding the outer area of the temenos wall is what seems to be a natural amphitheater from which onlookers could view whatever was taking place in the sacred precinct.

As they dug deeper into the structure and extended the range of the excavation, Adam and his associates kept trying to analyze what the edifice they were investigating could be. There was no chance that it could be an ordinary dwelling. It had no doors, no windows, and no floor. Houses of that period always had a floor, even if it was of pounded earth. And the fact that the structure was exactly centered over the circle of stones on Level II was significant.

The analysis of the pottery and bones was interesting, but still didn't answer the tantalizing question of exactly what they were dealing with in the Ebal dig.

Adam says: "In the past few years our knowledge of pottery of this period in the area of Manasseh has increased greatly. We can now say with considerable confidence that the site of Mount Ebal consists of two distinct levels to which two very similar groups of pottery are related: the earlier level from the first half of the thirteenth century B.C., and the later from the first half of the twelfth century B.C. Much of the later pottery is uniquely adorned on its handles with reed-hole decorations, peculiar to that period, and 'man's face' decoration. Both were discovered and studied during our survey in Manasseh, and had not been known before, or elsewhere. Now we consider these handles to be the clearest indication that the particular stratum in which they are found dates to the Israelite Settlement Period, and especially to the area of Manasseh.

"The fact is that the 'man's face' and the reed-hole punctures are the *only* decoration ever found on Israeli settlement-era pottery. In addition to Ebal, these decorations have been found in Wadi Farah and at Taanach, which were both considered to be Canaanite sites dating to the eleventh century B.C. With the dates established for Ebal, these would be the earliest findings of this decoration. It does not appear earlier, in the Bronze Age, nor later, in Iron Age II, which started about the time of Solomon, 1000 B.C.

"About seventy percent of the pottery vessels are large collar-rim storage jars, which are known to have been the principal storage vessels of the newly settled Israelites. About twenty percent of the pottery vessels are jugs and chalices. The balance are small vessels, mostly votive, specially made by hand for ritual use. We found only a small quantity of common domestic pottery, such as cooking pots." It is interesting to note also that the artistic endeavors of the people of Ebal were distinctly inferior as works of art or craft to the pottery found in the surrounding Canaanite sites of that era, let alone the sophisticated artwork of the Bronze Age and earlier. Furthermore, there were absolutely no representations of human or animal figures.

"In retrospect it seems strange," Adam says, "but the truth is that the finds I have just described did not suggest to us that the structure was an altar. That insight came only toward the end of the third season. Up to that time we remained in the dark as to what our mysterious structure was."

XXIV

A Sketch Solves
the Mystery

Adam and his team searched for parallels in other digs to guide their interpretations, but could find none. It seemed that the structure they were investigating was unique. They considered the possibility that they were dealing with a farmhouse or a watchtower and dismissed both of these ideas. The lack of doors or windows, for one thing, tended to exclude the possibility that the structure was some sort of habitation, as did the lack of substantial household pottery.

Zvi Lederman commented: "The irony of archaeology is that you spend your life looking for something unique, and then when you find it you must search for something just like it to compare it with."

"Then," Adam recalls, "the light dawned—in a flash. I remember it well. It was October thirteenth of 1983."

Zvi Koenigsberg was a student of the Bible and head of the local field school, which had supplied many volunteers for Adam's dig, and was a close friend of Zertal's. He himself had been working with Adam as a volunteer for several seasons.

Koenigsberg, along with the others, listened carefully as Adam outlined the problems of identifying the site. Suddenly, a young archaeologist named David Idan, who was touring the site, interrupted Adam's discourse to ask: "Why don't you think the opposite? Why don't you think the *filling* is the important part, rather than the building?"

"David's insight stunned me," Adam recalls. "I grabbed a Bible and opened it to Exodus 27:8, which describes the portable Tabernacle altar the Israelites were commanded to build in the wilderness: " 'Make it hollow, with boards. As you were shown on the mountain, so it shall be made.' "

"Then I went to the *Biblical Encyclopaedia* and looked under 'altar' and read as follows: 'The Tabernacle altar is described as having four walls. It was filled with earth and stones to its full height. On this filling the fire was burned. This construction is well known from Assyrian altars. That is why the portable altar is described [in the Bible] as being 'hollow with boards.' " [*Biblical Encyclopedia*, Hebrew edition, Volume 4, page 773] So, Adam reasoned, the structure we were investigating might be thought of as a container or "hollow" for the various layers of filling, which would be the surface on which a sacrificial fire could be burned.

David's suggestion set everybody's mind to working in a different direction. That evening, after a long day of excavating and washing pottery, Adam sat at a table in the field camp in Shavei Shomron and with a pen scratched on a tattered scrap of paper a rough sketch of what he thought the reconstructed structure they had been digging would look like, assuming it was an altar. He turned to Zvi Koenigsberg, who had been looking on as Adam drew the sketch and showed him what he had drawn.

"I took a look at his sketch, and got the shock of my life," Koenigsberg recalls. "Excusing myself hastily, I dashed to the synagogue library, grabbed a volume of the Mishnah off the shelves, and then ran the twenty yards to my home to call my wife, Ofra, and she saw the state of excitement I was in. All I said to her was one word: 'Come!' In the general hysteria, she didn't even realize she was barefoot, and ran down the road without thinking to put on her shoes. We ran together to where Adam was sitting and handed him the book."

Zvi opened it to a page he had marked in the Mishnah, Chapter Three in tractate *Middot*. This passage minutely described the Second Temple and all its structures. This particular edition had in it a drawing of the Second Temple altar as it was described in *Middot*.

"The drawing in the book," Zertal says, his eyes sparkling with the memory of this exciting moment, "was almost identical to the rough sketch I had drawn!" The biblical instructions in Exodus 20—not to use steps—fit in perfectly with the ramp on the Ebal altar and the one shown in the Mishnah drawing.

It was Adam's turn to be thunderstruck.

"You should have seen him!" Koenigsberg says. "He was in a state of ecstasy. We all were. Adam stared at this thing, and he could hardly believe it. It was incredible . . ."

"Suddenly it all became clear," Zertal says. "The filling and the structure were *together* one complete unit—an altar!"

As for confirmation of this new idea of what the Ebal dig was, Exodus 20:24–26 makes things even clearer in the instructions by Yahweh: "Make for me an altar of earth, and sacrifice on it your burnt offerings and your sacrifices of well-being, your sheep and your oxen; in every place in which I cause my name to be mentioned I will come to you and bless you. And if you make for me an altar of stones, do not build it of hewn stones; for by wielding your tool upon them you have profaned them. Do not ascend my altar by steps that your nakedness may not be exposed upon it."

The priests at that time wore short kiltlike skirts, which could indeed have been immodest when climbing high steps, since underwear had not yet been invented.

It must be noted that these instructions are given in the very first biblical mention of an altar, and it is said that the rule of the ramp should apply not in any one particular place but "at every place I cause my name to be mentioned."

"Beyond question, our site was a cultic center," Adam said. The more than fifty installations containing either animal bones and ashes (the remains of sacrifices) or votive pottery vessels (which must have once contained offerings) seemed to him to be irrefutable evidence of the religious nature of the site. A very small proportion of pottery anywhere on the site was ordinary cooking pots.

The nature of the bones, which were all kosher and, except for the fallow deer, all of sacrificial animals, further supported his conclusion. But the most exciting aspect of the new information was the identification of the pile of ancient stones he had unearthed as an altar—and an Israelite one by the evidence of the pottery. This pottery was characterized by the only two types of decoration that are strongly identified with the Israelites in the area of Manasseh:

reed-hole decoration and the "man's face" decoration, mentioned earlier, which shows the primitive outline of a human visage.

The puzzle of the thin surrounding wall was solved by reference to the description of the Second Temple altar in the portion of the Mishnah Koenigsberg had brought from the library. According to this description, the square Second Temple altar had two ledges surrounding it. The base of the altar was 32 cubits wide. (A cubit is about 18 inches.) One cubit from the base the altar narrowed to 30 cubits, leaving a 2-cubit ledge around it, or as the Mishnah calls it, "a surround." Five cubits higher, the altar narrows again to 28 cubits, leaving another two-cubit surround. The ledge created by the second narrowing curved around and down the ramp leading to the altar (see illustrations on page 125). The Mishnah calls it "a small ramp" made for the priest to ascend to "the surround."

"This is exactly what we had at our site," Adam said, "except that there is only one ledge or step instead of two. The step or ledge of our altar even curves around and goes down the ramp.

"Of course, the Second Temple was built about seven hundred years after our altar, but it now seems beyond doubt that the Second Temple altar, that of Herod, as it was described in the Mishnah, preserved ancient traditions concerning altar construction."

In Paul Johnson's *A History of the Jews* it is stated: "Herod took extraordinary care not to offend the religious scruples of the rigorists: for instance, for the alter and its ramp, unhewn stones were used, so that they would be untouched by iron. King Herod's temple, built on the ruins of Zerubbabel's, was located immediately on top of the old altar, preserving all of its stones and the ramp."

"Although the biblical descriptions of the altar built by the Israelites in the wilderness is not absolutely clear on this point, there is a hint that it, too, was constructed with a narrower block set on a wider base," Adam explained to me when he later described his identification of the altar.

"That evening," Zvi Koenigsberg told me, "Adam phoned up his old friend Professor Benjamin Mazar. He arranged that I go to Jerusalem the following day to pick him up and bring him to the site. The next morning was my first meeting with Mazar. I arrived at his home, and led him to the car. Suddenly, he stopped and said, 'Wait a minute! I forgot to get my Bible!' I said: 'Don't worry, you can use mine.' He smiled and said, 'Give me two minutes, and you'll see what is so important about my Bible.' I waited patiently downstairs, and when he came down and showed me the inner cover, I understood what he meant. The Bible itself was a simple, standard type, but the dedication on the inner cover explained things; it was a gift from his late brother-in-law, Yitzhak Ben-Zvi, second president of the State of Israel, a Bible scholar himself. Mazar explained that he never used any other Bible."

On the ride to the site, which Mazar filled with interesting anecdotes about the historical significance of the places they were passing, Zvi commented, referring to the discovery of the altar, " 'Professor, isn't it wonderful? We can prove the Bible!' He answered with a line that I have quoted interminably since: 'My young friend, we don't have to *prove* the Bible; we have to try and *understand* it!'

"That conversation was what started me off, in a serious way, to study the significance of the discovery," Zvi recalls. "We spoke about religion versus science in Bible study, and Mazar said to me that as far as he was concerned, these were two parallel lines that could never meet. I couldn't accept this, as truth, in my opinion, must be the same for all concerned. He threw me a challenge: 'Well, go ahead and try to prove your point! You have an excellent subject to work on!' [meaning the altar]"

Even Amihai Mazar, nephew of Benjamin Mazar and an archaeologist, who, at this writing, is doubtful of Zertal's identification of the site as being possibly Joshua's altar, makes the point that biblical references are often a valuable key to certain finds. Amihai Mazar says: "Would Zertal have identified this as such if he didn't know the biblical background?"

XXV

Do Altars Have Horns?

he Bible speaks of this altar's having 'a ledge' [Exodus 27:5]," Adam said. "Ezekiel's description of the imaginary future temple's altar is clearer [Ezekiel 43:14–17]: 'From the trench in the ground, to the lower ledge, which shall be a cubit wide: 2 cubits; from the lower ledge to the upper ledge, and which shall likewise be a cubit wide: 4 cubits; and the height of the altar hearth shall be 4 cubits. . . . It will have a number of ledges, creating a stepped tower.' "

As early as 1920 Albright suggested that the Israelite altar had a Mesopotamian origin ultimately based on the well-known ziggurats, of which the Tower of Babel may have been an early example. The alignment of the structure Adam had investigated, with its corners pointing to the four winds, now was of great interest, since the only place in which religious sites like this were so aligned in the ancient Near East was in Mesopotamia, the land from which, according to the Bible, Abraham first arrived in Canaan. Sir Leonard Woolley, digging in the ancient Hittite city of Alalakh, found not only the temple, but all of the buildings in the city aligned with the corners to the cardinal directions, and these buildings, which were ruined about the time of Joshua, had foundations going back before 3000 B.C. This was true also of Ur of the Chaldees, also excavated by Woolley, and believed to be the ancestral home of Abraham. The royal tombs in Ur were also laid out on these same compass points. The age of the ruins in this area predates the Egyptian dynasties.

The Bible tells us that Ahaz, a Judean king in the latter part of the eighth century B.C., ordered a new altar to be built for the Jerusalem temple, based on the plan of an altar he had seen in Damascus, where he had met the Assyrian king Tiglath-Pileser III. [2 Kings 16:10–16] This, too, suggests Mesopotamian influences on the orientation of the Israelite altar.

Sacred traditions tend to endure. It is only necessary to observe the antique Greek and Roman columns, or the medieval and Romanesque architecture of most churches built in recent centuries to become aware of this. The two ledges on the Second Temple altar mentioned in the Mishnah may well preserve an ancient tradition, and the ledge surrounding much of the altar on Mount Ebal may also reflect this tradition of the Mesopotamian altar built up with ledges.

The orientation of the altar's corners to the four winds is a definite Mesopotamian tradition, and the exactness of this orientation on the Ebal altar points toward its having been deliberate. This would indicate that the builders of this structure had roots in Mesopotamia. But why did the Second Temple and early Israelite structures have their *faces* aligned with the four directions instead of their corners?

Zertal says: "Perhaps altars associated with temples were oriented differently from open-air altars not associated with temples. In any event, it is almost certain that at the time of the Ebal site no enclosed Israelite temples had been built. Even the most elaborate Temple, the Second, was, in effect, an open-air temple. Only one small part, the Holy of Holies, was an enclosed structure, only used for one ceremony on one day, Yom Kippur. Therefore, it may fairly be assumed that the structure on Ebal was, in essence, really the First Temple.

"What do we know about altars from the Bible? The burnt-offering altar was used for animal sacrifices, as opposed to the smaller and portable altars used for incense offerings. Animal sacrifice was at the core of Israelite religious activities; but very few burnt-offering altars have been found so far in Israel. In fact Ebal is the *only* Israelite burnt-offering altar discovered to date; the other two Israelite altars discovered were much too small to have been used for burnt offerings, and of these three, Ebal is the oldest and the most complete.

"There seem to have been two kinds of burnt-offering altars," Adam explained. "One was associated with a temple, where, in the

Near East religious purview, God dwelled. The other might be called an independent burnt-offering altar, because it was not associated with a temple.

"There's plenty of controversy concerning this subject, as there seems to be with everything involving biblical archaeology, but it appears that the independent altar is part of what the Bible describes as a *bamah*, or high place, probably an open-air religious center where sacrifices were offered. For example, in I Kings 3:4 we learn that King Solomon went to Gibeon to sacrifice there, for it was the great high place (*bamah*). On that altar Solomon was said to have offered one thousand burnt offerings. Gold appeared to him there in a dream, and Solomon asked for, and was given by God, the gift of wisdom. And it was shortly after this that Solomon decided to fulfil his father David's dream and build the first temple in Israel. So the sacrifice at Gibeon was necessary because there was as yet no central temple at which Solomon could make his offerings to God.

"If this analysis is correct," Adam said, "our Mount Ebal site is an *independent* altar—not associated with a temple. But how could this be when, according to the Bible, there as yet were no Israelite temples?"

Koenigsberg, who has studied the subject for many years, provided this answer: "Our finds have proven that the biblical description of the Settlement era is certainly incomplete. The Bible was never intended to be a historical document. Each and every story or fable was there for a theological, and no other, purpose. So the fact that no temple is mentioned in the Bible at Ebal is irrelevant. What *is* relevant is that the Ebal find fulfills the four prerequisites of a temple, as listed by Maimonides."

Altars have been found throughout the near East—in Mesopotamia, Syria, Egypt, Anatolia, Greece, Cyprus, and the Aegean Islands. In Israel altars have been found from the early Bronze Age (3150 to 2200 B.C.) to the late Iron Age (800 to 586 B.C.). From the Bronze Age, altars have been found at Megiddo, Shechem, Hazor, and Nahariya. From the Iron Age, a Philistine altar was found at Tel Qasile, and the only two other Israelite altars were discovered at Tel Arad and Beersheba, but both were hundreds of years after the Israelite conquest and the time of Ebal.

Tel Arad was an Israelite fortress as far back as the tenth century

B.C., but at least 250 years after the time of Joshua, in the time of Solomon. In fact, an actual inscription was found there mentioning "The Temple of Yahweh," which must be referring either to the temple of Solomon in Jerusalem or to the temple to Yahweh built in Arad itself. Arad is listed in Joshua 12:14 as one of the towns defeated by Joshua. An earlier altar, not Israelite but probably Kenite, made of a single large unhewn stone, was found in the tell at Arad. Like other cities mentioned as being destroyed by Joshua, Arad had already been razed 1,500 years before Joshua's time and not reoccupied until 1200 B.C., when it became a Kenite settlement. It was then apparently a small, unfortified village built atop ancient Bronze Age ruins. Two altars connected with the Kenites were found in the center of the village, and were dated two centuries later, long after the presumed ceremony at Ebal. The Israelite altar was built of unhewn stones, as specified in the Bible, slightly to the north of the site. It measured five cubits by five cubits as specified in Exodus 27:1. Like the altar at Ebal, no horns were found. (Horns are a feature sometimes attributed to biblical altars.) The altar was filled with earth and clay, so it might have been used for animal sacrifices. This shrine to Yahweh was probably destroyed in the time of King Hezekiah (715 B.C.) in his campaign to eliminate all centers of worship except for the temple in Jerusalem. But although the temple at Arad was abolished, this was done with great reverence. Out of respect for their sanctity, the two incense altars that stood at the steps in front of the Holy of Holies were laid on their sides and covered with a layer of earth that completely concealed all traces of the former shrine, and the courtyard was covered by a fill about three feet thick that completely concealed the altar. This could be compared to the layers of stone and earth that covered the mound under which the Ebal ruins lay.

So we see that the only Israelite altars made of unhewn stones—Arad and Ebal—do not have horns, or at least none were found. From this considerable body of archaeological relics we get some idea of what ancient altars were like; but only a partial idea as to the form of the Israelite altar in particular. In general, Near Eastern burnt-offering altars, like the one at Mount Ebal, are square or rectangular structures of considerable size. Sometimes they have horns at the upper corners (as at Beersheba and Kition in Cyprus) and sometimes they do not (as at Arad). So the idea of having horns on the altar was not strictly an Israelite idea, but applied in other cults as well, yet not necessarily to all altars.

The altar at Beersheba *did* have horns, one of which was broken off, but it was small, certainly not a sacrificial altar, and was made of dressed stones, not natural untooled stones like the other two. It probably was used in a temple rather than out of doors. It dates to the time of Hezekiah, hundreds of years after the construction of Solomon's temple, and was destroyed, according to the Bible, because it flouted the tradition of centralization (of which more later). On one of the Beersheba altar's stones was incised a writhing serpent, well known as a symbol of Moses, indicating that it was an Israelite structure.

Large altars in other cults were ascended by stairs, where the means of ascent have been preserved. Unfortunately, there is no evidence of the means of ascent in the other Israelite altars so far discovered; at Ebal we have the ramp, which conforms to the instructions in Exodus 20:26. Some altars, like Ebal and Arad, have outer stone frames and are filled inside with stone, pebbles, or earth.

The two walls that almost meet in the center of the structure at Ebal may well have been built to make a stone pathway for the priests to the center of the altar since stones do not accept impurity. Incidentally, offerings could not have been burned on the limestone of which the altar is made because it tends to disintegrate under fire, so the offerings would have to be made either on the filling or on some pavement laid over it.

"Every other ancient altar that has been discovered thus far," Zertal comments, "has been identified with a temple, or, as at Beersheba, was in a city where we may suppose a temple existed in connection with the altar. Our altar alone seems to have been an independent altar in the countryside, not associated with a temple or even a settlement. This is probably because the Mount Ebal altar and its associated cult site were built in a very early period in the development of the Israelite religion and at that time there was as yet no temple. [There is no evidence either that at that time the Israelites had any permanent dwelling structures.] This site functioned in effect as an open-air temple, and almost surely is the first such cultic site—for the united tribes of Israel—that ever existed:

the place where the first rites of the tribes of the covenant were celebrated.

"We must remember," Zertal explains, "that as far as I can tell this site was functional for a relatively short time—perhaps some fifty years. It is doubtful that a temple could develop in such a short time. When the central place of worship moved south to Shiloh, the site at Ebal was abandoned and probably covered over at that time or soon after, and even at Shiloh no temple was built."

The Bible makes it clear that there were many independent Israelite altar sites; but during the religious reforms of King Josiah (the seventh century B.C.) these outlying ritual centers were destroyed. But the Ebal altar was so old, and in addition had been covered with earth for six centuries by the time of Josiah's reform, that it was probably overlooked, or perhaps even forgotten by the time of Josiah's reforms. In any event, since it had not been in use for many centuries, it would have posed no threat to Jerusalem. Incidentally, the Second Temple altar was much larger than any altars found so far, and ancient sources—the Mishnah, Josephus, and the Temple Scroll from the Dead Sea—all agree that it was larger than the other altars described in the Bible.

"In terms of its height—nine feet—and in terms of width and length, our altar is closer to the altar in Solomon's temple and Ezekiel's visionary temple than to the Tabernacle altar.

"But," says Zertal raising a finger judicially, "after discussing all this technical and historic data proving that we are dealing here with a burnt-offering altar in an Israelite cult center dating to the time of the Settlement, we come to the most intriguing question. Is this the actual altar related to the biblical traditions that describe Joshua building an altar on Mount Ebal?" His question was soon to receive a rude answer.

XXVI

Burnt Offerings

Aharon Kempinski, a former instructor of Adam's at Tel Aviv University, visited the site in 1982. As he arrived at the site, Kempinski stopped to look at the breathtaking landscape and commented, "O Palestine. How beautiful thou art!"

Kempinski stayed only about an hour, and left without comment concerning the dig. But his comment on "Palestine" should have been a clue to his attitude. Most Israelis do not care for the use of the term Palestine in connection with Israel. It is a word freighted with unpleasant overtones, because there is not and has never been a country called Palestine. The name is based on the term "Philistia," made up by the Romans after the Jewish revolts were put down, to further humiliate the Jews. The Philistines, aside from the Romans, were the most hated enemies of the Jews. Today the word is used frequently by Arab nationalists and others hostile to Israel as a way of denying that there actually is a state called Israel. Palestine was the official name of Israel and surrounding territory for only thirty years, under the British Mandate. Archaeologist Moshe Dothan, who visited Ebal about the same time as Kempinski, said in a speech before the International Congress of Biblical Archaeology: "We may conclude that the chronologically late [nineteenth century A.D.] and inconsistently used term 'Palestine' was apparently never accepted by any local national entity. It therefore can hardly serve as a meaningful term for the archaeology of this country [Israel]."

Adam interpreted Kempinski's use of the Palestine quotation as an indication of some hostility in regard to what he had seen on the

174

Ebal dig. He had a feeling that his former professor was not pleased with what he saw—and it turned out that this hunch was correct.

Zvi Lederman acted on the site as the devil's advocate, he told me during an interview at Harvard. He questioned and doubted every hypothesis, forcing Adam to give detailed explanations and parallels for his opinions.

"The main structure, which was all we had after the first season," Lederman says, "was quite well preserved; but it was covered with rocks and dirt. It was just a kind of heap of stones. So after that season we still had no real proof of what we were dealing with and I was nervous about Kempinski. His attitude was definitely negative. I could tell, because I knew him. I had been his student at Tel Aviv. His attitude was clearly hostile."

There was another problem when Yigael Yadin came to view the site, which was beginning to be talked about in archaeological circles. This was before many of the supporting finds were discovered.

"I clearly remember the day he came to the site," Lederman says, "because that year there was a special session in the Institute of Advanced Studies in Jerusalem. Famous scholars participated in it. Among them were Yadin, Abraham Malamat, Baruch Halpern, and Henri Cazelles, a well-known French archaeologist. During this visit to Ebal, Yadin examined the smallest details, and he was waiting for you around the corner, to trap you. He asked thousands of questions, and he was attacking Zertal, and there was a lot of tenseness in the air concerning not only the whole hypothesis but also the site itself. From a strict archaeological point of view, we don't even know the name of the mountain. Those with a purely archaeological view don't depend on biblical sources. They ask only: Is it an altar? Is it a cultic site or not? Basic archaeology. And on any detail, when he was arguing, he never admitted at any point, 'OK, you're right,' but he went on to argue another detail. Still, he couldn't really destroy our understanding of the site. Our basic archaeological understanding of the site. That's why he took so long. If he could invalidate our entire idea in fifteen minutes he would do so, and that's it. But in the end he didn't really buy Adam's ideas anyway, and Adam was very discouraged by this because he really respected Yadin."

The one big question Yadin had about the altar was "Where is the place where the ashes from the sacrifices were dumped outside the camp?" He felt that this had to be an integral part of the sanctuary if it were to be shown that it was a burnt-offering altar. He died in 1984. The season after he died, Zertal found a place that was filled with ashes, just outside the wall. "I wonder what he would have thought," Adam asks, "if he had seen our later finds." The year he died, Yadin, in a lecture before the International Congress of Biblical Archaeology in Jerusalem, described recent work in the Manasseh hill country and Ephraim and mentioned Zertal as having contributed "important survey work," which by implication indicated he approved what Adam had accomplished to date, though possibly not agreeing with his conclusions.

But the site was beginning to be well known around Israel, even though Adam as yet had made no official publication reporting his work. Among the people who visited the site were the former Commander in Chief of the army, Moshe Levi, and Arik Sharon. Benjamin Mazar came several times after his initial visit. But the political volatility of the site, in the heart of the occupied West Bank, would not allow anyone to comment for quotation.

Three weeks after Adam's first realization that the Ebal site was probably an altar, shortly after Mazar's visit, the first public mention of that idea appeared in the Sunday, November 3, 1983, edition of *Haaretz*, Israel's leading newspaper. It had all sorts of repercussions, archaeological, religious, and political. But all of this was before anyone knew about the important finds that had come up in the 1983 season.

One of the most important finds of that season was made by a volunteer working in one of the installations outside the altar itself. She held up a tiny bit of metallic material and shouted, "Hey! Look what I found!" Adam ran over and took the tiny bit of metal from her. He was able to identify it almost immediately as a gold earring of Egyptian design that probably had been placed in the pit as an offering. This gave indication that the settlers or builders of the altar site might have some connection with Egypt, which fits with the Exodus tradition concerning the origins of the Israelites, but is fiercely disputed by the Mendenhall theorists, who cling to the idea that Canaan's occupation was a purely local revolution. Later finds intensified this argument.

XXVII

A Biblical Minefield

At the end of the summer season of 1984, Zertal wrote an article for the *Biblical Archaeology Review* that described his dig on Mount Ebal. The title, devised by the editor, Hershel Shanks, was: "Has Joshua's Altar Been Found on Mount Ebal?" It appeared in the January–February 1985 issue of the magazine.

Toward the end of the article Zertal responded to possible objections to his theory that the Ebal site is Joshua's altar. Answering those who criticized his identification of the Ebal site as the altar mentioned in the Bible because it was not exactly on the peak of the mountain, and because Gerizim was not visible from its summit, Zertal argued that the Bible itself suggested that the altar was not to be built on the very peak by using the Hebrew letter *beth* to describe the location. A *beth* used in this way as a prefix is usually interpreted as "in" rather than "on top of." This usage actually occurs twice in reference to the Ebal altar, in Joshua 8:30 and in Deuteronomy 27:4.

In Deuteronomy 11:29, where the instructions for pronouncing the curses are given, we are told that they are to be pronounced *al* Mount Ebal, that is, *on* Mount Ebal. This shows that the use of the *beth* in the other cases had real significance.

Zertal acknowledged that biblical archaeologists here had trouble to date finding archaeological confirmation of Bible stories. In fact, excavations at sites where the Bible placed some of Joshua's most important victories have proved that there does not seem to have been a military conquest of Canaan. Joshua apparently never "fit the battle of Jericho," because the site, when excavated, showed no military destruction, and indicated that in any event the wall collapsed hundreds of years before his time. Digs at Ai, Arad, and other sites also showed no military destruction dating from Joshua's time.

But in the case of Ebal, for the first time in archaeological history, a site clearly identified in the Pentateuch has presented a number of important factors confirming the Bible story.

The fact that the altar was found on the exact mountain named in the Bible seems unlikely to be mere coincidence. Its identification as a purely Israelite site, with no evidence of other cultures, adds weight to the argument that it is the biblical altar of Joshua, and the date of the site coincides exactly within the commonly accepted date of the Israelite settlement in Canaan.

But is it *Joshua's* altar? We have to date no proof that any of the pre-Solomonic patriarchs existed. But it is clear that the Israelites were taken by their leader to this particular mountain for religious reasons and nothing else. Lacking contrary evidence we can fairly assume that leader was Joshua. Zertal's conclusions are powerfully convincing, and they lead also, based on the trail of Israelite pottery up the Jordan and across into Shechem, to the conclusion that (with the exception of the biblical version of the crossing of the Jordan near Jericho) the route of the Exodus after Mount Sinai was much as described in the Bible. This is the most important confirmation of a portion of the Pentateuch ever discovered. It is the *only* scientific confirmation found to date.

But Adam, with the caution of a serious scientist, resisted stating in the *BAR* article that he was positive he had found the Israelite altar. He felt he should hold off making an ultimate statement until he could complete several more seasons of digging.

However, the article stirred up a storm of controversy among archaeologists and biblical scholars that is still going on.

XXVIII

Did Joshua

Really Conquer Ai?

I n the issue of *BAR* following Adam's revelations, questions concerning the historicity of the Book of Joshua and Joshua's exploits early in the Settlement Period were raised by an archaeologist named Ziony Zevit, who had excavated a place called Khirbet-et-Tell. It is widely believed to be the site of Ai, the second city Joshua was supposed to have destroyed [Joshua 8:3–29] following his victory of Jericho and just before he arrived at Ebal.

There had already been two major digs at this site, and the archaeological evidence of these excavations was clear. In the early Bronze Age, around 3000 B.C., there had been an unwalled village on the site. This later developed into a major walled city that covered some twenty-eight acres. That city was destroyed between 2550 B.C. and 2350 B.C. After that the site remained unoccupied for more than 1,100 years.

The top of the hill, abandoned since the Late Bronze Age, was resettled as a small unwalled village in early Iron Age I—the time of the Israelite settlement led by Joshua. It seemed to have been remodeled once during that time, but never fortified. The village was deserted again sometime after 1125 B.C. There was no further ancient occupation of the site. Since there was essentially no city on the site for Joshua to destroy, when did the battle of Ai take place, if ever? If it was one of Joshua's feats, one would have to move the time of the Settlement back to 2300 B.C., which does not fit any known evidence. Indications are, therefore, that there was no military activity at all there in Joshua's time, or at best a minor skirmish with local seminomadic tribes. So the Ai story, told in dramatic detail in Joshua 8, is as unconfirmed archaeologically as the battle of Jericho.

Though there was no sign of the battle of Ai, Israelites did eventually build a village there that covered some six acres, and utilized, as was often done, the remains of the city that had existed on the site in the dim past, even making use of some of the still-standing fortifications. According to population studies of that time made by archaeologists, there probably were 160 to 200 people per acre in this area in the early Iron Age, so a six-acre village would have had about 960 to 1,200 people, including women and children. The Bible states that Ai was not only defeated by Joshua, but ruined and burned to the ground. There is no evidence of any such destruction on the site. Zevit's conclusion: After the eventual abandonment of the village, around 1050 B.C. a "realistic folk story about the battles emerged among the local peasantry.

"The original stimulus for the story may have been a local bard's desire to spin a reasonable tale about the impressive ruins at the top of the hill," Zevit surmises. "Perhaps in retelling the story the ancient poet connected his explanation of the ruins with the local hero, Joshua, who, in these stories, led the successful attack.

"It is reasonable to assume," Zevit adds, "that the ancient historians considered the story of the conquest of Ai to be true. Otherwise their work would be a sham."

"What we see then, in the conquest accounts in general," Ai-explorer Joseph A. Callaway concludes in a March–April 1985 *BAR* article "and in the Ai account in particular, is a rather free use of ancient sources expanded and interpreted to speak to the needs of future generations. At the same time, there was enough respect for the traditions that no effort was made to synthesize them into a harmonious narrative without repetitions, numerical inaccuracies and contradictions. This faithfulness in preserving traditions that did not always agree in details is, to me, evidence of their authenticity, and it says something about the people who preserved these traditions. I do not believe they would spin a tale out of whole cloth about some landmark such as the mound at Ai. Instead they worked with ancient oral and written traditions handed down from generation to generation. During this period the history of places such as Ai and Gibeon yielded to theological constructs that built up layers of interpretation like strata in a tell, forever concealing the real events themselves." But other aspects of the Joshua legend were confirmed by new finds that year.

A second Egyptian earring was discovered at Ebal in 1985, in the context of an offering. Naboth, Zertal's eight-year-old son, who was on the site that day, as he occasionally was, picked it up as though it were a piece of foil or some glittery litter, and just threw it away. The workers who had noticed this were appalled. Metal objects in the dig were rare, and gold, in particular, retains its luster even after being buried for millennia, so the crew knew this was something important.

A volunteer remembered the occasion vividly: "Everybody was going berserk until we found it again." But ultimately the golden object was located and studied in connection with the rest of the finds.

The Bible mentions offerings of gold and silver (which was then more valuable than gold, but not as valuable as iron) in the passage on the golden calf, where offerings, including earrings, were melted down to build the calf-idol. [Exodus 32:3–4]

In that same season in 1985 Zertal's team dug up a gateway in the temenos wall. It consisted of two parallel walls perpendicular to the main wall, twenty-three feet apart. Three wide steps led up the slope and through the gateway. The entrance was beautifully paved with large, flat stones, which create a very wide and precisely detailed processional entrance. This is not the sort of entrance that would exist in a farming village or an ordinary residence. Says Adam: "No parallel to this entranceway has ever been found in Iron Age Israel. This beautiful entrance emphasizes the significance of Mount Ebal as a cultic center."

Within the temenos or sacred precinct, Adam's team that season found some stone installations that were different from those already found. They were mostly built of small flat stones and were arranged in three groups. In some were found pottery vessels but no ashes or trace of fire. Originally, the vessels probably contained some kind of offering, Adam believes—perhaps grain or oil. In other installations there were ash and animal bones but no pottery.

The pottery found in these new installations was of a type studied and found in great quantities during Adam's survey, uniquely adorned on its handles with the reed-hole decoration and "man's face" design.

But the most exciting aspect of the 1985 season was the finding of a second scarab, also at Level II, the earlier level, where the scarab with the snake decoration had been found the previous year. This one was a faience scarab with a white glaze, issued to honor Thutmoses III. Brandl translated the hieroglyphic inscription on it as "Thutmoses III, lord of many troops." It was found in one of the stone installations just north of the Ebal altar. After checking with Brandl, Zertal was able to date this scarab to the thirteenth century B.C., which again pinpointed the period of the altar without any serious possibility of doubt. The scarab shows what looks like a capital B in the center (see illustration on page 121), which is actually a double composite bow held by a kneeling archer on the far left of the scarab. The Egyptians must have been proud of this bow, which was of a compound construction that made it very powerful.

The cartouche of Thutmoses III appears at the far right. At the top is a crawling salamander, an Egyptian symbol of abundance. This scarab was very important and very rare. In the first place, only four others with parallel inscriptions are known to exist, according to Brandl; but only one of them has the same details, such as the location and shape of the hieroglyphics, and only one comes from an archaeological context.

The one that is exactly like Zertal's scarab is in a private collection, and nobody knows its exact origins. In fact, Brandl uses the Zertal scarab to authenticate the earlier find, since previously this arrangement of signs was unique.

The second item to which he is comparing Zertal's scarab, Brandl says in his official report, is also of unknown provenance and has a slightly different arrangement of the characters but is similar to Zertal's finds in that it has archer and cobra decorations.

A third, also of unknown provenance, is in the British Museum, and also differs in details, though it is basically similar.

The fourth, which comes from a tomb at Tell el-Farah (South) is the only one besides Zertal's found in an archaeological context, but it is somewhat different. The compound bow is now a simple bow, and there are differences in the inscription and design. The dating of this scarab is confirmed both by its early Iron Age pottery assemblage, and by two other scarabs and a seal bearing the name of Rameses II.

Because of its rarity it is highly unlikely that this second scarab could have existed, as some critics suggested about the previous one, in a Canaanite market. Second, the fact that both scarabs were found *in situ* in the second or oldest level of the ruin makes the date all but unchallengeable. The rareness of the scarab makes it likely that it originated in Egypt rather than being available for local trade.

During that same season of 1985, a stone-carved object was found in almost perfect condition in a natural dent in the bedrock at the bottom of the altar. It was an interesting seal carved of limestone in the form of a truncated prism, carved on four sides, and with a perforation so that it could be worn on a string around the neck. Says Brandl in his report: "This simple stone seal would seem to join a gradually expanding group of stone seals dated to the end of the Bronze Age and the beginning of the Iron Age." It could have appeared, says Brandl, as early as 1250 B.C. It probably was used as an identification marker.

In the same indentation, which measured about five feet by five feet, were found two large stone hammers and a cultic vase. The "vase" was 4.75 inches high, and was either a chalice or an incense burner, made of a light black volcanic stone not known in the area. These items were placed in the hollow before the filling of the main structure, so Zertal dates them to Level II. This chalice seemed to have been sculpted from a single stone. The black stone from which it was carved was porous, with air holes. Since there were no sources for this type of stone in the Manasseh hill country, Zertal feels it may have been imported from Golan or the Transjordan. (This sort of stone artifact is what we were looking for during my field trip in the Wadi Malich.)

"The chalice," Zertal observed in his preliminary report, "is similar in shape to a group of cultic stone vessels discovered in the Egyptian temple at Sarabit-el-Hadam by Flinders Petrie, who wrote them up in 1906. It has been found in Egypt, and nowhere else."

Petrie identified them as altars. He said those he found probably were used for offerings of incense. One showed signs of burning in its upper part. The uniqueness of this group, Petrie observed, suggested that it belonged to a Semitic cult of incense altars, differing from the elongated Egyptian ones. It is reasonable to assume, Petrie estimated, that the dates of the Semitic altars were during the thirteenth to twelfth centuries B.C. In other words, they were used in Egypt, probably not by Egyptians but by a Semitic people of the time of the Israelite settlement.

But if some of the Israelites came from Egypt, which tribes were they? George W. Ramsey, in *The Quest for the Historical Israel*, says: "The Biblical traditions suggest principally the *Josephite* tribes (Ephraim and Manasseh), and most scholars assume this to have been the case. Since Moses is claimed for the tribe of *Levi* and since numerous Egyptian names (e.g., Moses, Hophni, Phinehas) are found in the tribe of Levi, many have concluded that the Levites were also present." This question is still being hotly debated in both biblical and archaeological circles.

XXIX

Not an Altar— a Watchtower?

On March 31, 1984, about five months after the newspaper publicity on his dig, Zertal appeared on Israeli television in a presentation detailing the finds on Ebal and his conclusions. As a counterbalance, the program included an interview with Binyamin Zedakah, the spokesman for the Samaritan sect, which is ardently opposed to the identification of Ebal as the site for biblical rites. Zedakah claimed that his TV statements had been unfairly edited, and his verbatim comments were published in *Haaretz* a few days later. Actually, to doubly ensure a balanced presentation, the TV station included another interviewee, Anwar Nuseiba, who has died since recording the interview. Nuseiba, who was not an archaeologist and had never been to the site, was chairman of the East Jerusalem Electric Company, a staunch Palestinian nationalist, and one of the primary spokesmen for their cause. Asking him about the find was about as relevant as asking an Imam to solve a problem in nuclear physics. Nuseiba insisted that the Ebal site was Hivite rather than Israelite, and used this attribution to negate any spiritual claims to the area that Adam's find on Mount Ebal might engender.

But a more virulent attack was published just one year later. An article appeared in the January–February 1986 issue of the *Biblical Archaeology Review* by Aharon Kempinski, Zertal's former professor. Kempinski launched a savage attack on Adam's identification of

Ebal as an altar, his story headlined: JOSHUA'S ALTAR—AN IRON AGE I WATCHTOWER. This was the article I had seen published in the Samaritan newspaper when Zvi and I had visited a Samaritan home on Mount Gerizim.

Kempinski opened by recalling his only visit to the site in 1982. He contended that even during the first season rumors had spread that Zertal had found Joshua's altar. He felt that Zertal had believed this from the beginning. Kempinski wrote:

"When we arrived at the site and walked around it, it appeared to us to be the remains of a small settlement enclosed by a wall. In the center of the village was the major structure—the building or the base of a tower. Zertal had already identified this structure as an 'altar.' Only half of it had been excavated at the time. A large collar-rim pithos, or storage jar, typical of the Israelite settlement period, appeared sunk into the floor *inside* the structure. The pithos was resting against a small, thin wall.

"After visiting a newly excavated site, I usually write for my own files a short report with some sketches of what I saw, since it often takes years before anything is published. This habit sometimes proves very useful. It did in this case, for I drew the pithos *in situ*. In the report published in the *BAR*, nothing is mentioned about this pithos *inside* the structure. One would hardly expect to find a whole storage jar inside an altar—if it were an altar!"

Kempinski went on to say that when he looked inside the structure he could see no signs of deliberately laid layers of fill. "As a matter of fact the 'fill' inside the structure looked more like the normal debris or remains usually found after a building has been destroyed. My impression, looking at the structure, was that it had two rooms, with storage installations in each room at opposite corners."

After having read Zertal's article, Kempinski said: "I am more than ever convinced that what Zertal found on Mount Ebal is simply a three-phase village from Iron Age I, the so-called Israelite settlement period. These three-phase villages are not at all rare during Iron Age I; on the contrary, they are quite common between 1230 and 1000 B.C."

To prove his case Kempinski analyzed Zertal's drawing of the

site and how he envisioned three phases of the site from
his own point of view. First: seminomadic occupants in tents,
who had left behind the pits or small installations. Second: a
two- or three-room house. Third: events following the destruction
of phase two, perhaps by the Canaanites from nearby Shechem
or possibly by the Philistines, who invaded the area in about
1070 B.C.

"Or was this phase destroyed in an intertribal clash?" Kempinski asks. "In any event the phase-two settlement was destroyed,
thus demonstrating the need to improve security with a watchtower.

"In phase three," Kempinski continued, "a watchtower was built;
debris was probably added to the inside of the phase-two building to
increase the podium for the watchtower—a common feature of Iron
Age watchtowers . . . the remains were also used for the courtyard of
the watchtower."

Kempinski went on to cite several digs that he felt had similar
patterns: Giloh, Izbet Sartah, Hazor, Tell Beit Mirsim, and Tell
Masos, which had been Kempinski's own dig. (He did not mention
that all of his findings at Tell Masos were later discredited by other
archaeologists.)

"Zertal," Kempinski says a bit later, "sees a ramp leading up to
the 'altar.' But the altar in Solomon's Temple had steps, and steps
lead up to the altar at Tell Dan and extend along the altar's entire
width." [Author's note: This was an eighth or seventh century B.C.
altar, long after the time of Solomon.]

Kempinski concluded that Zertal's ramp is too narrow to serve for
mounting to an altar with sacrificial animals (a bit over three feet)
and was simply the remains of a collapsed wall. As for the cultic
installations, Kempinski conceded that their identification as such
might be correct, but commented that such cultic activity would
hardly be surprising. "Evidence of cultic activity in Iron Age I was
found in the cult room at Ai and at the so-called bull site recently
excavated by Amihai Mazar. In our excavation at Tell Masos we also
found buildings where cultic activities had occurred. Almost every
Iron Age I settlement has one or more cultic installations. But the
discovery of pits in which cultic activities took place—such as on

Mount Ebal—is not proof that Joshua's altar was built on top of the pits."

Kempinski then took on the question of the fill, which he takes to be "merely the destruction debris from the destroyed watchtower. Or it could have been fill deliberately laid to create the surface . . . on which to build the tower at a later date."

As to the bones found on the site, Kempinski says that if Zertal were to excavate modern rubbish pits from nearby Nablus he would not find any pigs either, since Muslims do not eat pork. The bones found by Zertal, says Kempinski, "simply reflect the faunal conditions in the area and the diet of the people involved. In short, there is no basis whatever for interpreting this structure as an altar."

He blames what he calls Zertal's "mistaken identification" on uncritical reading of the Bible. "He placed the passages in Deuteronomy 27 and Joshua that supposedly describe an altar on Mount Ebal. Actually the earliest version of the text probably placed the altar on nearby Mount Gerizim, which is where the Samaritan version of the Pentateuch places it."

Kempinski further extended his criticism: "According to our understanding the Deuteronomistic school was active during the eighth and seventh centuries B.C. and the earliest edition of the Book of Joshua was written in the seventh century B.C. For the purposes of argument, however, it does not matter if these dates are off by 100 or 150 years. If the original texts of Deuteronomy and Joshua had references to Mount Ebal rather than Mount Gerizim, surely there would be some remains on Mount Ebal from the period when these texts were written. Yet we have Zertal's word for it that there is not a single sherd from the period of the Israelite monarchy, that is, after the 11th century B.C. . . .

"It is tempting to agree with Zedakah [the Samaritan spokesman] that the earlier version of Deuteronomy 27, as well as Joshua 8, referred to Mount Gerizim and not Mount Ebal."

Kempinski concluded his attack with a little homily on archaeology in general: "Biblical archaeology is not simply field archaeology using the Bible as a guidebook. Biblical archaeology must also be based on a sound grounding in the scholarship of Biblical studies. Without this basic knowledge of the development of The Scriptures, Biblical archaeology can easily be transformed from a science to a theology. In short, without realizing it, Adam Zertal is strangely playing a role in the longstanding theological drama that was set up by the Samaritans and the Jews. A drama that was first played at the beginning of the Hellenistic age in the center of Jerusalem and the Samaritan center of Shechem."

XXX

Zertal Strikes Back

dam was appalled at what seemed a vicious, poorly researched and reasoned, and definitely political attack on him
and his find. It was possible that his old professor was still
smarting from the rejection of his Tell Masos dig as a biblical Israelite site by the archaeological community, which undermined much
of Kempinski's earlier work. Fortunately, the editor of the *BAR*,
Hershel Shanks, as he frequently did, sent Kempinski's article to
Adam for comment before publishing it. As a result, Adam's response appeared side by side with Kempinski's attack. It was
headed: HOW COULD KEMPINSKI BE SO WRONG?

Zertal was loaded with material for his rebuttal, since Kempinski
had not kept up with later developments at the Ebal dig, which by
now had convinced most of the archaeological establishment that it
was indeed the first and only Israelite cultic site from the time of the
Settlement that had ever been found in Israel. In his introduction
Zertal comments: "Although Dr. Kempinski's article begins with
archaeology, it is quite obvious that his ideological attitude preceded
his purely archaeological examination. His ideas about the dating of
Deuteronomy and Joshua, together with his 'new' ideas concerning
how the Pentateuch was 'corrected' by the Jews . . . point to a very
clear preconception of what ought to be found on Mount Gerizim
and Mount Ebal."

Zertal tabled the Samaritan argument for the moment to take on
Kempinski's archaeological criticisms. Pointing out that since
Kempinski based his criticism entirely on his 1982 half-hour visit,

and had never communicated since with Adam concerning the progress of the dig, he was obviously unaware of all the new finds.

In the first place, he denied Kempinski's contention that in 1982 he already regarded the site as Joshua's altar. "True," he wrote, "many indications pointed from the very beginning to the site's special character; among these were the absence of any remnants of exposed architecture; the special style of the enclosure wall encircling a vast empty area; the strange location of the site, across the middle of a ridge, etc. None of these factors apply to Iron I villages in the Hill Country, so we assumed that we were not dealing with a settlement or a regular village.

"The first announcements concerning the discovery that the site was an altar did not occur until November 3, 1983, in the newspaper *Haaretz*, exactly a year after the time that Kempinski alleged that the news was already in the Israeli daily press."

As regards the collar-rim jar Kempinski saw sunk into the floor inside the altar, Zertal said that he had emphasized clearly "that the installations at the bottom of the structure represent an earlier phase, and the large structure itself represents a later phase—both from the same Iron I period."

That collar-rimmed jar, along with other finds that Kempinski did not know about, belonged to Level II, the earlier phase. "It is hard to understand what he means when he says this find contradicts our conclusion that the later altar buried the earlier cultic structure—including the jar!"

Zertal had no trouble dealing with Kempinski's contention that the altar site had already been discovered by French archaeologist Victor Guérin. "If Kempinski would just read Victor Guérin, he could easily learn that Guérin never claimed that he discovered the location of this altar. Guérin wrote: 'In order to find this precious monument [i.e., Joshua's altar] I have thoroughly explored the southern plateau [of Mount Ebal] with the northern as well; but all my explorations were in vain.' "

As to Kempinski's "three phase" hypothesis, Zertal gave the actual stratigraphy as proof that Kempinski's idea did not hold water. In the first place, the site had only *two* levels, not three. There were no signs that any nomadic or seminomadic tribes had ever occupied

the site. And if people had lived there, there would have been food-
and water-storage containers on the site. There were none. Also a
regularly inhabited site would have had a defensive wall around it.
No such wall was found by Zertal in any of the strata. Instead a ritual
temenos wall was found at the older level and a revetment wall was
laid on the western slope only. The later stratum, Level I, was
completely surrounded by a temenos wall, creating a sacred religious
area.

As to the debris being the result of normal destruction, Zertal
pointed out that no signs of destruction of any kind had been found
at Ebal. The transition from Level II to Level I had to be viewed as
a planned decision to expand the site as a ritual center.

In fact, efforts to reconstruct a complete vessel from the pottery
sherds found on the site were futile, indicating that the fill was
comprised of material gathered from a wide area before the construction of the altar.

I myself discovered, in a conversation with Dr. Stager at Harvard,
that Kempinski's claim that Zertal's find was a watchtower was
highly improbable since no Israelite watchtower from the early Iron
Age has ever been discovered.

As to the ramp, Zertal wrote: "Is it a ramp or isn't it? It is true that
many of the Biblical and Mishnaic terms are not clearly understand-
able today. The main reason for this is the lack of good archaeological evidence showing the exact meaning of the terms. This is
particularly true regarding cultic terms, since little, if any, Israelite
cultic architecture has been unearthed. But I claim that the discovery of a full-scale untouched and very early Israelite cultic center
enables us to study afresh the whole issue. In this context, it is clear
that a ramp to climb up an altar was used since the 12th century B.C.
in Israelite religious architecture, and that the Mishnaic description
of the Second Temple altar is validly based on much earlier proto-
types. Moreover, it is now beyond doubt that Israelite altars maintained an old tradition and remained relatively unchanged for 1,100
years. The phenomenon of the persistence of architectural details is
well known in cultic and religious architecture."

Zertal went on to point out that, aside from scriptural evidence,
structurally the ramp "cannot under any circumstances be a wall.
The steps that provided access to the courtyard show that there

could never have been a freestanding wall where the ramp is, because there were no walls on the western (outside) line of the courtyards."

As to the fill, Zertal answered that he had spent two weeks excavating it, and found it to be composed of deliberately laid strata. If it were comprised of debris, Adam reasoned, it would have been all jumbled together, earth, ashes, bones, and pottery.

"It is beyond my understanding how a supposed scientist can rely on his one-hour visit to the site three years ago, not knowing the whole problem, to analyze this fill. A clear indication that the fill consists of deliberately laid strata is the fact that, from the hundreds of sherds found in the fill, not one complete vessel could be restored. Moreover, since no destruction occurred during the history of the Mount Ebal site, from where would the inhabitants have taken the ashes in order to fill their new (and unnecessary) watchtower?"

Zertal then took up Kempinski's comments on the bones by quoting from Kolska-Horowitz's faunal osteological report: "When compared to other Iron Age habitation sites, some interesting differences are apparent between Ebal and the others. The first is the difference in the emphasis of the species present. *Equids* [the genus that includes horses, donkeys, etc.], pigs, carnivores and gazelle (both wild and domesticated) are absent at Ebal, but present at Iron Age sites of Lachish, tell Qasile, tell Miqneh, tell Dan, Hazor, tell Michal, Shiloh, Beer-sheva, tell Masos and Isbet Sartah. The species represented and their frequency suggests that only edible animals were present at Ebal, while at other sites animals possibly used for other purposes (such as *equids*) are present. The specific absence of gazelle and pig remains is of interest considering their presence in the immediate area of the site, both in antiquity and today. This is further emphasized by the high frequency of fallow deer, which share a similar environment to wild pig, though the latter does not appear to have been hunted in Ebal.

"An aspect which further highlights the difference between Ebal and habitation sites is the number and distribution of burnt or scorched bone from Ebal (28 bones forming 9% of the diagnostic bone sample) compared with 8 bones (0.8%) from the Iron Age levels at the City of David (from the sample there of approximately

1,000 bones). Waponish has reported that 15% of the *equid* material (total of 65 bones) from tell Jemmeh had cut marks and burning."

The osteological report states that Zertal's sample had a slightly higher proportion of burned bones than other known sacrificial sites. "However," Kolska-Horowitz continues, "the most salient feature of the burnt material from Ebal in the altar area (17 of the 28 bones, or 61% of the total burnt bone samples from the site) indicates a different pattern of animal utilization at Ebal than that found at Iron Age habitation sites. It is suggested that the Ebal faunal assemblage represents a narrow range of activities either in function or time. The absence of animals prohibited for consumption but frequent at other Iron Age sites suggests conformity with Biblical tenets."

Although this report does not mention it, there was also an absence of dog bones, which had been found in other Iron Age sites.

Zertal now took on Kempinski's comments concerning the cultic nature of the Ebal site, which was crucial. If the site was Israelite, from the early Iron Age and cultic in nature, it was, even without the Joshua concept, a unique and extremely valuable find in biblical history.

When I asked Zertal his reaction to Kempinski's comments, he said he had been totally astonished by such a factually incorrect and ignorant attack on his work.

In the first place, he pointed out to me (and wrote in an article in *BAR*), there were features that made it all but impossible that the Ebal site was anything but a religious precinct; the fact that the only architectural connection between the courtyard and the altar was via the ramp is an example.

Also Kempinski did not even deal with the secondary ramp and surround which could not be explained by any function except that of an altar.

The fact that there were installations containing clay vessels that did not match up with those found in this period or any other was ignored by Kempinski, as was the absence of features that had been found in Iron Age I villages. There were no buildings supported by single columns of stone, nor were there storage bins for food and water, which would have been required to support an ordinary settlement. There were also no buildings of the three- or four-room design that had been regarded as common to early Israelite Iron Age I houses. And if the Ebal site had been a dwelling, it would have had an entrance and a floor, neither of which exists at Ebal.

Zertal sums up what he has found on Mount Ebal this way:

In the last quarter of the thirteenth century B.C., as verified by the two unique scarabs found at the site, an Israelite cultic center was founded on the third ridge of Mount Ebal, looking northwest toward Wadi Farah.

It is now clear, says Zertal, that this site was used in its earliest level for fire-related religious activities both at the central sites and in the surrounding areas.

About fifty years later, according to Zertal's estimates, a much larger and more elaborate structure was built on the site. A large burnt-offering altar was built directly over the center of the earlier basic structure. It was surrounded by an inner temenos wall. The altar complex includes courtyards and installations, as well as ramps and a surround leading to the top of the altar, which is about ten feet high. There were no structures besides that altar inside the inner temenos wall. A wide ceremonial gateway was built into the inner wall; beyond it was a larger wall, which can be regarded as the outer temenos wall, thus creating one area within another.

"No doubt," Zertal says, "this ritual center was intended for the gathering of a relatively large number of people. The evidence for this lies in the special location of the enclosure in a way that the viewer could see the ceremonies on the altar from outside the enclosure wall."

Zertal believes that this center existed for a relatively short time in archaeological terms—perhaps fifty years. But the site was never actually destroyed. Instead it was abandoned while in a complete and undestroyed state, first having been covered with a protective layer of stones and earth. It was this covering that made it possible for the Ebal site to survive to this day.

But why *was* it deserted? The answer is not yet known. But the fact that it was covered over before being abandoned meant that Zertal now had a complete untouched ruin of an Israelite religious site from the time of the Settlement, the first of its kind ever discovered—one that could be studied and analyzed by scholars of all Bible-based religions in terms of interpreting early Bible stories.

"The desertion of the site resulted in the fact that we now have a complete and untouched Israelite cultic center from the time when monotheism began."

That should have settled the hash of Adam's detractors. But it didn't.

XXXI

Two Egyptian Earrings

dam was still having trouble getting complete acceptance of his ideas from the archaeological establishment. Many, if not most, were by now becoming convinced that Ebal was an Israelite cultic center from the time of the Settlement, but before they would say anything publicly they were waiting for the publication of Zertal's full report. This takes time and money. Many archaeologists don't publish until many years, or even decades, after their dig. Many die before having published. At this writing (1990) the full Ebal report has just been published.

In the summer of 1986, after Kempinski's attack had appeared, Zertal made several provocative finds on the Ebal site. He discussed them in a report called *Excavations and Surveys in Israel 1986*, the Archaeological Newsletter of the Israel Department of Antiquities and Museums. Beneath the paving of the courtyard that had been built in connection with the altar he found burned material including bones of sacrificial animals, and store jars, all on the bedrock level. They appeared to represent the remains of sacrifices made before construction of the larger altar, and certainly supported the contention that this was a sacred site.

So the structure could be linked in time to the area where the older level had a similar pavement. More bones and pottery of early Iron Age I were uncovered in the open space near the altar, but not in it.

It was in this same period, Zertal reported, that the two earrings, the gold and the silver, were found, further strengthening the connection between the Israelites and Egypt.

It must be admitted, however, that the earrings did not necessarily prove that the Israelites actually *came* from Egypt, since, because of the frequent occupations by Egypt of the area, no doubt artifacts of that nation, or decorations inspired by the Egyptians, existed in the Shechem Valley before the arrival of Joshua and his followers. There was always the possibility that they were of local origin or could have been available in a Shechem marketplace.

But the scarabs discovered that season were a different matter, once Brandl had confirmed that they were extremely rare and could not possibly have appeared in a local market. Therefore it seemed almost certain that they had come from Egypt with the fleeing Israelites, probably the property of an influential Israelite who had traveled with the people of the Exodus. This, at any rate, is my conclusion. Adam, with his usual caution, has not gone so far in connecting the scarabs with the Exodus Israelites; but who but a ranking Israelite would possess such a thing, and be so dedicated that he had it placed as an offering in the altar?

Opposite the complex of ramps ascending toward the top of the altar the pavement was interrupted by masonry compartments about six by six feet which also contained pithoi and storage jars *in situ*. This provided a paved open space, with the area containing pithoi at its center in front of the base of the altar structure.

As in previous years, there was no evidence of destruction during the transition between the two levels.

So we have large, paved areas, probably meant for processions and assembly of people (worshipers?) in a place where there was no substantial evidence of any town or village. Where did these people come from, and why, if not for a religious assemblage? And why was a pavement necessary if nobody lived on the site?

By now Zertal was ready to publish his conclusions in a scientific paper, but found difficulty in financing the publication and production of his final report. In the end he had to return to his alma mater, Tel Aviv University, which agreed to publish it. But that publication faced endless delays, and other archaeologists tended to withhold their opinions until they could see Zertal's scientific summing up. Meanwhile Kempinski kept the dispute alive by responding in the July–August 1986 *BAR* to Adam's comments. He did not really succeed, however, in destroying Zertal's thesis.

There were other letters in the *BAR* bearing on Zertal's find. The Ebal matter had stirred up a storm. One letter from a notorious firebrand in the profession, Anson F. Rainey—like Kempinski a professor at Tel Aviv University—labeled Zertal's altar as "fabrication of wishful thinking and partial evidence."

Citing the location of the site as unsuitable, among other things, Rainey says: "Only the very gullible will continue to support Zertal's theory. All the facts are against it. The question must be raised about *BAR*'s editorial policy. Don't the professionals on your advisory board ever get consulted? Is it your intention to pander to the sensational at the expense of scientific honesty? I speak for several professionals who agree about Zertal's site but who probably wouldn't take the trouble to write. But I speak especially for myself. The Zertal altar on Ebal is a blatant phony."

Adam replied angrily in the next issue to Rainey's heated attack. First, he pointed out, that as a former student of Rainey's at Tel Aviv University, he was well aware that the professor was not a specialist in archaeology, but rather a teacher of Semitic languages.

Zertal pointed out that Rainey had not visited the site, and apparently had not even read the published material, including Zertal's and Kempinski's articles in *BAR*, and he had never spoken or communicated with Adam.

"Since the scientific report is to be published soon, hopefully in 1987 [He was wrong there. It finally appeared in 1989] there is no value in continuing this kind of a debate. Every serious scientist is invited to visit the site and discuss the discovery with me."

In fact a great many of the leading archaeologists including Yigael Yadin, Benjamin Mazar, Frank Moore Cross and Lawrence Stager of Harvard, and others had done exactly that. No one who had seen the later finds seemed by now to have any doubt that this was an important archaeological site from the Settlement Period, but most preferred to wait before going public with an opinion.

XXXII

Zertal's Conclusions

I n 1989 Zertal published his official report, under the auspices of Tel Aviv University. Here are his conclusions from an advance copy of his scientific report:

Until the emergency survey of 1967, the archaeological material bearing on the Settlement Period was scarce. Only three excavations in the Manasseh hill country revealed a layer of Iron Age II—Shechem, the Dothan Valley, and Tell el-Farah (North), which is Tirzah. Only the Tirzah dig has been published so far, Zertal observed, so it could not be said that the area has been extensively surveyed. Only four minor surveys preceded the 1967 emergency project. During the course of that emergency survey the entire area was examined and a preliminary picture emerged according to which the emergency surveyors suggested a "new Settlement process identified with the settlement of Ephraim and Manasseh."

In a preliminary paper bringing the project up to 1988, Zertal reported that he covered three quarters of the Manasseh hill country, and conducted two excavations—the fortified tell of Aruboth-Narbata and the cultic site on Mount Ebal.

From his research it was apparent to Zertal that the Iron Age I population of the Manasseh hill country was the largest in all of Canaan. This was confirmed by the number of towns discovered in the area and their built-up surroundings. From his explorations Zertal could conclude that two thirds of the Israelite population of Canaan during the eleventh century B.C. (25,000 out of 40,000) lived in the Manasseh hill country and one third of the sites explored were located there (100 out of 300). This is even more striking when you realize that the Manasseh territory is only a small part of Canaan as a whole.

This presents a challenge to the traditional view of biblical and archaeological scholars. Viewing the situation in Canaan as researched by Zertal raises the question: What caused this profusion of settlement at this particular time?

One of the basic problems faced by Zertal and his team was to examine the historical and archaeological background of the Israelite settlement process. How did the people of the preceding periods behave in the same ecological setting? What was the reality that faced the Israelite settlers? The cultural world of "Greater Canaan" was created during the Middle Bronze II period in the first half of the second millennium B.C. Undoubtedly this world was also the background for the Israelite settlement following the Exodus. Zertal chose therefore to begin with this period.

Pottery of Middle Bronze II was found at 135 sites in Manasseh during Adam's survey. This indicated an extremely dense population for a rural area. The finds indicate a population at that time even greater than the ultimate Israelite population that became dominant by 1000 B.C. and made it one of the most populated areas in Canaan.

These Israelites were probably descended from those settled in the coastal plain where the settlement process in Middle Bronze II had its genesis.

Zertal tells us that the new settlers established themselves on the. fringes of the internal valleys of the eastern streams, such as the Wadi Farah. The remains discovered of most of these settlements show that they were fortified. These areas were chosen in preference to the mountains, the inner hills, or the desert area because of the abundance of fertile ground available in the well-watered valleys. Zertal estimates that by the end of the sixteenth century B.C. the population in these areas was about 30,000.

During the course of the American expedition directed by G. E. Wright at Shechem (1956–1966), the monumental fortifications of the city during Middle Bronze IIB and IIC periods were uncovered. Wright suggested that "the enormous effort to create this impregnable fortress during the Hyksos Period indicates that during the seventeenth–sixteenth centuries B.C. Shechem was a city-state which controlled the hill country from Megiddo to Gezer."

The American excavators related the two massive destructions that were inflicted on Shechem in the beginning of the Late Bronze era (1550–1400 B.C.) to the Egyptian eighteenth dynasty of Ahmose or possibly Amenhotep I. The settlement picture complements the excavations of Shechem very well, indicating the importance of this then-flourishing area during that period, as well as the massive destructions that followed. This indicates that the fighting pharaohs of the eighteenth dynasty wanted to turn the central mountain region around Shechem into a wilderness because of the great difficulties they were having in controlling the area. The Egyptian interests centered on the coast, the valleys, and the transportation routes. The mountains produced no wealth for them.

After this destruction, and the eventual abandonment of the area in the sixteenth century B.C., the region did not revive quickly. Zertal found pottery of all stages of the Late Bronze era in only thirty-three sites. Only one of the four sites that preceded this period survived. It can be assumed that the Mediterranean forest cover that had been cleared in various parts of the area by the people of the Middle Bronze period (2200–1550 B.C.) grew up again to cover vast areas.

"Only the inner valleys, which in our opinion were covered by a forest park of Tabor oak, continued to be partially cultivated. This forest, convenient for grazing, was one of the major attractions for the Israelite settlers," Zertal states.

During the Late Bronze period population returned to some of the fortified tells built hundreds of years earlier in the Middle Bronze era. The location of these tells, adjoining fields, water sources, and highways was certainly a source of attraction to the population that continued to live in them after the Egyptian conquest. Despite the decline of settlement during this period, the Manasseh hill country remained the major area of the Shechemite princedom of the El Amarna era (1400–1360 B.C.) with the dynasty of Labaya at its head. It is noticeable that even in this period of generally sparse settlement in the area, settlement in Shechem itself was dense.

So the political and economic situation on the eve of the Israelite settlement was as follows: The 2,000-square-mile area of the Manasseh hill country was mostly unpopulated, but there was some settlement of the Canaanite populace, whose livelihood was agriculture, in the inner valleys. (This is why we were looking particularly for Late Bronze pottery when we trudged over the slopes of these valleys earlier.) However, they were only partially cultivated, and the mountains that comprised 50 percent of the total area were covered by Mediterranean forest. The fringe of the desert attracted seminomadic groups who herded their flocks and watered them in the perennial streams. These water sources were controlled directly or indirectly by the resident Canaanites.

Eleven tells have been found that were built during the Israelite Settlement Period. *All were unfortified at the time they were built.* Apparently what fortifications they developed were built more than two hundred years later, during the Israelite Kingdom period of David and Solomon. The rest were built on existing tells, and in slightly more than half the cases (twelve out of twenty-three) the last settlement on these sites had been during the Middle Bronze Age, at least three hundred years earlier, and the sites had been abandoned until the arrival of the Israelites. Only nine of all the tells of the Late Bronze period found contained Israelite Settlement Period pottery, and these were generally from the later part of the Israelite settlement in the eleventh century B.C.

"We may assume, therefore," Zertal writes, "that the Israelite settlers 'went up' to the Canaanite cities only at a later stage of the process and that the existing population adopted the material culture of the new rulers. In both cases, decidedly, the direct continuity between the two periods is negligible. This factor has great importance when analyzing the origins of the new population."

A review of the few sites actually excavated in the area confirms the conclusions Zertal reached. The excavators of Tell el-Farah (North) have so far published results dealing only with the Iron Age. But even this preliminary report mentions that in two places the excavators found remnants of the Late Bronze Age. But the Israelite pottery found was of a much later date, around the tenth century B.C., or at the earliest, the end of the eleventh. "It seems, therefore," Zertal concludes, "that the city remained deserted during at least the entire twelfth century B.C., and that only afterward the Israelite settlers of the tribe of Manasseh went up to it."

Ancient Shechem was notable for plentiful springs, fertile ground, and the fact that it was the most important junction of the highways traversing the central mountains. There has been a problem in understanding Shechem during the early Iron Age because the results of excavations there have not yet been fully published. Some details are available, however, from preliminary articles and books. The excavators at Shechem from 1956 to 1966 reported two levels of destruction, which can serve as a starting point for any discussion of the history of the periods we are talking about here. The first destruction, in which both the acropolis and the city were partially destroyed, was dated to the second half of the fourteenth century B.C. The historical background of this event is unclear, but it may be related to the internal strife among the Canaanite city-states of that period. It was a time when Egyptian power was beginning to weaken and city-states were perhaps struggling for dominance. The El A-marna letters of the period discuss problems with locals whom they call *habiru*, which some scholars believe may mean the Hebrews. It was, I later found, the time when the Egyptians were also having a great deal of trouble with the Hittites invading from their strongholds in what is now Turkey.

In any event, after the first destruction, the city underwent a slow revival in the thirteenth to the twelfth centuries B.C., without being harassed by the Egyptians. By this time, according to the excavators, the material culture was identified with the early Iron Age. But the city itself was not refortified, and the second level of destruction, the harsher one, occurred during the second half of the twelfth century B.C. and was related by Wright and his researchers to the destruction of the city described in the Bible during the reign of Abimelech. "Abimelech fought against the city [Shechem] all that day. He captured the city and massacred the people in it; he razed the town and sowed it with salt." [Judges 9:45] Afterward Shechem remained desolate until the time of King Solomon.

"In our opinion," Zertal states, "the level between the fourteenth-century destruction and the twelfth-century destruction was under the control of the Hivite Shechemites." This relates to the purchase of land in Shechem from Prince Shechem, son of Hamor, in Jacob's time.

But the other important affirmation for the existence of Hivite

Shechem, says Zertal, is the establishment of the cultic center at Mount Ebal. "Apparently Shechem continued to be a cultic center during this period as well for the indigenous mountain population, whereas the Israelites—who represented a new foreign element in the area—chose to build their central holy place on the heights of Mount Ebal, on virgin ground, near the hallowed traditions of Hivite-Canaanite Shechem, but at the same time at a distance from it."

To Zertal the most important conclusion of his survey is that the settlement process was essentially *dynamic*. On the basis of pottery finds it appears that the settlers moved north along the east bank of the Jordan and then west across the Jordan near the village of Adam and up the region of the Wadi Farah and ultimately Shechem and Ebal. To date, such movement has been discussed only on the basis of biblical references rather than on actual archaeological evidence.

According to Zertal's findings, the Israelite settlements did not have their own independent water supplies until the tenth century B.C. So it appears that in their effort to gain independence as quickly as possible they first made agreements to obtain the water from local Canaanites. Only later did they achieve these independent goals by means of their military and political superiority.

Zertal's pottery finds indicate that the next settlement of the Israelites was in the inner valleys of these eastern-slope rivers, which also include Zebabde and Tubas and the valleys surrounding Shechem. These valleys form a kind of a belt along the eastern edge of the inner part of the slope. Many Israelite settlements were established, which necessitated the Israelites coming into contact with the Canaanites. In the Tubas Valley, for instance, the Israelite site of Khirbet Inon was only a short distance from Khirbet A-Dir, where Zertal found many remnants of the Late Bronze Age. In the Zebabde Valley the major Canaanite site was Khirbet Sheikh Spirein, and in that very valley Israelite settlements such as Zebabde and Khirbet Nahom were founded on adjacent sites. This indicated at that stage an excellent coexistence between the two populations, since the Israelite settlement sites were based on grazing and grain agriculture on available ground, which necessitated the cooperation of the Canaanites. Besides, and perhaps more significant, the Canaanite

ownership of the water source required a special agreement giving
permission to the Israelites to use the water.

"We may assume," Zertal writes, "that the first stage of settling
in the eastern valleys involved grazing in the forest park, a remarkable remnant of which still exists near the village of Zirin in the
Zebabde Valley."

Gradually the economy of that area became predominantly agricultural. Settlement sites spread out to the nearby valleys where
water was available.

With the changeover to permanent agriculture, settlement sites
began to appear also in the central valleys. A large number of Israelite settlement sites were discovered along their fringes, some built
on older Middle Bronze sites and some on virgin ground.

After about one hundred and fifty years of growth and development, the Israelites began the final phase of the settlement process—
the ascent to the mountains. The increasing population of the
prosperous valley settlements necessitated the cultivation of new
lands. But the new settlements were so far away from the main
villages that it became a problem to get to the fields and to guard the
animals and crops, which caused the newly developed areas to break
off from their mother-villages.

The undeveloped land that could be utilized was mainly in the
mountains, so the settlers began to spread out in that area. Because
of the ruggedness of the terrain it became necessary to clear the
Mediterranean forests that covered them. The ascent to the mountains was a crucial factor, which determined the economy and the
history of the people for many generations to come. "In our opinion
this process was well-defined in the Bible," says Zertal.

The major problems faced by the early Israelite settlers in the
mountain areas was one of water. In the past such noted archaeologists as Aharoni and Albright have assumed that the Israelites obtained their water from the limestone cisterns found so commonly in
Iron Age Israelite settlement. But Zertal has found that these all
date to a later time, at least as far as the Manasseh settlement is
concerned.

"This does not coincide with our finds," Zertal observed. "Apparently in the majority of Israelite towns settled during the twelfth
and eleventh centuries B.C. in areas of porous limestone, no cisterns

were hewn for water storage, and the supply of the precious liquid did not rely on this method." The flowing water sources, according to Zertal, were controlled by the Canaanite owners of the area, and this made it necessary for the Israelites to deal with the local people for the water, which they stored in the pithoi, the collar-rimmed jars found so abundantly in the area. The water was hauled in by pack animals—almost certainly burros.

Because of this situation, Zertal reasons, it would have been important to the Israelites to make compacts with the local inhabitants concerning rights to the water sites as well as permission to pass through the land peacefully. Such agreements are not unusual in the area even today. Local landowners enter into agreements with Bedouins and other pastoral nomads passing through. Coexistence was the key word for the Israelites of Canaan at this time.

Zertal calculates that the occupation of the inner valleys, the second stage of the settlement process, must have made such agreements necessary. This is one of Zertal's most important conclusions as affecting the process of the settlement or "conquest" of Canaan: "From the very beginning of scientific research it has been accepted that the settlement of the Manasseh hill country was carried out by peaceful means, and this conclusion was repeated in every paper dealing with the period. But during the course of our research it has become clear for the first time to me that the water-dependency factor was *the* crucial point which made coexistence imperative. It may be assumed that in other parts of the central mountains similar conditions did not exist, and the Canaanite settlement was weak and much more limited. This enabled in those situations an emphasis on forceful conquest of the Canaanite sites, but this, in our opinion, was much later than the events we are dealing with in the Manasseh hill country."

The concept here, that until the tenth century B.C. the Israelites did not have control of their own water supplies, brings into question many of the existing theories concerning the Settlement Period. It now seems that in the beginning the Israelites got their water through agreements with the local Canaanites, but later were able to ensure their water supply through the acquisition of their own land by military or political means. But this was long after the time of Joshua—hundreds of years.

A careful reading of biblical sources could indicate that at least some of the local Canaanites were absorbed into the Israelite culture, which, according to the Bible, as well as Zertal's finds, is much as it is today, with local farms producing a spectrum of Mediterranean produce such as olives, citrus fruits, figs, winter and summer grains, and a wide variety of beans and peas. In ancient times grapes were also widely cultivated, but because Muslims do not drink wine, this aspect of local agriculture diminished. In addition, such livestock as sheep, goats, and cattle were raised. The presence of cattle, which do not thrive under nomadic practices, is an indication of the fact that the Israelites were gradually becoming sedentary. The cultivation of olives also indicates the same fact because the olive tree takes seven years to mature and requires annual pruning to produce adequate fruit. This would have been impossible for a nomadic people.

Ecologists estimate that twenty-five head of cattle would be required to support each person in the community in those days. The main economic revolution in methods of cultivation, Zertal says in his report, was the result of the fact that the Israelites were gradually moving up into the mountains, and as they did so, they were cutting down existing forests in order to make room for grazing and growing crops. One result of this deforestation was ultimately the disappearance of the fallow deer from the area.

The developing farm community required sophisticated changes. A system of paths and roads had to be built to transport the crops to market. In addition to leveling the forest, it was necessary to terrace the land to prevent slippage and water runoff. Places had to be developed where the crops could be processed—wine and olive presses were needed as well as protected storage areas for the crops. This in turn involved development of market villages and systems of barter for many of the farmers who grew only one crop—oranges or figs, for example.

The Ebal site gave Zertal invaluable insights into the culture, social organization, and religious customs of the Israelite settlers. But the most important element was the cultic nature of the site.

The offering installations discovered in and around the altar on both levels certainly can be read as further support for the idea that this was a religious site. The bringing of religious offerings of valuable possessions, or sometimes such humble presentations as oil or grain, were typical of cultic practices even among the people of the Bronze Age in this area.

Some authorities have identified Ebal with the destruction visited on the area by Abimelech, but there is no destruction level at Ebal. The fact that the site was apparently abandoned peacefully, Zertal reasons, makes this impossible. Also because of the difficulty of access to the site, Zertal argues, it is almost impossible to imagine that this would be the principal cultic center of what had by then become the important Israelite capital of Shechem.

Defining his own conclusions about the site, Zertal wrote: "The excavation expedition suggested seeing the main complex as an Israelite burnt-offering altar within a holy enclosure (temenos), which together comprise a biblical 'high place.' Since no other burnt-offering altars have been discovered to date by archaeologists, we must rely for comparison on detailed descriptions in the Bible and the Second Temple literature, which describe the burnt-offering altar of the Temple in Jerusalem. According to these descriptions, the altar was an especially large structure, built with unhewn stones, surrounded by two outer gradings, and approached by means of steps or a wide ramp. So a graded or multi-levelled structure was formed which Albright and others convincingly suggested was a compact copy of a Mesopotamian ziggurat. The basis of the biblical description of the altar is found in the description of the future temple in Ezekiel 43:13. . . . The striking architectural similarities between the structure and the descriptions of the altars of the first and second temples prove that this structure underwent almost no changes over a 1,200 year period, which is a factor typical of holy structures.

"The discovery of Mount Ebal," Zertal continues, "exposed new and previously unknown data on the cultic beginnings of the Israelite settlement period. The site was built in such a way that a large audience could participate; the southwestern enclosure wall, facing the hilly valley adjoining the site, was built especially low for this purpose. The large size of the outer enclosure also hints at the participation of a sizeable audience. The site demanded extensive organization: transport, storing and preparation of food and water. Apparently, already at this stage, there existed a political and religious leadership which supervised the establishment of the site and the cultic activities within it. The practice of bringing offerings and placing them in installations was adopted from Canaanite ritual, and possibly there were prestigious families or patriarchal extended families who gave their offerings, as the practice described in Shiloh (I Samuel 1:24)."

Regarding ecological findings connected with the site, Zertal found there was evidence that the Mediterranean forest park mainly consisted of the common oak and the Israeli pistachio. This would fit with the presence in this area of fallow deer, which preferred this type of forest.

The fact that the "high place" in Ebal was enveloped in a mountain covered with a forest correlates with the assumption that already at this stage the ascent to the mountains had begun, though on a limited scale.

But the most important aspect of the Ebal excavation, of course, was its connection with the Bible, about which Zertal had some interesting things to say in his report.

XXXIII

A New View of Exodus

The argument over the origin of the settlers in Canaan following the Exodus has been the subject of serious splits in the scientific world recently, as we saw briefly in Chapter XVII. The big problem is the disparity between biblical descriptions of the event and archaeological evidence as interpreted by various scholars. There are also earnest disputes concerning what the archaeological evidence means in terms of the ethnic and religious origins of the early inhabitants of Canaan, and what these identities represented in antiquity. To begin with, Zertal says, prior to the dig at Ebal there were three schools of thought on the origins of the people of Israel in Canaan, each suggesting an explanation making use of different methods. The school that suggests that there was a uniform conquest, subscribed to by Albright, Wright, Yadin, Malamat, and others, sees the biblical description as being basically historically credible, although it may have undergone some changes and editing through the years.

The second school of thought, founded by Alt and Noth, sees the Israelite settlers as seminomads who arrived from Transjordan by a slow process of searching for alternative grazing areas.

The third school—the "sociological" theory, founded by Mendenhall and somewhat supported by Norman K. Gottwald—suggests that the origin of the majority of the Israelite population is the Canaanite city-states. This population moved to the hill country, which was empty of other settlement, and by means of various sociological and economic processes, established their new settlements.

Zertal's survey of the Manasseh hill country was the most extensive ever attempted and covered the areas of heaviest occupation by
the Israelites during the time of the settlement.

Actually, the Manasseh hill country and the northern part of the
central mountain region are not mentioned directly in the tale of
conquest in the Book of Joshua. Conquered cities were mentioned
in an offhand manner in the lists of Joshua 12, according to which
the cities of Hepher and Tirzah (verses 17 and 24) were conquered, and the obscure story of the battle at Bezek occurs in
Judges 1:5–7.

The Israelites, says the Bible, engaged the people of Bezek in
battle, "and defeated the Canaanites and the Perizzites. Adoni-
Bezek fled, but they pursued him and captured him; they cut off his
thumbs and his big toes. And Adoni-Bezek said: 'Seventy kings,
with thumbs and big toes cut off, used to pick up scraps under my
table; as I have done, so God has requited me.' They brought him
to Jerusalem and he died there."

(This would make the battle an anachronism, as the Israelites did
not conquer Jerusalem for several hundred years, according to the
Bible and archaeological findings. This would definitely tend to
exclude Joshua from this gory conflict, one of many that had so
distressed me on first reading the biblical story of Joshua.)

In the early stages of his survey Zertal had suggested identifying
Hepher with Tel-Muhaphar in the northern part of the Dothan
Valley, which is in the center of the Manasseh hill country. Tirzah's
location long ago was established as Tell el-Farah (North) by Albright in 1931 and was confirmed by the excavations of De Vaux in
1956. This is generally accepted, but the circumstances concerning
the capture of these two cities are unclear. They depend largely on
what the attitude is toward the list of Joshua 12, which describes the
defeat of some thirty-one Canaanite kings, and its dating. The finds
at Tell el-Farah showing the destruction of the city are dated in the
Late Bronze Age, just before Joshua's period, but unfortunately the
results of that dig have not yet been fully published, so our knowledge of the circumstances of the destruction is limited. But it seems
as though this destruction, if done by the Israelites, would have to
have taken place much later, during or following the time of

Joshua—and therefore it is unlikely that the razing of Tirzah was one of Joshua's accomplishments. These conclusions did much to settle my concerns about the bloody nature of the Israelite occupation of Canaan.

Zertal feels that Mendenhall's "sociological" theory certainly deserves careful scrutiny. Archaeological finds to date have at least allowed the possibility that the founders of the new villages were local Canaanites who left the city-states by means of the four patterns suggested lately by Gottwald, and made a pact, whose nature is unclear, with nomadic tribes from Sinai. These tribes would have brought with them Egyptian traditions, and a deity of desert origins—Yahweh—who overcame the Canaanite gods by a competitive process.

The Manasseh hill country is particularly useful as a place to base these sociological theories. Its topography and animal life fit the criteria for an area that allows escape from the cities, shelter, and the establishment of new settlements. Since the area is so near major Canaanite city-states in the valleys and on the coast, it lends a certain credence to the Mendenhall theory. But Zertal, after a careful examination, found that the theory did not hold up to the factual evidence he and others have uncovered.

One of the most prominent features of the settlement of the Manasseh area is the movement from east to west—the dynamic process discussed earlier. If the large city-states in the Yizrael Valley and the Sharon were the major sources of the "retreating" Canaanite population—those leaving the city-states to settle in the mountains—the direction of the expansion of this new population would have been from the north and the west into the Manasseh hill country, and this is not the case. "Our archaeological finds," Zertal points out, "indicate a movement from the Jordan Valley toward the mountains, similar to the biblical view."

Another important point raised by Zertal is that of chronology. "We found no factor in the history of Canaan that indicates a 'farmers' rebellion' and related processes, specifically during the thirteenth century B.C. The period that was ostensibly suitable for such a process, for which we have authentic historical record, is the El Amarna period of the fourteenth century B.C. During this era, the hold of Egypt on Canaan weakened. The rivalry among city-states had reached its peak, and the activities of the *habiru* are mentioned as one of the most serious problems faced by the Egyptians. As long as more established chronological data were unavailable to research, it was logical to predate the beginning of the Israelite Settlement Period to the fourteenth century B.C. as did Aharoni and others. Once the established dating of the Israelite settlement was set at the middle of the thirteenth century B.C., allowing the 'pulling back' of the date of the appearance of the Israelites to no more than a few decades, the supporters of the 'sociological' theory are forced to suggest special historical circumstances, which would justify the feasibility of their models specifically in the thirteenth century B.C., one hundred years or more after El Amarna. We should add that in the Manasseh hill country no dated archaeological evidence was discovered that would indicate a settlement process during the El Amarna period. In this case we should also note that this area is one of those most suited for examining the hypothesis, because of the repeated mentions of the *habiru* in relation to Labaya, Prince of Shechem."

So, Zertal asks, what *is* the origin of the settling population in the Manasseh hill country in the early Iron Age?

"Our finds," Zertal concludes, "generally support the approach of Alt and Noth and others, according to which the settlers were of foreign origin, in a seminomadic state, and entered Canaan in the process of searching for alternative grazing areas.

"The absence of enduring physical remains such as architecture and pottery has made it nearly impossible for modern archaeology to pinpoint physical cultures of the nomads. Therefore we developed our model on the ecological and archaeological finds alike: the type of economy that suits the climatic botanic and topographical conditions, along with the earliest pottery forms. This examination indicates that the desert fringe of Manasseh is most suited to alternate grazing. The westward movement in toward the mountains, already established by the pottery finds, enabled us to reconstruct the Israelite settlement process."

Zertal has had the assistance of an interesting document in reconstructing the events of the thirteenth century in the Manasseh hill country. This is part of the continued publication of material in the Mari archives. Mari is a large ancient city in Syria where an enormously valuable archive of some 25,000 cuneiform tablets were found in 1933, inscribed with economic, legal, and diplomatic texts dating back as far as 3000 B.C. Mari tablets have an important place in the history of the Israelites since they refer both to the *habiru* and the tribes of Benjamin. Both of these people have been associated by scholars with the early Hebrews.

Recently the Mari tablets presented a broad picture of the Amorite tribes, who inhabited the desert fringe of the Euphrates and Tigris basins. There are apparently important points of similarity to the model for settlement theory proposed by Zertal. The Amorite culture was also represented by a combination of livestock grazing and agriculture. They were nomadic as well as permanent settlers. Various types of economic and political coexistence prevailed between them and indigenous population and authorities, including military service. On the whole, correct relationships existed between the Amorite nomads and the city dwellers. The Amorite penetration was mainly during the periods of weakness of the ruling regime, which is very similar to the weakness of the Egyptian rule during the thirteenth century B.C.

In the Euphrates Valley and its desert fringes we find a continuous process of Amorite settlement and incorporation into the local population. Indeed, the process in Mari and in Mesopotamia in general resembles the usual model of nomadic penetration into more fertile areas, and it is difficult to ignore the resemblance here.

"On the other hand," Zertal argues, "it is difficult to accept Alt's ideas about the continuation of the settlement process into the mountain areas. His theory was written in the thirties with almost no archaeological or ecological data at his disposal; the balance of his description of Israelite settlement in Manasseh and other parts of the central mountain region is no more than intelligent guesswork. He rightfully claimed that the important stages wherein the tribes and families wandered into the central mountain region are little mentioned in the Bible, since they lack the dramatic stages which typify conquest and war. This necessitates dependence on other sources for information. The archaeological tools at our disposal today en-able a reconstruction of the process, along with the biblical source, which contains, in our opinion, considerable and accurate information that has not yet been sufficiently tapped to date."

The Bible certainly tends to support the Transjordanian origins of the Israelites. In a recent analysis of the Book of Genesis, Benjamin Mazar came to the conclusion: "These obscure traditions are a source that reflects a period during which the children of Israel—a pact of shepherd tribes relating to the ancient father of Jacob—who resided in the Jordan Valley, and especially the Succoth Valley, assembled and spread from there to Gilead to the east and up to the mountain area of Shechem in the west."

Many scholars, including De Vaux and Le Maire, have concluded that the area of the Valley of Succoth, the Gilead, and the Manasseh hill country are vital links in the chain between the patriarchal era and that of the conquest. Le Maire even dates the patriarchal stories, particularly those relating to Jacob, to the Israelite Settlement Period itself. The patriarchs, he theorizes, existed very shortly before the time of Joshua. He feels that the area of wanderings and settlement of the sons of Jacob, in addition to the Transjordan, was the valley of Tirzah, which Adam included in his survey, and the northeast portion of the Manasseh hill country. The origin of the sons of Jacob, who are an important part of the people who entered Canaan from the east during this period and represented the original nucleus for the creation of "the pact of the Israelite tribes," is in upper Mesopotamia. As far as dates go, Le Maire connects the journey of the sons of Jacob westward to Canaan with the disappearance of the Mithani kingdom and the invasions of King Adadnireri I, king of Assyria in the early part of the thirteenth century B.C., less than fifty years before Joshua. The Assyrian king conquered Haran on the Euphrates, Abraham's putative home, and Carcamesh in northern Syria.

"One way or another," Zertal comments, "this dating fits well with the dates we have determined by archaeological methods as the beginning of the Settlement Period of the tribes of Manasseh [led by Joshua]."

In his summation of these ideas, Zertal says, "The settlers who entered the Manasseh hill country during the thirteenth century B.C. came mainly from outside the country. They were seminomadic

during their early stages. Their major source of penetration was from
the Succoth Valley through the desert fringe of Manasseh (Wadi
Farah and Wadi Malich) and on to the inner mountains of which
Shechem is the center. The population adopted part of the Canaanite material culture, a natural process for a nomadic population beginning to settle. There are clear signs that the origins of this
population was in the upper Euphrates Valley—Aram Naharaim. As
a result, the stories of the patriarchs and the Israelite settlement
should be observed as though looking through a kaleidoscope illu-
minating the background of the area in a fragmentary and sometimes
disordered fashion. These traditions underwent extensive revisions
and editing over a period in some instances as far back as hundreds
of years. But the very persistence of these important traditions and
their solid historic nucleus now enables an examination of the beginnings of the Israelite tribes in the patriarchal traditions in general,
and in the tradition of the settlement of Manasseh in particular."

The altar Zertal found on Ebal gave positive archaeological confirmation to the story of Joshua, which had until then been supported only by the Bible story. The presence of Mesopotamian
influences, which were found nowhere else in Canaan, indicates that
the design of the altar was inspired by the memory of the Israelites'
origins in Mesopotamia.

An interesting parallel to Ebal is the temple first excavated by
H. J. Franken at Deir Allah, in 1960, which is identified with the
biblical city of Succoth. This temple was found without an adjoining
residential site, as was the case at Ebal. It is believed it was a central
open-air cultic site for nomadic non-Israelite tribes. It was destroyed
by an earthquake in the twelfth century B.C. The appearance of
temples and cultic sites of this type—that is, not attached to a city—
is not rare in Canaan and other places, and apparently the site at
Ebal fits this very category, which supports the idea that Ebal was
actually the first Israelite temple in the time of the conquest.

Another point in examining the relationships between the
Canaanite population and the Manasseh hill people is the settlement
of the Israelites in the internal valleys, and the Canaanite ownership
of the water supply and the Israelite dependence on it, which indicates a coexistence between the Canaanites and the Israelites. This
situation contradicts the social-revolution theory, since obviously

hostile relations would develop between the local farmers who ran away from the city-states and the rulers of the city-states themselves.

A third argument against the sociological theory involves the site at Ebal. The discovery of an Israelite "high place" with an altar, whose origin differs from the architecture of the Canaanite cults, necessitates the conclusion that the "retreating" Canaanite population adopted an entirely new cultic form at the earliest stages of its existence. Societies in the ancient world, and in the modern one as well, says Zertal, do not easily discard existing cults, and it should be expected that at least an echo of Canaanite cult would be found in the Ebal site, which is certainly not the case. The Mesopotamian roots of the structure type do not fit with the idea of a meeting between the local population and nomadic elements with Egyptian traditions.

"The tradition of Mount Ebal," Zertal says, "appears twice in the Bible as a significant ceremony, including the building of a cultic site and altar as well as making a pact, immediately following the entrance into Canaan. [Deuteronomy 27:1–15; Joshua 8:30–35] Scholars have dealt at length with the difficulties of the Deuteronomistic story, but in our opinion, no doubt can be cast on its historical authenticity. We should remember that we are dealing with an important tradition of the northern tribes situated near Shechem and at the heart of the territory of the House of Joseph, near the important cultic site of the northern part of the central mountain region. It may be assumed that the Judaic priests, responsible for the writing and editing of the book of Deuteronomy, attempted to forget this tradition, and only its importance saved it from extinction."

Zertal goes on to cite Alt's evaluation of the ceremony on Ebal: "But if an entire category of the Israelite law fits into the scene described in Deuteronomy 27, this provides strong support for the view that the account is not simply the product of the writer's imagination, having no relation to reality, but preserving at least the recollection of a sacral action that actually took place at one time in Israel. The recently established view that this same sanctuary of Yahweh at Shechem was visited and used in common by the whole federation of Israelite tribes, and may perhaps have been their only sanctuary in Palestine, brings the scene in Deuteronomy 27 quite within the bounds of historical possibility." [Alt:1966 125–126]

The historical authenticity of the Ebal ceremony is agreed on also by Benjamin Mazar, Sternagel, Noth, and many others. Zertal says that his find is confirmed by biblical sources in at least three areas: the dating, the geographic location, and the nature of the find.

XXXIV

The Mystery of Gilgal

But if this *is* Joshua's altar, how does it fit with the biblical location of Gilgal in relationship to Jericho? In the Bible it says first: ". . . the people came up from the Jordan . . . encamped at Gilgal, which is on the eastern border of Jericho." [Joshua 4:19] As we know, British archaeologist Dame Kathleen Kenyon stated that there was nothing in Jericho in Joshua's time except the ruins of a Bronze Age city, and earlier ruins underneath it. It had been sacked many hundreds of years, perhaps a millennium, before Joshua got there. Neither she nor any other archaeologist has been able to locate any place that conforms to the Bible's description of the location of biblical Gilgal. So maybe there is some other angle to this Gilgal business. There are four different Gilgals mentioned in the Bible. If the mound on Ebal was Joshua's altar, then this Gilgal must be someplace else—not adjacent to Jericho—but somewhere in the valley of Shechem.

Might Joshua's Gilgal have been along the Wadi Farah? Adam's survey had showed a large concentration of Israelite pottery of Joshua's time along Wadi Farah. The Gilgal near Jericho would make no sense if Joshua was on his way to Shechem. Besides, no Israelite remains have been found in that area. On the other hand, according to instructions to Joshua in Deuteronomy and the Book of Joshua, Shechem is the ancient home of Jews: Abraham, Isaac, Jacob, Joseph. It was historically the central site of Israel.

" 'And when Yahweh, your God, has brought you into the land which you are about to enter and make your own, you shall set the blessing on Mount Gerizim and the curse on Mount Ebal. These mountains as you know are on the westward road in the land of the Canaanites who live in the plain, opposite Gilgal, near the Oak of Moreh. . . .' [Deuteronomy 11:29–30]"

So now the Bible places Gilgal where it *should* be if Joshua were going to Ebal—"on the westward road . . . near the Oak of Moreh." Wadi Farah, a cool green-fringed stream that I had seen earlier from Mount Kebir, runs from the Shechem Valley below Elon Moreh on a curving route eastward to the Jordan.

Gilgal is an ambiguous term. It means "a circle of stone" or "a pile of stones." It was at first used to describe a holy site. This was a place where the people would stand up before God in times of peace and war. Others feel that the term *gilgal* refers to structures that remained as holy ground from previous times, and already were considered sacred places in the eyes of the Canaanites.

In the Bible the first Gilgal mentioned is the one on the eastern side of Jericho. This is just after Joshua dries up the waters of the Jordan so that the priests can carry the Ark across on dry land. Joshua 3:16 says that "the upper waters stood still and made one heap over a wide space—from Adam to the fortress of Zarethan." But later in this passage, the Bible locates this Gilgal site clearly: "The people crossed opposite Jericho."

The name of the city of Gilgal is mentioned as a memory of the place where Joshua circumcised all those born in the desert. Moses had decreed, remember, that none of the older generation except Joshua and Caleb would be allowed actually to enter the Promised Land. When the new generation had been circumcised, Yahweh said to Joshua: " 'Today I have taken the shame of Egypt away from you.' That place has been called Gilgal until now." [Joshua 5:9]

According to Ernest Sellin, who first dug up ancient Shechem in 1917, the entrance to the land of Israel was not via Jericho and Ai, as the Bible has it, but through the ford over the Jordan at Adam, which is where Joshua dried up the Jordan waters. The village of Adam has been identified with Tell el-Damiya, near the confluence of the Jabbok River with the Jordan. At this point a deep ditch is formed in the river, and its eastern bank consists of earthen walls, whose bases are easily eroded by the stream. A sudden collapse of the banks may have produced an obstruction to the normal flow of the water. A similar phenomenon has occurred more than once in more recent times, namely in 1267, 1906, and 1927, according to Gonzales Baez-Camargo in his book *Archaeological Comment on the Bible* (Garden City, N.Y.: Doubleday-Galilee, 1986). The Gilgal where the Israelites camped at first is not the Gilgal previously described, he claims, but Gilgal Adet. The tradition about the camp at the Gilgal next to Jericho, he thinks, was born during the period of the kingdom when the kings of Judah were in opposition to the rulers of Israel and the Gilgal near Shechem had a bad name.

Another place mentioned as Gilgal in the Bible is related to the blessing and the curse on Mount Ebal and Gerizim: "Are they not across the Jordan? etc." Since Elon Moreh is near Shechem, it stands to reason that the site of Gilgal is near Shechem. But Shechem is not in the plain. However, according to the *Archaeological Encyclopedia of the Holy Land,* the word for "plain" can also be interpreted as "oak."

What we have here, as presented by Zertal, is the idea that the entrance of the Herbrews into Canaan was in the area of Adam's Bridge and not near Jericho. This theory is supported by the frequent accidental damming of the Jordan at this point, conforming to the biblical account of the Israelites crossing the stream on dry land. The survey has pointed out that there were many, many more settlements—sixteen times as many, approximately—in this general vicinity than in the south, where the tribes of Ephraim and Benjamin settled. In light of this, Zertal assumed that Gilgal would be near Shechem and not near Jericho. In fact, no site identifiable as biblical Gilgal has been found near Jericho.

Zertal observes: "It is self-evident that the natural way to get from the Transjordan (the east bank) to Mount Ebal is via the route of Wadi Farah and not via Jericho and the Gilgal near it. The archaeological dating in the Wadi Farah matches the biblical description, which deals with the beginnings of the settlement. The location of Mount Ebal is beyond question, and the name of the mountain, along with that of Gerizim, had been well preserved in Samaritan tradition which began during the Persian-Hellenic period—around 300 B.C."

In fact, during the course of his survey in Wadi Farah, Zertal *has* discovered a site fitting the biblical description, containing elements that conform entirely to what the Gilgal should contain: an elliptical camp whose outer walls are made of piles of stones, with large quantities of sherds only of Iron Age I, identical to the kind discovered at Ebal. However, since a lack of funding has prevented an organized dig there to date, one cannot yet draw final conclusions.

XXXV

What the Ebal Altar Means to History

The time of the occupation of Canaan, when the Ebal altar was built, was exactly the time of the Trojan War—about 1250 B.C. At first I thought of this as an enigmatic coincidence, until I ran across the Hittite story in following up on the legend of the *Iliad*.

These were the same Hittites cited so often in the Bible, and just about no place else until 1906. They were believed to be another one of those biblical fables, or else a very small group that soon disappeared. But in 1906 Hugo Winckler, an anti-Semitic German archaeologist, who was ironically financed by a Jewish philanthropist, discovered a store of cuneiform tablets in the village of Bogazköy in central Turkey, about ninety miles east of Ankara. It turned out that the place where these tablets were found was the site of the capital of the Hittite empire.

It was discovered on translating the tablets, which were in several ancient languages including Akkadian and Sumerian, that the Hittites had indeed been an important early people. They had ruled the Fertile Crescent for centuries, had introduced iron, and had probably invented horse-drawn chariots (which the Assyrians and Egyptians were later to improve upon, to the sorrow of the Israelites). They also introduced the horse, which they had captured and tamed in Russia, to the Middle East. This, combined with the chariot, gave them overwhelming military superiority. Their extensive documentation of, and interest in, their own past caused the Hittites to be dubbed the inventors of history.

The fall and sack of Troy by Greek invaders in northwest Turkey is thought by many to have been a sign of the imminent collapse of the Hittite Empire, which for five hundred years or so had dominated Asia Minor. It is possible that a massive plague, perhaps related to the plagues mentioned in many parts of the Pentateuch and Joshua, contributed to the downfall of the Hittites, as well as the rigors of their battles with the Egyptians. In addition, a massive earthquake in the area at about that time may have contributed to their downfall. (Might this have been the earthquake that dammed up the Jordan so that Joshua could cross on dry land?)

But despite their prominent place in ancient history, the Hittites had fallen into a crack in the historical matrix as far as the Bible was concerned. In the time of the patriarchs they had not yet invaded the Holy Land, and by the time of Joshua they were exhausted. The Hittites, under their last great leader, Mutawallis, had fought a major battle against Egyptian forces led by Rameses II at Kadesh on the Orontes (not the Kadesh-barnea of Moses) and the conflict had weakened both Middle Eastern giants. In fact Rameses himself came near to losing his life in the conflict. Although the Egyptians claimed a victory in the battle, it was in essence a debilitating stalemate for both sides. It now appears that the Hittites had at least as good a claim to victory as the Egyptians, but the Egyptian version reached historians at an earlier date.

In any event the battle of Kadesh on the Orontes, fought in 1296 B.C., is the first historic battle between the two powers that we are able to reconstruct with accounts from both sides. Winckler ultimately found a tablet giving the Hittite version of the battle. The upshot was that sometime between 1280 and 1269 B.C. Rameses II married the daughter of the Hittite king in the newly founded city of Rameses in the Nile Delta, and made her his chief wife. This marked the peak of Hittite power. From the reign of the weak king of the Hittites, Tudhaliyas IV, which ran from 1250 to 1220 B.C., Hittite power withered away, making the lands of Canaan, Mesopotamia, and Anatolia easy prey for marauding tribesmen, almost certainly including the Israelites. In 1190 B.C. Hattusas, the capital of the once mighty Hittite Empire, was overrun and burned to the ground.

Since the Bible, until Winckler's discovery, was the only source of information about the Hittites, they became a mighty people almost lost to memory. But if they had sustained their power there might have been no occupation of Canaan and no Trojan War. The reason the Hittites, whose empire had extended at times from Turkey to Egypt, seemed less than giants to the Israelites is that at the time of the Exodus they were the tired tag end of a dying major power, depleted by its wars with the Egyptians and the mysterious Sea People, as well as the invading Philistines. They also were greatly weakened by a serious plague that afflicted them as well as the Egyptians. In fact, at the time of Joshua's occupation of Canaan, the crumbling Hittites and the weakened Egyptians had their hands full with onslaughts that descended on both nations from many more backward peoples who were on the move again over vast areas. As a widespread pattern of destruction shows, invading hordes engulfed Cilicia and the whole of the Levant—Mersin, Tarsus, Aleppo, Carcamesh, Alalakh, and Ugarit—as they did the once powerful Canaanite towns in Israel and Judah.

The exhaustion of the two former dominant powers, Egypt and Hatta (as the Hittite nation was known), was evident in northern Canaan, which, in the thirteenth century B.C. after the fall of the Hittites, became a power vacuum, ripe for occupation by Joshua's legions—or settlers, depending on one's point of view. It was *not* a coincidence that the events of the *Iliad* and the conquest of Canaan took place at the same time, because both incidents occurred for the same reason—the weakening of the Hittites and the weariness of the Egyptians.

"Two dynamic societies, Israel and Greece, rose from the ruins of the ancient Near Eastern world," comments biblical historian Frank Moore Cross. "Evidently the static and hierarchical societies of the Fertile Crescent had grown old and moribund. Israel was born in an era of extraordinary chaos."

But, Cross points out, the remnants of the Hittite power survived to oppress Israel. "In biblical terms," Cross comments, "the iniquity of the Amorites is not yet complete."

A by-product of the rise of these two societies, the Israelites and the Greeks, became perhaps their most important contribution—the invention of the alphabet as we know it today, adapted by the Greeks from the Hebrew. The events of the Iliad preceded Homer by 750 years, but it was the subsequent invention of the alphabet by Semitic peoples and its adoption in about 800 B.C. by the Greeks that made the writing of his epic possible. Meanwhile in the Indus Valley, in what is now Pakistan, where Hinduism was being developed at that very same time, the written language of Sanskrit was being evolved from the Aramaic version of the same alphabet. It is interesting to note that the only major civilization in the world at that time aside from the Mediterranean and the Indus Valley was the Shang dynasty in China, and it was at that same time that *that* early dynasty collapsed. No connection between these events can be made, but it is known that the Chinese already had made contacts with lands to the west from whom they learned the art of ironworking at a very early time.

In any event, the success of the Israelites' occupation of Canaan no doubt had more to do with their timing, and their talents as farmers and negotiators, than their superiority as warriors, at least in Joshua's time. Farming can sustain a much larger population in a given area than would be fed by previous systems of hunting and gathering, or nomadic herding.

But, as was pointed out in a recent book called *Archaeology and Language* by Colin Renfrew (Cambridge University Press, 1988), a transition to agriculture will naturally lead to a spreading from the center of origin. The people migrate in a piecemeal fashion, and generally peacefully. When all the land in their area is in use, they look beyond to the next floodplain or, in the case of the Israelites, to the potentially fertile hills of Canaan. Since a farming community can support ten times the population of a nomadic or hunter-gatherer one, the farming communities gradually spread out, absorbing the previous inhabitants. The Israelites' use of the hollowed-out plastered water cisterns and the clearing of previously unusable land undoubtedly had more to do with their relentless advance into Canaan than did the supposedly marauding armies of Joshua. Joshua himself gives the direction for settlement to the Josephite tribes when they complain that he has allocated their family too small a share of the acquired lands.

" 'Why have you assigned us as our portion a single allotment and a single district, seeing we are a numerous people whom the Lord has blessed so greatly?'

" 'If you are a numerous people,' Joshua answered them, 'go up to the forest country and clear an area for yourselves there, in the territory of the Perizzites and the Rephaim, seeing you are cramped in the hill country of Ephraim.'

" 'The hill country is not enough for us,' the Josephites replied, 'and all the Canaanites who live in the valley area have iron chariots, both those in Beth Shean and its dependencies and those in the valley of Jezreel.'

"But Joshua declared to the House of Joseph, to Ephraim and Manasseh, 'You are indeed a numerous people, possessed of great strength; you shall not have one allotment only. The hill country shall be yours as well; true, it is forest land, but you will clear it and possess it to its farthest limits. And you shall dispossess the Canaanites, even though they have iron chariots and even though they are strong.' " [Joshua 17:14–18]

"We have already shown by means of literary sources and the new archaeological finds alike that Ebal and Shechem were the national cultic centers of the Israelite tribes during the early part of the Israelite settlement," Zertal stated in his preliminary report. "The approximate date that the Ebal site was abandoned coincides, more or less, with the establishment of the cultic center at Shiloh. Upon the destruction of that center by the Philistines or near that time, the cultic center at Jerusalem was built by David and Solomon. The movement of cultic centers from north to south along the backbone of the central mountain must be connected with the transfer of the national center of gravity from Manasseh to Ephraim and later to Judah, Benjamin, and the house of David. Apparently the most feasible explanation for this movement is the connection between it and the order in which the tribes settled and consolidated."

What does all this mean? Let's sum up. This is the Gospel according to Zertal.

First: about the Exodus and the conquest of Canaan. What really happened? In the beginning of the thirteenth century B.C., with the weakening of the Egyptian and Hittite power, there were no major cities or military powers to oppose the entry of the Israelites into the land. Prior to this time there had been no nation of Israel as such, but only a loosely organized association of tribes joined by family ties and by common acceptance of the worship of Yahweh.

In the first half of the thirteenth century B.C., a group of Israelite tribes, who originated probably in Mesopotamia but some of whom had their most recent origins in Egypt, and traditionally led by Moses, allied themselves in a Covenant with Yahweh as their only God. This was the beginning of monotheism as we know it today. The Israelite tribes, probably belonging to the houses of Joseph and Levi, left Egypt and migrated up the east bank of the Jordan to the plains of Moab, where according to the Bible Moses died and turned over leadership of the Israelites to Joshua. Joshua led his people over the miraculously dry bed of the Jordan at the town of Adam. He ascended the Wadi Farah to a place near the site of Tell el-Farah, where the Israelites established a camp that would serve as the base for their further penetration of Canaan at a place they called the Gilgal. From the Gilgal the Israelites traveled the few miles to Mount Ebal, where Joshua built an altar and conducted for the twelve tribes assembled there the rites described in the Bible: the first religious ceremony of Israel as a nation.

The occupation of Jericho and Ai took place probably sometime after the Ebal ceremony—a very long time, possibly in the era of the Book of Judges—and under peaceable terms since both places were undefended at the time, and probably uninhabited. Following this period the tribes of Israel, sometimes under the leadership of a man called Joshua in the Bible, went on to occupy the hill country of Ephraim, Judah, Galilee, and the Gilead, following the plan described in the Bible to some extent, except that again, at least during the lifetime of Joshua, there were almost no bloody military victories, but rather peaceful occupation, sometimes in virgin land or cleared forest land, sometimes on the site of ruined cities, and sometimes by agreement with the local inhabitants. Many of the hilltop areas were covered with thick scrub that had heretofore made it unusable by farmers and herders, but the Israelites cleared off these overgrown sites, terraced them to conserve water, and claimed them as their own—much like the homesteaders in America's early West. In developing previously unusable land, according to Albright and Aharoni, the Israelites ultimately made use of a device for storing water—the plastered sunken cisterns—which made possible settlement away from established water sources, but this was a later development.

In his book, *The Archaeology of the Israelite Settlement* (Israel Exploration Society, 1988), Israel Finkelstein, a colleague of Zertal's, characterizes the Mount Ebal dig as "one of the most important ever undertaken in the land of Israel." Finkelstein completely agrees with Zertal's conclusions about the peaceful early settlement of Canaan and the development of the water supply that made it all possible.

This is the most plausible scenario for the early settlement of Canaan by the Israelites, according to the latest archaeological research. At present there is no credible evidence of the existence of an Israelite nation before Iron Age I. According to the surveys conducted by Zertal and Finkelstein in the hill country of Manasseh and Ephraim, literally hundreds of settlements were in place within the first hundred years of the arrival of the Israelites. Somewhat later sites identified as Israelite proliferated in Judah, the Galilee, the foothills of the Shephela, and the Negev desert. Most of these sites were completely unfortified, adding credence to the peacefulness of this occupation.

To sum up the evidence for Mount Ebal as the most important and only relic of early Israel:

1. The ruin is dated very close to the year 1250 B.C. This is attested to by the pottery, the scarabs, the seal, and the dating of the bones.
2. The site is Israelite according to the pottery, which is consistent with pottery found along the east bank of the Jordan, and along the Wadi Farah. It contains pottery designs (the reed-hole punctures and the man's face) that are unique to Israelite pottery of the era.
3. The site is a religious one. The offering installations, the ashes with sacrificial remains, the isolation of the site, the lack of any other purpose to which it can have been put, as well as the altar itself, point to this.
4. The altar is on Mount Ebal, a place well confirmed and geographically identified in the Bible, with an ancient tradition.

5. No idols or decorations were found on the site other than the man's face and reed-hole decorations associated with Israelite pottery. If the Israelites had simply revolted against the Canaanite rulers, why would they not have taken the more decorative and evolved Canaanite pottery with them, rather than relying on the primitive and unadorned pots found in the Israelite sites?

In regard to Zertal's pottery finds indicating Israelite origins in Egypt, three points of Egyptian origin should be noted: 1. The monotheistic concept introduced by Akhenaten in the period just before Moses. 2. The practice of circumcision antedating the Exodus in Egypt. 3. The use of a portable wooden Ark to carry the godhead into battle.

I found that the most respected archaeologists I have spoken to, including Benjamin Mazar, Lawrence Stager, and Frank Moore-Cross, as well as Amihai Mazar, basically agree on the above points concerning Ebal. Amihai Mazar cited Zertal's discovery at Ebal in his contribution to the book *Biblical Archaeology Today*, published by the Israel Exploration Society in 1985.

Michael Coogan, a highly respected archaeologist, formerly of Harvard and now at Stonehill College, developed four criteria for identifying a cultic site from archaeological remains:

1. *Isolation*. "In most cultures," Coogan notes, "there is a continuous separation between the holy and the profane. Architecturally, this finds expression in a temenos wall, which separates a holy place from its immediate context, whether natural or settled."

2. *Exotic materials*. "The special function of cultic sites will normally result in the presence of material not typical in other contexts," Coogan writes. "So we are likely to find unusual objects such as miniature vessels, figurines, or expensive objects." The proportion of exotic objects to ordinary ones such as cooking pots will be higher in a cultic site, in Coogan's opinion.

3. *Continuity*. In multiperiod sites, the cultic function of the site is likely to be retained from period to period. The outstand-

ing example of this is the Temple Mount in Jerusalem, which has retained its cultic character for nearly three thousand years.

4. *Parallels.* Questionable cultic sites are likely to have parallels, if they are truly cultic, at other unquestionably cultic sites. Thus, Coogan says, "Building plans, altars, pedestals, and the like should show resemblance to cultic installations known from written or non-written sources."

The Mount Ebal site fit in well with his criteria, in Coogan's estimation. In terms of his "isolation" criterion, Ebal certainly qualifies. "There are no other Iron Age sites on the mountain. This site is therefore isolated."

As for the pottery, 70 percent of the vessels were collar-rim storage jars; 20 percent were jugs and chalices. He found it significant that while a number of miniature vessels were found, there were very few cooking pots common in all residential sites.

As to continuity, although the site is of one period, it did have two phases, both apparently cultic, and Zertal, Coogan observes, cites a number of archaeological and literary parallels to other cultic sites.

Coogan's conclusion: "In view of the absence of significant numbers of elements of the ordinary domestic ceramic repertoire and the presence of miniature vessels, the isolation of the site from contemporary settlements, and some of the parallels adduced by Zertal, I tentatively concur with his interpretation of the function of the site as cultic."

But Coogan questions whether the site is Israelite. He admits that it is in an area assigned to the tribe of Manasseh in the Bible, and it is from the period of the Israelite conquest. But he says this does not mean that it is necessarily Israelite.

"What distinguished the Israelites from their non-Israelite contemporaries was metaphysical, not physical," Coogan contends, "the acceptance of Yahweh, the God of Israel, and the concomitant allegiance to fellow Yahwists."

Coogan goes on to say: "The biblical record makes it clear that as Israel developed in Canaan it grew in part by the conversion of individuals and groups who had not been part of the original nucleus. . . . Just as Israelites could commit apostasy by yoking themselves to such deities as Baal Peor, so non-Yahwists could commit themselves to Yahweh and his adherents and join Israel."

Coogan argues that there is no difference between Yahwist Israelite pottery and Yahwist Canaanite pottery.

Coogan's conclusions: Given the demonstrable continuities between the Late Bronze Age and the Iron Age, and the complicated biblical picture of the origins of Israel, it is methodologically questionable to label specific exemplars by a designation that is religious and political. Only toward the end of the Iron I period do distinct national cultures emerge; until then it would be wise to avoid labels such as Israelite or Canaanite unless there is conclusive evidence for using them."

The cultic installation on Mount Ebal was not necessarily Israelite, Coogan concluded, "and it is misleading and ultimately unhelpful for the larger historical task of a biblical archaeologist . . . to presume that [it was] Israelite."

Finally, Coogan considers the possibility that Mount Ebal may have been a "local Canaanite shrine which was also (or later) used by Israelites, or at least it was 'Israelitized.' "

But Canaanite cities did *not* have the same pottery as Israelite sites, and Israelite pottery in Zertal's survey followed a certain dynamic trail up the Jordan, across and up the eastern valleys, and then south. Coogan's arguments on this issue seem tenuous to me, and to other more qualified experts. I remember a visit to the small museum in Kedumim, where I observed the sophisticated Late Bronze Mycenean-originated pottery, so different from the coarse reddish Iron I ware at Ebal. The cultural and physical difference is striking. But Coogan has a point about the metaphysical difference. If you remember, the Ebal site is open for all to view, whereas the cultic practices of its major contemporaries, both Egypt and Mesopotamia, were conducted in enclosed shrines, visible only to the practicing priests. This is an extremely important point philosophically, since it represents the more abstract nature of the Israelite religion.

In an interview at his home in Jerusalem, Benjamin Mazar confirmed to me his strong opinion that the ruin on Mount Ebal is one of the most important finds in biblical archaeology: "The period of the dig on Mount Ebal is clear. This was the end of the thirteenth century, which is the period of the occupation . . . and it treats with the well-known tradition that Ebal was the site of a ceremony at the time of [the Israelites'] arrival in this part of the country, and that's all. You don't need more for it to be of utmost importance . . ."

I asked him about the material on Level II on the bedrock, the earliest part of the structure.

"The earliest level is clear. There is no question at all. The second period [the part of the structure Zertal characterizes as an altar], what it is, if it is a structure, or if it is something else is not yet absolutely proven, but it doesn't matter, because what Zertal did is fantastic. He worked very hard on this project. . . . It is clear that these kinds of structures in the later period are altars. So we certainly must take this into account."

"How much later do you think the structure identified as the altar was put down on the original bedrock site?" I asked him.

"Immediately. Shortly after the first installation.

"Ebal is important if only because it deals with a tradition that in this specific place a ceremony was held by the entire nation of Joshua. A tradition which is connected with the name of Joshua. Joshua is the symbol of the entire country. Now you understand that whoever wants to believe in the biblical story, believes in it, and who doesn't, doesn't. It is plain, speaking about Ebal, that this altar is connected to that tradition. I think that is a cultic center. This alone is wonderful in connection with the tradition."

"Do you think they would have built a noncultic structure on top of a previous holy site?"

"It is certainly not likely, and the scarabs are very important in the dating—very."

"What do you think of the contention of Kempinski and others that the structure on Ebal is a watchtower?"

"The term 'tower' in Hebrew is *migdal*. This also has the meaning of a religious tower. It can also have a political meaning. To be specific, this kind of structure is not a watchtower as Kempinski says. This is a structure, but we don't know exactly what; but it certainly might be an altar. . . . We are dealing here with tremendous material. We are not speaking just of fantasies; but of . . . something real."

Professor Lawrence Stager of the Harvard Museum of Semitic Studies disposed of Kempinski's watchtower argument in one sentence: "If it is a watchtower, it is the only one from Iron Age I ever found; although there are plenty from Iron Age II.

"If the ruin on Mount Ebal is what Adam says it is, the effect on archaeology and biblical studies will be revolutionary," he added. "We'll all have to go back to kindergarten. But that's a big 'if.' "

What Stager is talking about is the fact that almost all Western philosophy developed only after science, in the seventeenth century under the leadership of Hobbes and Spinoza, began to formulate the idea of different sources for the Pentateuch. This negated the historical credibility of the origins of the Old Testament in general and the Pentateuch in particular. From this era on, many scholars believed that the Bible was historically valid only after the time of David, and that all that preceded—the Pentateuch—was fable.

The discovery at Ebal, along with the findings of the survey regarding the entrance of the Israelites into Israel, goes a long way to disproving almost all previous scientific theory about the occupation of Canaan. The Deuteronomistic concept that almost everything in the Bible was written in Josiah's or Hezekiah's time does not hold water if Ebal is the site of Joshua's altar, or of the first Israelite ceremony.

The striking similarity between the biblical description and the archaeological finds at Ebal, especially the idea that the site was built "in" the mountain, makes it nearly impossible to assume that these chapters were written some six hundred years later, by people who certainly had no interest in playing up the role of a holy place outside Jerusalem. This is even more striking in light of the fact that the site was deliberately covered up and never mentioned again in the Bible. The Book of Deuteronomy never mentions Jerusalem specifically as the "place that he will choose," and, in light of the finds at Ebal, the biblical description certainly lends credence to the impression that the "place" referred to is, indeed, Ebal.

Since Deuteronomy is generally agreed to be the last book of the five, that means that the entire Pentateuch may now be dated as having been recorded near the times of the occurrences themselves. There may or may not have been some editing here and there, but that is relevant only to a few scholars. The historical relevance—the fact that this story really took place in some form—is of much greater importance. Even Professor Friedman, in *Who Wrote the Bible?*, says

that Deuteronomy comes from basically one source. (He credits only
a few sentences to someone he calls Dtr 2.)

"The correlation between the Ebal find and the Bible has important repercussions for the entire research of the Israelite period,"
Zertal states. "Over the last few decades extreme views have taken
root, which see the biblical traditions relating to the beginnings of
the nation as mainly relatively recent additions, and in any event of
little historical value. The creditability of the tradition of Ebal should
result in a renewed and more intensive study on the dating and
creditability of many parts of the books of Deuteronomy and Joshua,
which have been relegated until recently by many scientists to the
world of mythology."

Philosophically, of course, the greatest impact of the identification
of Ebal as Joshua's altar should be the negation of religious funda-
mentalism of all kinds. The fact that even Jewish tradition did not
preserve its knowledge in an absolute manner means that no one, to
date, has an absolute knowledge of what is considered to be the basis
of all Western religion. No one can legitimately make the kind of
statements you hear every Sunday on TV from the Christian Fundamentalists concerning the exact words of the Bible. This would also
tend to confound the profoundly literal interpretations of the words
of Mohammed insofar as they are based on the Bible. It all comes
down to what Professor Mazar told Koenigsberg on that fateful day:
"We don't have to *prove* the Bible; we have to understand it!"

This idea, probably more than anything else, makes the find on
Mount Ebal so interesting, since, if the Bible *is* viable historically,
but earlier historians have misinterpreted it, then, as Professor Stager
implies, all Western philosophy is due for an overhaul.

So now comes the big question: *Is it Joshua's altar?*

The problem here is that there is, so far, no archaeological evidence that Joshua ever existed (or Moses, Abraham, Jacob, and
Isaac, for that matter). We can only conclude that the place, the
time, and the people fit the biblical tradition. If there *was* a Joshua,
this was certainly his altar. If not, it was the earliest Israelite place of
worship ever discovered in Canaan, under whatever leader the people of Israel had at the time of their entrance into the Promised
Land. As such, Ebal was the place where the nation of Israel was
born.

But Zertal's archaeological confirmation of the probable route of the Exodus has equal significance in disproving the theories of those who argued for years that there never was an actual Exodus. Johnson wrote in *The History of the Jews*: "So the sojourn in and Exodus from Egypt, and the desert wanderings that followed, involved only part of the Israelite nation. Nevertheless this phase was of crucial importance in the evolution of their religious and ethical culture. Indeed, it was the central episode in their history, and has always been recognized by Jews as such, because it saw emerge for the first time, in transcendent splendor, the character of the unique God they worshipped, his power to deliver them from the greatest empire on earth and to give them a bounteous land of their own; and it also revealed the multitude of his exacting demands which in return he expected them to meet. Before they went to Egypt, the Israelites were a small folk, almost like any other, though they had a cherished promise of greatness. After they returned, they were a people with a purpose, a programme, and a message to the world."

> The Lord appeared to Abram and said, "I will assign this land to your offspring." And he built an altar there to the Lord who had appeared to him . . . [Genesis 12:7]

The modern implications of this passage are enormous. One has only to look at the bitter political struggle within the Jewish community of Israel today, between what are called right and left.

The right sees the current state as a philosophical continuity of the ancient Jewish nation, basing the right to the land on the historical connection. The left sees it more as an offshoot of the nationalistic groups that developed during the nineteenth century, with only vague undertones of the ancient connection.

While gathering material for this book I had occasion to spend a night in the Arab village of my driver in Israel. The inhabitants of the village came to Israel in 1948 at the time of the Israeli War of Independence. There were seven brothers and their families—a unit much like those of the pastoral Israelites at the beginning of the Settlement Period. Everyone in the village was part of one nuclear family. The brothers took over an Arab village that had been abandoned by its residents who fled into Syria. It reminded me very much of the common heritage in the Old Testament of Judaism and Islam. The village was relatively neat and self-sufficient. There were sheep and goats in the upland pastures that returned to the courtyard of their owners in the evening driven by children, old women, and dogs. This was in the narrow strip of land that lies between the Mediterranean and Samaria. In the hills above we could glimpse the outlines of sprawling Arab villages.

"If Jordan moves back into that area," I said, indicating the brooding blue hills Adam had admired as a child, "you could all move back and live in an Arab nation. Would you be happy with that?"

"It is all the same to us where we live as long as we have peace and freedom and money. I own my car. It is a Mercedes-Benz. I own my house. The Israelis do not come into our village. When my wife gives birth next week she will be cared for by the Israeli health plan. I do not especially love the Israelis. I vote, but I am treated as something less than an Israeli. But would I be better off as a Jordanian citizen, or even a Syrian or an Iraqi? I do not think so. Is Samaria really Jordan or Palestine or Israel? It is not my affair. I have my car, my goats, my children. This village is ours. That is what matters to me and my family." At that moment I dared to hope that, as unlikely as it seemed, the modern Israelis and Arabs could share a territory with local autonomy, with the settlers, as in the old days of the Bible, occupying their new settlements on the reclaimed hilltops, and the Arabs occupying the existing villages. It seems a remote dream today, but remember we are dealing with a land that reckons time by millennia.

The solution to the question of whether Samaria and Judea are historically Arab or Israeli is answered, in great part, not only by the Bible but by the astonishing find at Ebal, a site that was intended to be, in the words of Moses, the very birthplace of Israel: "This day you have become the nation of the Lord your God."

On a visit to the Ebal site just after the last digging in 1989 I rode to the ruin in a hired jeep, so crowded that some of us had to sit on the roof. The way was through the gate of an army base, which surmounted the peak of Ebal, and out the other side. Atop the peak were tall antennas sending and receiving messages, one assumes to all parts of the world.

But as I looked down into that peaceful hazy valley, buffeted by a fiery wind so strong I had to tuck my hat in my belt to keep it from flying away, I wondered: If the occupation of Canaan some 3,250 years earlier had been a peaceful one, as all research indicates, and if the people who settled there had been a tribal coalition, relatively unknown to the great powers of that time, then how had it come to be that the monotheistic religion first dedicated on this hill had become the dominant religious theory of the world and retained that dominance for more than 3,000 years? And what would happen in the near future when the identification of this altar became widely known? How would religious leaders of the three major faiths descended from the ceremonies on Ebal respond?

The site, and indeed the entire land, is like a deed of purchase dating back 3,300 years. And there is more blood being spilled today in the battle for control of ancient Canaan than probably was spent in all of Joshua's battles.

Select Bibliography

Aharoni, Yohanon. *The Archaeology of the Land of Israel*. Philadelphia: Westminster Press, 1978.

Aharoni, Yohanon. *The Land of the Bible*. Philadelphia: Westminster Press, 1979.

Alt, A. *Essays on Old Testament History and Religion*. London: Oxford University Press, 1966.

Barnett, R. D. *Illustrations of Old Testament History*. New York: British University Press, 1962.

Barthel, Manfred. *What the Bible Really Says*. New York: William Morrow, 1982.

Bevan, Edwyn. *Ancient Mesopotamia*. Chicago: Argonaut, 1968.

Ceram, C. W. *The March of Archaeology*. New York: Knopf, 1958.

Champion, Sara. *Dictionary of Terms and Techniques in Archaeology*. New York: Facts on File, 1980.

Cornfeld, Gaalyah. *Archaeology of the Bible, Book by Book*. San Francisco: Harper & Row, 1976.

De Vaux, Roland. *Ancient Israel*. New York: McGraw Hill, 1961.

Dowley, Tom, ed. *Discovering the Bible*. Grand Rapids: Marshall Pickering/Eerdsmans, 1986.

Finkelstein, Israel. *The Archaeology of the Israelite Settlement*. Jerusalem: Israel Exploration Society, 1988.

Frank, Harry Thomas. *Atlas of the Bible Lands*. Maplewood, N.J.: Hammond, 1984.

Friedman, Richard Elliott. *Who Wrote the Bible?* New York: Summit Books, 1987.

Gottwald, N. K. *The Tribes of Yahweh*. New York: Orbis, 1979.

Grant, Michael. *The Ancient Mediterranean*. London: Weidenfeld and Nicolson, 1969.

Israel Academy of Sciences and Humanities. *Biblical Archaeology Today*. Jerusalem: Israel Exploration Society, 1985.

Jacksonville Art Museum. *Rameses II*. Provo, Utah: Brigham Young University, 1985.

Johnson, Paul. *A History of the Jews*. New York: Harper & Row, 1987.

Keller, Werner. *The Bible As History*. New York: William Morrow, 1956.

Levin, Meyer. *The Story of Israel.* New York: G. P. Putnam's Sons, 1966.

McEvedy, Colin. *The Penguin Atlas of Ancient History.* Baltimore: Penguin Books, 1967.

May, Herbert J., ed. *The Oxford Bible Atlas.* New York: Oxford University Press, 1962.

Mazar, Benjamin. *The Early Biblical Period.* Jerusalem: Israel Exploration Society, 1986.

Mendenhall, George E. *The Tenth Generation.* Baltimore: Johns Hopkins Press, 1973.

Negev, Abraham. *The Archaeological Encyclopedia of the Holy Land.* Nashville: Thomas Nelson, 1986.

Noth, Martin. *The History of Israel.* Oxford: Blackwell, 1960.

Packer, J. I., Merrill C. Tenney, and William White, Jr. *All the People and Places of the Bible.* Nashville: Thomas Nelson, 1980.

Packer, J. I., Merrill C. Tenney, and William White, Jr. *Daily Life in Bible Times.* Nashville: Thomas Nelson, 1980.

Packer, J. I., Merrill C. Tenney, and William White, Jr. *The World of the Old Testament.* Nashville: Thomas Nelson, 1980.

Pearlman, Moshe. *The First Days of Israel.* New York: World, 1973.

Polzin, Robert. *Moses and the Deuteronomist.* New York: Seabury Press, 1980.

Ramsey, George W. *The Quest for the Historical Israel.* Atlanta: John Knox Press, 1981.

Rappoport, Angelo S. *Myth and Legend of Ancient Israel,* rev. ed. 3 vols. Hoboken, N.J.: Ktav Publishing House, 1966.

Starr, Chester G. *Early Man.* London: Oxford University Press, 1973.

Woolley, C. Leonard. *A Forgotten Kingdom.* New York: Norton, 1968.

Woolley, C. Leonard. *The Sumerians.* New York: Norton, 1966.

Woolley, C. Leonard. *Ur of the Chaldees.* New York: Norton, 1965.

Wright, G. E. *Biblical Archaeology.* Philadelphia: Westminster Press, 1962.

Bibles Consulted

Tanakh. New York: Jewish Publication Society, 1985.

The Jerusalem Bible. Garden City, N.Y.: Doubleday and Company, 1966.

The Holy Bible, 1611 Edition, King James Version. Nashville: Thomas Nelson, 1982.

Holy Bible from the Ancient Eastern Text (*Peshitta*). San Francisco: Harper & Row, 1968.

Index